Indigenous Peacebuilding in South Sudan

This book explores the indigenous peace cultures of the major ethnic groups in South Sudan (Dinka, Nuer, Anuak and Acholi) and analyses their contribution to resolving the civil war.

The book utilises qualitative narrative inquiry ethnographic methods to explore the indigenous institutions and customs (customary laws, beliefs and practices) employed in resolving ethnic conflicts and argues for their application in civil war resolution. This book contributes to the decolonial literature/knowledge by discussing the subtle norms; the role of youth, women and elders; and the concepts of resilience and proximity and their significance in peacebuilding. The book shows that for sustainable peace to happen, subtle roles and disputants' indigenous knowledge should be part of national peace negotiation strategies.

This book will be of interest to the following: 1) Students of Conflict Studies/Peacebuilding, Development and African Studies. 2) Scholars of indigenous knowledge on African customs, women, youth and elders. 3) NGOs, peacekeepers or actors operating in the local communities in the Horn of Africa and sub-Saharan regions.

Winnifred Bedigen is a Lecturer in International Development at the School of Politics and International Studies, University of Leeds, UK.

Routledge Contemporary Africa

Popular Protest, Political Opportunities, and Change in Africa
Edited by Edalina Rodrigues Sanches

The Failure of the International Criminal Court in Africa
Decolonising Global Justice
Everisto Benyera

African Identities and International Politics
Frank Aragbonfoh Abumere

Quality Assessment and Enhancement in Higher Education in Africa
Edited by Peter Neema-Abooki

Media Ownership in Africa in the Digital Age
Challenges, Continuity and Change
Edited by Winston Mano and Loubna El Mkaouar

Policing and the Rule of Law in Sub-Saharan Africa
Edited by Oluwagbenga Michael Akinlabi

Tonga Livelihoods in Rural Zimbabwe
Edited by Kirk Helliker and Joshua Matanzima

Women Writers of the *New* African Diaspora
Transnational Negotiations and Female Agency
Pauline Ada Uwakweh

Indigenous Peacebuilding in South Sudan: Delivering Sustainable Peace Through Traditional Institutions, Customs and Practices
Winnifred Bedigen

For more information about this series, please visit: https://www.routledge.com/Routledge-Contemporary-Africa/book-series/RCAFR

Indigenous Peacebuilding in South Sudan

Delivering Sustainable Peace Through Traditional Institutions, Customs and Practices

Winnifred Bedigen

LONDON AND NEW YORK

First published 2023
by Routledge
4 Park Square, Milton Park, Abingdon, Oxon OX14 4RN

and by Routledge
605 Third Avenue, New York, NY 10158

Routledge is an imprint of the Taylor & Francis Group, an informa business

© 2023 Winnifred Bedigen

The right of Winnifred Bedigen to be identified as author of this work has been asserted in accordance with sections 77 and 78 of the Copyright, Designs and Patents Act 1988.

All rights reserved. No part of this book may be reprinted or reproduced or utilised in any form or by any electronic, mechanical, or other means, now known or hereafter invented, including photocopying and recording, or in any information storage or retrieval system, without permission in writing from the publishers.

Trademark notice: Product or corporate names may be trademarks or registered trademarks, and are used only for identification and explanation without intent to infringe.

British Library Cataloguing-in-Publication Data
A catalogue record for this book is available from the British Library

Library of Congress Cataloging-in-Publication Data
Names: Bedigen, Winnifred, author.
Title: Indigenous peacebuilding in South Sudan: delivering sustainable peace through traditional institutions, customs and practices / Winnifred Bedigen.
Description: Abingdon, Oxon; New York, NY: Routledge, 2023. |
Series: Routledge contemporary Africa | Includes bibliographical references and index. | Summary: "This book explores the indigenous peace cultures of the major ethnic groups in South Sudan (Dinka, Nuer, Anuak and Acholi) and analyses their contribution to resolving the civil war. The book utilises qualitative narrative inquiry ethnographic methods to explore the indigenous institutions and customs (customary laws, beliefs and practices) employed in resolving ethnic conflicts and argues for their application in civil war resolution. This book contributes to the decolonial literature/ knowledge by discussing the subtle norms, the role of youth, women, and elders, the concepts of resilience and proximity, and their significance in peacebuilding. The book shows that for sustainable peace to happen, subtle roles and disputants' indigenous knowledge should be part of national peace negotiation strategies. This book will interest NGOs, students and scholars of indigenous knowledge, women, youth, conflict and peacebuilding, African Studies and Development in the Horn of Africa and sub-Sahara regions"– Provided by publisher. Identifiers: LCCN 2022050865 (print) | LCCN 2022050866 (ebook) |
ISBN 9780367561642 (hardback) | ISBN 9780367679439 (paperback) |
ISBN 9781003133476 (ebook)
Subjects: LCSH: Peace-building–South Sudan. | Youth in peace-building–South Sudan. | Women in peace-building–South Sudan. | South Sudan–Ethnic relations.
Classification: LCC JZ5584.S74 B44 2023 (print) | LCC JZ5584.S74 (ebook) |
DDC 327.1/7209624–dc23/eng/20230103
LC record available at https://lccn.loc.gov/2022050865
LC ebook record available at https://lccn.loc.gov/2022050866

ISBN: 978-0-367-56164-2 (hbk)
ISBN: 978-0-367-67943-9 (pbk)
ISBN: 978-1-003-13347-6 (ebk)

DOI: 10.4324/9781003133476

Typeset in Sabon
by Deanta Global Publishing Services, Chennai, India

Contents

	List of figures	vi
	Introduction: Why Indigenous Peacebuilding in South Sudan	1
1	Ethnic Conflicts and Civil Wars	14
2	Indigenous Peacebuilding, Peace Theories and the South Sudan Justice System	35
3	Narrative Inquiry	63
4	Socialising through Food and Etiquette in Peacebuilding	87
5	Indigenous Communities, Institutions and Peacebuilding Methods	107
6	The Role of Youth (*Monyomiji*) in Indigenous Peacebuilding	132
7	The Role of Women (*Honyomiji*) in Indigenous Peacebuilding	161
8	Social Capital, Resilience and Proximity in Peacebuilding	188
9	Summary and Conclusion	202
	Index	223

Figures

1.1	The Location of Ethnic Communities Under Study	16
1.2	The Complexity of Sudan Inter-Ethnic Conflicts and Civil Wars 1983–2013	31
2.1	An Illustration of Nilotic Lwo Conflict Resolution Foundations	36
2.2	The Basic Requirements for Indigenous Peacebuilding	37
2.3	The Nilotic Lwo Indigenous Peacebuilding System	38
2.4	Present–Past, Past–Future Concept	40
2.5	Conflict Cause, Types and Resolution	45
2.6	Prophet Ngungdeng's Rod	47
2.7	The New Sudan Judicial System—Court Hierarchy	52
2.8	Indigenous Court Levels Disputes or Crimes and South Sudan Judicial Hierarchy	53
2.9	Nilotic Lwo Indigenous Court Levels and Types of Disputes or Crimes	56
2.10	Indigenous Courts, Mechanisms and Crimes or Dispute Types	57
2.11	The Dual Justice System and Judicial Hierarchy	58
2.12	The South Sudan Judicial system and Nilotic Lwo Indigenous Courts	59
3.1	Narrative Inquiry Descriptive Design	66
3.2	An Indigenous Conflict Resolution Process	69
4.1	Features of Nilotic Lwo Societal Customs	88
4.2	The Nilotic Lwo Indigenous Peacebuilding Features in Socialising	90
4.3	Boo Plants	96
4.4	Kaal Seeds	96
4.5	Sesame Seeds	97
5.1	Acholi Community—Ongwen for Traditional Justice	114
5.2	Why Ongwen Is Facing Trial at The Hague	118
5.3	Nyono Tong Gweno Ritual Setting	123
6.1	Monyomiji Hat	136

6.2	Cultural and Modern Monyomiji	137
6.3	Preparation for Kwero Merok Ritual	154
7.1	Nilotic Lwo Women and War	169
7.2	Nilotic Lwo Women, Local Resources and Capacities in Peacebuilding	170
9.1	The Proposed Sustainable Indigenous Peacebuilding Model	204
9.2	Components of an Indigenous Conflict Resolution	208

Introduction
Why Indigenous Peacebuilding in South Sudan

Introduction

The role of indigenous peacebuilding in the South Sudan conflict and similar environments in the sub-Sahara region has become a hot topic in the recent decade (Allen, 2006; Bedigen, 2017; Belay, 2015b; Bradbury et al., 2006; Leonardi et al., 2010; Simonse and Kurimoto, 2011). Starting from the Rwanda *Gacaca* post-civil war peacebuilding, Somali elders forums, Darfur *Judiyya* system, the hybrid frameworks (such as South Africa's Truth and Reconciliation Commission (TRC), including Sierra Leone's *Fambul Tok*), indigenous institutions, customs and practices are being considered significant in the delivery of sustainable peace (Adebayo et al., 2014). Its potential is not only evident in post-conflict situations. One has to look at the *Mato Oput*, which was utilised in the Northern Uganda civil war for peacebuilding between the victims, ex-combatants and communities, even at the intensity of the Lord's Resistance Army (LRA) incursions (Allen, 2006).

This book conceptualises indigenous peacebuilding situations in communities emerging from inter-ethnic conflicts and civil wars. It does so by identifying and conceptualising the 'indigene-centric' or the core set of indigenous institutions, customs and practices that underpin the historical and foundational peace values existent in the Nilotic Lwo ethnic groups and the South Sudan justice system. The argument is made that indigenous peacebuilding is largely responsible for ethnic co-existence and sustainable peace that can be applied to civil war situations and/or at national levels.

Indigenous peacebuilding is comprised of a peculiarly African form of socialism (that emphasises the community peace or non-violent values rather than individuals or other forms of political or non-indigenes social organisations). Additional research (see Chapter 8) indicates that this form of socialism is supported by proximity, resilience and social capital. Indigene-centric or social organisation is equally a peculiar type of indigenous institutional governance that emphasises African notions of kingship, chieftaincy, clan and family systems to the exclusion of other forms of civil representations (Bedigen, 2017, 2019; Jok et al., 2004). The result is a peculiar type of peacebuilding—often characterised by a plethora of political, social and economic activities guided by indigenous non-violent norms or processes that include:

First, the involvement of all community members in storytelling, mediation and negotiation. Second, compensation, forgiveness, offering amnesties to perpetrators (war criminals). Third, rehabilitation of perpetrators, victims and whole communities through cleansing rituals. Fourth, disarmament processes that are characterised by physical burning/destruction of weapons of war. Fifth, inter-communal socialising events such as sports (hunting, fishing, wrestling, dancing), digging, harvesting, inter-marriages and child naming socialising ceremonies aimed at maintaining peace and preventing future violence.

Antithetical to indigenous peacebuilding is the conventional/international methods that have dominated peacebuilding in post-conflict situations. For instance, some writers indicate there has been a 'conspiracy not to see' the potential of local resources for peacebuilding (Srinivasan, 2021:6). In this context and from 1983 to 2015, the international organisations, namely the United Nations (UN), African Union (AU) and regional governments through the Intergovernmental Authority on Development (IGAD), have led and implemented conventional (liberal peace) methods of peacebuilding. They majorly include negotiation and mediation that have at times culminated into peace agreements, power-sharing and the deployment of peacekeeping forces (Mac Ginty, 2010; de Waal, 2014; de Waal and Flint, 2005). Such attempts have not delivered sustainable peace in the region due to its non-contextual structures. Such include the 2005 Comprehensive Peace Agreement (CPA) for Sudan. In his work, Mac Ginty (2010:1) argues that such 'liberal peace is often inflexible, ethnocentric, ministers to conflict manifestations rather than causes,' thus, making it incapable of addressing the underlying factors that have historically contributed to ethnic animosities.

Consequently, millions of South Sudanese people lost their lives, experienced crimes against humanity, faced the destruction of civilian and government property and were displaced into neighbouring countries, such as Kenya, Ethiopia, Chad, Congo and Uganda (Allen, 1994; Allison, 2016:3; Iyob and Khadiagala, 2006; Jok and Hutchinson, 1999; Prunier, 2005). In support of conventional incapability in providing sustainable peace, Simon Allison (2016:1), in his article entitled 'South Sudan's rebel leader: "I am a hero. I am a victim"', indicates that:

> the Intergovernmental Authority for Development, the regional body, along with international heavyweights including China, the United Kingdom and United States – seems misplaced. The international community is out of ideas when it comes to South Sudan, and has less influence in Juba than ever before.

This book, therefore, proposes an alternative, the indigenous peacebuilding through indigenous institutions, customs and practices (Jeong, 2005). These are, at times, referred to as traditional, grassroots, local, people-to-people, bottom-up or peace from below. In doing so, it examines the Nilotic Lwo traditional institutions, customs and practices that communities have historically utilised to resolve inter-ethnic conflicts and maintain peace. This is because civil war crimes are similar to those atrocities historically experienced by the Nilotic Lwo ethnic groups under study, when they engaged in inter-ethnic conflicts among themselves and with their neighbours (Grawert, 2014:144; Schomerus and Allen, 2010:20). In addition, these civil wars (in 1955, 1983, 2010 and 2013) were fed by inter-ethnic conflicts, where ethnic militias remained loyal to their ethnic political leaders (Leonardi et al., 2010:11; Sørbø, 2014). This study focuses on 1983–2015 inter-ethnic conflicts and civil war crimes, suggesting their sustainable resolution.

In this book, the word 'indigenous' is applied to peoplehood (Corntassel, 2003) or socio-cultural native norms of cultural or traditional institutions, customs and practices (Ineba, 2000; Mbiti, 1970). At times, the word 'traditional' will be applied to the native norms that have evolved over time (Bradbury et al., 2006; Jok et al., 2004). Traditional institutions, systems or structures refer to structured social systems (Machar, 2015). Examples of these include: *Gurtong* 'To blunt the spear,' *Mato Oput* 'Drinking bitter herbs,' *Judiyya* 'local Muslim justice system' and *Monyomiji* 'owners or fathers of the village' or indigenous institution. Customs are obligatory community laws and practices that the community has derived from individuals' and community's economic, social and political experiences to guide the society (Jok et al., 2004). Practices are ceremonies and rituals utilised in maintaining and rebuilding lives/communities. Examples include *Gomo Tong* 'Bending the spear,' *Cieng* 'putting in order,' *Mabior* 'a young white bull.'

Reasons for Indigenous Peacebuilding in South Sudan

Why should we be interested in indigenous peacebuilding in South Sudan? After all, conventional involvement has often realised a vast improvement, ranging from the 2005 Comprehensive Peace Agreement (CPA) that led to South Sudanese gaining self-determination, independence and, on the large scale, the 2013 civil war that has just ended (Grawert, 2014; Srinivasan, 2021). The cessation of hostilities within ethnic communities, militia groups and government forces; the commencement of restructuring the political system through power-sharing; plans for disarmament and demobilisation; and the massive involvement of humanitarian, development or post-war reconstruction programmes may suggest that there are many positives about South Sudan peace situations. However, this mission is peculiar for many reasons:

First, looking back to the conclusion of a 17-year first Sudan civil war (1955–1972), a conventional negotiation approach was utilised in achieving the Addis Ababa Agreement in 1972 (Agreement, 1972). However, this civil

4 *Introduction*

war was largely fed by inter-ethnic conflicts between black Africans from the South and Arabs in the north. The conventional negotiations and mediation approaches that were utilised ignored indigenous cultures, traditional institutions, customs and practices. In subsequent peace processes, indigenous/traditional aspects of negotiations and mediation approaches have been utilised. However, they are often implemented through political means akin to conventional culture.

Moreover, life in intermittent conflicts and post-civil wars remains extremely desperate, for most South Sudanese communities, classed with deeply dysfunctional inter-ethnic relations, violence, chronic poverty and underdevelopment (Mac Ginty, 2010). Such shreds of evidence demonstrate that conventional peace processes are not sustainable. For instance, the failure of this agreement directly led to the second Sudan civil war (1983–2005) (Ali and Matthews, 1999; Beswick, 1991). Further, respect for sovereignty and fear for intervening in tribal disputes implied that international intervention took longer to implement. It is important to note that inter-ethnic conflicts and civil war are closely linked, but the latter is more politically embedded. At the same time, the former is more culturally motivated. An intervention approach must incorporate indigenous concepts (indigene-centric), which should first address the indigenous root causes of conflict, then political, economic and other related issues (Ineba, 2000). This might mean applying socio-cultural ceremonies and rituals in peace processes.

Second, there were many dimensions of inter-ethnic conflicts and the civil war experiences by Sudan and South Sudan. That is to say, ethnic, regional, national and international levels of conflicts fall under the categories of State–People, People–State and People–People models of conflict (Prunier, 2005:76–80; de Waal and Flint, 2005:64). As such, peacebuilding attempts have attracted various approaches, most of which ignore ethnic conflict causes or resolution methods. Similar to many other conflicts in Africa, authors, Ogot (1999), Barash and Webel (2002:186), Laremont (2002) and Ramsbotham et al. (2005), indicate that interventions at both national and international levels have revolved around suppression, conventional negotiation and mediation. These interventions excluded holistic indigenous approaches, which, according to Jeong (2005), are vital in contemporary peacebuilding. Bearing in mind that inter-ethnic conflicts fed into these civil wars, the Sudan and South Sudan governments individually or in partnership with regional governments and/or the international community or agencies responded in various ways found to be unsustainable. Exclusively, conventional or politically influenced counter-insurgency, diplomacy and power-sharing, negotiation, peace agreements and mediation (Iyob and Khadiagala, 2006). Note, at times, some of these conventional approaches minimally integrated grassroots participation. De Waal (2014) points explicitly to practitioner William Lowery's grassroots peace works. It is essential to highlight that much as conventional approaches are widely utilised, their implementation in the South Sudan situation has not produced sustainable peace, which brings to question their efficiency in dealing with ethnically influenced civil wars.

Third, the economic capacity of Sudan and South Sudan has had a significant impact on war, peace and peacebuilding. De Waal (2014), in his work on the causes of civil war in South Sudan, indicates that economic interests have often overcome the passion for peace, for example, the continued aerial bombings in the oil-rich Nuba Mountains and Abyei areas (Arya, 2009; Reeves, 2012; Totten, 2015). Likewise, the 2013 civil war, which became known as the Dinka–Nuer inter-ethnic conflict, was blamed on the poor management of national resources. Whereas inter-ethnic conflicts could have ceased at the onset of the second civil war due to the greater need to fight the common enemy—the Arab north (Reinton, 1971), the economic reasons meant that both ethnic and civil wars continued to feed into each other, worsening the level of violence. For example, South Sudanese ethnic groups, the Dinka, Nuer, Shilluk, Acholi, Toposa, continued to engage in ethnic disputes over property, murder, physical assault and domestic violence (Evans-Pritchard, 1940; Jok et al., 2004; Reinton, 1971).

Moreover, Prunier (2005) indicates that political manipulation from within and from Libya meant that the economically deprived South Sudanese were easily recruited into militia groups by promised economic gains. While some people joined the Khartoum government forces or militia with expectations of certain benefits, some interviewees highlight that recruitment into militia groups was not an outsider manipulation but that some homegrown militia members simply wanted self-sustenance during the war. Further, continued political indifference within the Sudan People Liberation Movement/Army (SPLM/A) and aspiration for the government positions by some of its leaders led to its split and intensified conflicts (de Waal, 2014). Here, I note that ethnic, political and economic motives cause disputes, suggesting that a resolution should be drawn from the traditional institutions, customs and practices as these are foundational to the indigenous social, political and economic lifestyles (Ineba, 2000).

Fourth, indigenous peacebuilding exists in the South Sudan justice system, which comprises both state and customary laws. Francis indicates, 'Peace anywhere must be made by the people who live there' (Francis, 2004:43). Adding, Galtung (1996) expounds on this ideology of sustainable peace by indicating that peace culture should embrace language, customs, art, ideology, religion and practices to guarantee permanent and lasting peacebuilding. Indigenous traditions, customs and practices are significant because they consist of peacebuilding approaches 'grounded in the local social context' (Belay, 2015b; Machar, 2015:3). For example, customs such as *Cieng*, *Mabior* and *Mato Oput* are Dinka–Nuer's daily experiences. Wa Thiongo (1986) indicates that these cultures are rich in conflict prevention, peacemaking and peacebuilding values—thus, their norms could be useful at national levels.

Moreover, most western scholars have widely documented the perceived 'inadequate' status of indigenous peacebuilding. They are keen to disregard the historical contributions indigenous peace cultures make in ethnic/community peacebuilding when government institutions are not functional (Bedigen, 2020). Some western scholars argue that indigenous mechanisms lack efficiency compared with western-style justice systems (Mansell et al., 1995). For instance, Mansell et al. (1995) refers to Gacaca as a state-manipulated system that is instead furthering the political ambition of the ruling government. Such campaigns have led to the dominance of conventional/international institutions in the region's peace processes and western-led post-conflict reconstruction programmes. For example, in the post-genocide Rwanda, around 200 NGOs, most of which were externally linked, became crucial in the post-conflict peacebuilding (Bedigen, 2017). Indigenous peacebuilding is not certainly exempt from weaknesses. Authors (Jeong, 2005; Mazurana et al., 2005) point to their powerlessness in the face of violent conflicts, violation of human rights and the fact that they operate with a limited sphere of applicability under an efficient justice system and within an inherent conservativeness that leaves them open to abuse by their own members.

Aims of the Book

The purpose of this book is to examine the indigenous peacebuilding approaches, i.e. the traditional institutions, customs and practices of the Nilotic Lwo in delivering sustainable peace in South Sudan. To achieve this, I pose the following questions:

i) What indigenous peacebuilding approaches do the Nilotic Lwo (Dinka, Nuer, Acholi and Anuak) have to intra-ethnic and inter-ethnic disputes resolutions?
ii) How do people who have knowledge and experiences in indigenous approaches to ethnic conflict resolution and the civil war understand them?
iii) How can these indigenous approaches be utilised to deliver sustainable peace during conflict and in post-civil war situations?

I have previously considered the traditional conflict resolution of the Nilotic Lwo of South Sudan that is utilised in inter-ethnic and usefulness in the civil war resolution. The analysis showed how such mechanisms could be employed in conflict prevention, peacebuilding and peacemaking. This approach was used to give an understanding of the Nilotic Lwo traditional conflict resolution cultures and helped narrow the gap with the westernised concepts of traditional methods by Lederach (1996, 1997, 2012), Galtung (1996, 2004) and Ramsbotham et al. (2005). An in-depth study has shown that some indigenous practices have been modernised to suit contemporary inter-ethnic and civil war contexts. It is suggested that indigenous methods are an antidote to westernised concepts, contributing to the failure of conventional interventions in the region. Their inclusion in the national peace processes can deliver sustainable peace (Bedigen, 2020; Jeong, 2005; Latigo, 2008). Some recent examples of indigenous methods utilised in the region's civil war and post-conflict or civil war situations include the *Mato Oput*, *Mabior* and *Gacaca* courts.

Objectives

i) To explore Nilotic Lwo (Dinka, Nuer, Acholi and Anuak) indigenous conflict resolution peace cultures.
ii) To explore inter-ethnic conflicts, Sudan and South Sudan civil war and analyse conflict resolution attempts.
iii) To examine interviewees' narratives on the Nilotic Lwo indigenous methods of addressing conflict.
iv) To examine the usefulness of these methods in delivering sustainable peace in the South Sudan civil war situation.

Outline of the Book

Chapter 1: Ethnic Conflicts and Civil Wars. This chapter will give a contextual background to the causes and course of ethnic, inter-ethnic conflicts and the civil wars in South Sudan. It will analyse ethnic conflicts that fed into civil wars and highlight failed conventional conflict resolution attempts from 1983 to 2015. Furthermore, details will be given here about the research question, methodology, rationale and key arguments pursued in the book.

Chapter 2: Indigenous Peacebuilding, Peace Theories and the South Sudan Justice System. The purpose of this chapter is to familiarise the reader with the indigenous (at times referred to as traditional, grassroots, bottom-up, local or people-to-people) approaches to peace and conflict resolution. To help identify research gaps, it will review the literature on the current peace theories propounded by Lederach (1997), Galtung (1990, 1996) and Ramsbotham et al. (2005). Also, this chapter will utilise a cultural theory lens to give an understanding of the limitations of peace theories and note the pragmatic nature of Nilotic Lwo cultures in conflict resolution. Further, the chapter will provide an overview of the South Sudan justice system that starts from customary law courts. It will argue that it demonstrates the potential for traditional justice and conflict resolution in a civil war situation.

It will explore the concept of sustainable resolution, Nilotic Lwo societal customs, beliefs and practices. It will argue that ceremonies and/or rituals are marginalised or under-represented traditional peace and conflict resolution concepts in conventional grassroots peace theories considered in this

8 Introduction

study. Exploring indigenous practices will contribute to knowledge in this area, suggesting a holistic approach.

Chapter 3: Narrative Inquiry. This chapter takes us through the research process and highlights the significance of using qualitative narrative inquiry or stories in indigenous research. Through face-to-face focus groups and online interviews, interviewees told their stories and life experiences that confirmed data from the literature review and brought to light new information. Interviews provided opportunities to identify more comprehensive perspectives suitable for generalising concepts or themes (see the summary of themes/concepts).

In view of cultural theory, some ethnographic and anthropological concepts came to light during the narrative inquiry process. Rather than the commonly used statistical methods in social research, this book argues for qualitative ethnographic aspects, including narratives and observations of interviewees' everyday lives, practices, rituals, symbols, inter-connections or relationships, customs, values and beliefs.

Chapter 4: Socialising through Food and Etiquette of Peacebuilding. The purpose of this book is to examine the indigenous peacebuilding approaches, i.e. the traditional institutions, customs and practices of the Nilotic Lwo in delivering sustainable peace in South Sudan. The previous chapter demonstrated that investigation was conducted through narrative inquiry ethnographic methods such as in-depth interviews, focus groups and online interviews. The sample includes the Nilotic Lwo migrant community in the UK and Africa. They narrated their experiences and views. I explored with experts who have the knowledge and experience in inter-ethnic conflicts, civil war, indigenous peacebuilding or peace studies. In their narratives, it became more apparent that socialising through food, food sharing and following the code of conduct is significant in indigenous peace processes. These foods are symbolic but possess nutritional healing values. The purpose of this chapter is thus to discuss socialising through food, food sharing and associated rituals and ceremonies.

Chapter 5: Indigenous Communities, Institutions and Peacebuilding Methods. This chapter aims to discuss the second aspect of findings, i.e. indigenous communities, institutions and methods. In discussing these three aspects and providing a deeper appreciation of indigenous peacebuilding, some contrasts with conventional approaches and protocols are highlighted. Such includes the role of institutions such as the International Criminal Court (ICC) and its unsustainable justice process and the involvement of peacekeeping forces in conflict zones. It argues that such international conventions ignore the significance of community and relationships, enacted through peacebuilding ceremonies and rituals such as the *Nyono Tong Gweno* ritual 'Stepping on Egg.' The crucial role of elders in conducting a peacebuilding ritual, *Ekisil* and *Akigath* ('Breaking of bones' and prayers), is demonstrated.

Chapter 6: The Role of Youth (*Monyomiji*) in Indigenous Peacebuilding. Unlike conventional peace interventions that relegate youth to studentship, this chapter aims to discuss findings on the Nilotic Lwo traditional youth roles in war, peace, peacebuilding and post-conflict reconstruction. This chapter will discuss how youth take over community responsibilities when they have learnt their traditional duties. In doing so, I continue to discuss a case study: The contribution to knowledge on traditional roles of youth (*Monyomiji*) in conflict resolution. In discussing these findings, I shall draw from interviewee narratives on *Monyomiji*, its meaning, importance and youth roles in traditional conflict resolution. Youth duties and responsibilities to be discussed include initiatives, apprenticeships, participation, leadership, mediation and involvement in conflict resolution rituals such as the Kwero Merok 'cleansing of ex-combatants' ritual.

Chapter 7: The Role of Women (*Honyomiji*) in Indigenous Peacebuilding. Conventional peace theories from which this study is derived talk about the involvement of women in local peace processes, but they do not explore the significance of their traditional and domestic roles. In this chapter, I continue to discuss the findings on the traditional roles of women or *Honyomiji* and mothers in Nilotic Lwo conflict resolution processes and post-conflict reconstruction. The argument here stresses that the Nilotic Lwo communities' functionalities are dependent on women's traditional roles. It demonstrates that women play a significant role in ensuring that customary laws, beliefs and practices are at the core of peace and conflict resolution processes. It highlights that within the boundaries of women's traditional roles are organisation, facilitation, peace education, leadership and decision-making in traditional conflict resolution processes.

Chapter 8: Social Capital, Resilience and Proximity in Peacebuilding. This chapter provides additional information to the original thesis. It discusses three main concepts (i.e. social capital, resilience and proximity) concerning migrant perspectives. These concepts have been analysed in other disciplines but are less known in peacebuilding, yet subtle ways indicate their existence in the peoples' everyday lives. This chapter highlights refugees' reflections on their past, present and future concerns. Such includes the steps some have taken regarding peacebuilding between South Sudanese ethnic groups in the diaspora, residents in South Sudan and the state. While this chapter seeks to argue that resiliences in a conflict-prone zone are inbuilt in peoples' cultures, beliefs and practices, proximity in the refugee settlements, Internally Displaced Peoples' Camps (IDPCs) or diasporas is essential in maintaining peacebuilding networks and developing young peace actors. Adding, this chapter recognises that these two concepts are dependent on social capital.

Chapter 9: Summary and Conclusion. The purpose of this book is to examine the indigenous peacebuilding approaches, i.e. the traditional institutions, customs and practices of the Nilotic Lwo in delivering sustainable peace in South Sudan. In conclusion, this chapter will provide an overview of the main findings and recommendations based on study objectives stated earlier.

Key Arguments Pursued in This Book

The key arguments pursued in this book revolve around three areas. First, conflicts are part of human nature, and those parties involved should be at the core of peacebuilding. Second, any resolution should holistically be indigene-centric. That is, it should include the indigenous people, institutions, customs and practices. Third, where ethnic conflicts influence national instabilities, a resolution should initially focus on the ethnic factors, then workable elements are modified to suit peacebuilding at national levels. Fourth, it is recognised that South Sudan has experienced protracted conflicts, and due to the overwhelming humanitarian crises that overflow to the neighbourhoods, external agencies and institutions can work with and are led by local institutions to build peace.

The Theoretical and Empirical Contributions of the Book

There are many theoretical contributions this book makes. First, it suggests that peacebuilding in post-conflict environments should be indigene-centred at local and national levels. Second, by utilising the qualitative narrative method, this book provides a close link that has been forged between theory, method and data—contributing to ethnographic and anthropological methodologies. It argues this particular method is crucial in researching indigenous communities. Third, by exploring intra- and inter-ethnic conflicts, civil wars and subtle peacebuilding norms, this book successfully integrates the research results into existing bottom-up peacebuilding theories. Thus, it suggests doing so enables sustainable peace at national levels. It adds that the sociological contribution of norms, including resiliences, proximity and social capital, is clearly shown to contribute to sustainable peace, unlike the politically led measures. Fourth, the indigene-centric focus redirects empirical research in peacebuilding to commence from the local/community level or the disputants' cultures/beliefs/practices. Overall, it is suggested that new peacebuilding initiatives should not seek to 'westernise' indigenous peacebuilding by excluding indigenous key attributes.

Bibliography

Adebayo, A.G., Jesse, J.B. and Brandon, D.L. (Eds.), 2014. *Indigenous Conflict Management Strategies: Global Perspectives*. Lanham, MD, Lexington Books. Retrieved from https://rowman.com/ISBN/9780739188040.

Ali, T. and Matthews, R.O. 1999, Civil war and failed peace efforts in Sudan. In T. Ali and R. O. Matthews (Eds.), *Civil Wars in Africa* (pp. 193–220). Kingston and Montreal, McGill-Queens University Press..

Allen, T., 1994. Ethnicity and tribalism on the Sudan-Uganda border. In K. Fukui and J. Markakis (Eds.), *Ethnicity and Conflict in the Horn of Africa* (pp. 112–139). London, James Currey.

Allen, T., 2006. Trial Justice: The International Criminal Court and the Lord's Resistance Army London and New York, Zed Books.
Allison, S., 2016. South Sudan's rebel leader: 'I am a hero. I am a victim' Maverick, South Africa. Retrieved April 21, 2014, from http://South Sudan's rebel leader: 'I am a hero. I Am a vi...' (dailymaverick.co.za).
Arya, S., 2009. Sudan–conflicts, terror, and oil. *Journal of Defence Studies*, 3(4), pp. 64–78.
Barash, D.P. and Webel, P.C., 2002. *Peace and Conflict Studies*. London, Sage.
Bedigen, W., 2017. Traditional conflict resolution: The Nilotic Lwo of South Sudan (PhD thesis). Leeds, Leeds Beckett University.
Bedigen, W., 2019. Youth (Monyomiji) and conflict resolution in the South Sudan Civil War. *Journal of African Cultural Heritage Studies*, 2(1), pp. 18–35.
Bedigen, W., 2020. Significance of societal customs in the South Sudan Civil War resolution. *Journal of Peacebuilding and Development*, 15(1), pp. 3–17.
Belay, T., 2015a. Armed conflict, violation of child rights, and implications for change. *Journal of Psychology and Psychotherapy*, 5, p. 202. doi:10.4172/2161-0487.1000202.
Belay, T., 2015b. Conflicts, conflict resolution practices and impacts of the war in South Sudan. *International Journal of School and Cognitive Psychology*, S2, p. 013. doi:10.4172/ijscp.S2-013.
Beswick, S.F., 1991. The Addis Ababa agreement: 1972–1983 harbinger of the second civil war in the Sudan. *Northeast African Studies*, 13(23), pp. 191–215.
Bradbury, M., Ryle, J., Medley, M. and Sansculotte-Greenidge, K., 2006. *Local Peace Processes in Sudan: A Baseline Study*. London, Rift Valley Institute.
Corntassel, J., 2003. Who is indigenous? 'Peoplehood' and ethnonationalist approaches to rearticulating indigenous identity. *Nationalism and Ethnic Politics*, 9(1), pp. 75–100.
de Waal, A. and Flint, J., 2005. *Darfur: A Short History of a Long War*. London, Zed/International African Institute.
de Waal, A., 2007. *War in Darfur and the Search for Peace*. Cambridge, MA, Harvard University Press.
de Waal, A., 2014. When kleptocracy becomes insolvent: Brute causes of the civil war in South Sudan. *African Affairs*, 113(452), pp. 347–369.
Evans-Pritchard, E.E., 1940. The Nuer: A Description of the Modes of Livelihood and Political Institutions of a Nilotic People. Oxford, Oxford University Press.
Francis, D., 2004. *Rethinking War and Peace*. London, Pluto Press.
Galtung, J., 1996. *Peace by Peaceful Means*. London, Sage.
Galtung, J., 2002. Peace journalism – A challenge. In W. Kempf and H. Luostarinen (Eds.), *Journalism and the New World Order: Studying War and the Media* (Vol. 2). Göteborg, Nordicom, pp. 259–272.
Galtung, J., 2004. *Transcend and Transform: An Introduction to Conflict Work*. London, Pluto Press.
Grawert, E., 2014. *Forging Two Nations Insights on Sudan and South Sudan*. Addis Ababa, OSSREA.
Hutchinson, L., 1999. Evaluating and researching the effectiveness of educational interventions. *BMJ: British Medical Journal*, 318(7193), pp. 1267–1269.
Ineba, B.-M., 2000. *A Cultural Approach to Conflict Transformation: An African Traditional Experience*. Term Paper. Written for the Course: "Culture of Peace and Education" taught at the European Peace University. Austria, Stadtschlaining.

Iyob, R. and Khadiagala, G.M., 2006. *Sudan: The Elusive Quest for Peace*. Boulder, CO, Lynne Rienner Publishers.
Jeong, H.-W., 2005. *Peacebuilding in Postconflict Societies*. London, Sage.
Jok, A.A., Leitch, A.R. and Vandewint, C., 2004. *A Study of Customary Law in Contemporary Southern Sudan*. Rumbek, South Sudan, World Vision International.
Laremont, R.R., 2002. *The Causes of War and the Consequences of Peacekeeping in Africa*. Portsmouth, N.H.: Heinemann.
Latigo, J.O., 2008. *Northern Uganda: Tradition-Based Practices in the Acholi Region*. Stockholm, International Institute for Democracy and Electoral Assistance.
Lederach, J.P., 1996. *Preparing for Peace: Conflict Transformation across Cultures*. Syracuse, NY, Syracuse University Press.
Lederach, J.P., 1997. *Building Peace: Sustainable Reconciliation in Divided Societies*. Washington, DC, United States Institute of Peace Press.
Lederach, J.P., 2012. The origins and evolution of infrastructures for peace: A personal reflection. *Journal of Peacebuilding and Development*, 7(3), pp. 8–13.
Leonardi, C., Moro, L.N., Santschi, M. and Isser, H.D., 2010. *Local Justice in South Sudan (Peaceworks Number 66)*. Washington, DC, United States Institute of Peace.
Mac Ginty, R., 2010. No war, no peace: Why so many peace processes fail to deliver peace. *International Politics*, 47(2), pp. 145–162.
Machar, B., 2015. *Building a Culture of Peace through Dialogue in South Sudan*. Juba, South Sudan, The SUUD Institute.
Mansell, W., Meteyard, B. and Thomson, A., 1995. *A Critical Introduction to Law*. London, Cavendish.
Mazurana, D., Raven-Roberts, A. and Parpart, J. (Eds.), 2005. *Gender, Conflict and Peace Keeping*. Oxford, Rowman and Littlefield Publishers.
Mbiti, J.S., 1970. *Concepts of God in Africa*. London, SPCK.
Ogot, B.A., 1999. *Building on the Traditional: Selected Essays 1981–1998*. Nairobi, Kenya, Anyange Press.
Prunier, G., 2005. *Darfur: The Ambiguous Genocide*. London, Hurst & Company.
Ramsbotham, O., Woodhouse, T. and Miall, H., 2005. Contemporary Conflict Resolution: The Prevention, *Management and Transformation of Deadly Conflicts*. 2nd edition. Cambridge, Polity Press.
Reeves, E., 2012. Sudan: Aerial military attacks on civilians and humanitarians: 'They Bombed everything that moved', 1999–2012. *African Arguments*. Retrieved March 21, 2014, from http://africanarguments.org/2012/01/18/they-bombed-everything-that-moved-aerial-military-attacks-on-civilians-and-humanitarians-in-sudan1999-2012-by-eric-reeves/.
Reinton, P.O., 1971. Imperialism and the Southern Sudan. *Journal of Peace Research*, 8(3–4), pp. 239–247.
Schomerus, M. and Allen, T., 2010. *Southern Sudan at Odds with Itself: Dynamics of Conflict and Predicaments of Peace*. Development Studies Institute, London, London School of Economics and Political Science.
Simonse, S. and Kurimoto, E. (Eds.), 2011. Engaging 'Monyomiji', bridging the gap in East Bank Equatoria. In Proceedings of the Conference 26–28 November 2009. Nairobi, Pax Christi Horn of Africa, pp. 2–129.

Sørbø, G.M., 2014. Return to war in South Sudan. *Norwegian Peace Building Resource Center*. Retrieved from https://www.ciaonet.org/attachments/24871/uploads [Accessed: 4 December 2015].

Srinivasan, S., 2021. *When Peace Kills Politics: International Intervention and Unending Wars in the Sudans*. London, Hurst & Company.

Totten, S., 2015. *Genocide by Attrition: The Nuba Mountains of Sudan* (Vol. 1). London, Transaction Publishers.

wa Thiong'o, N., 1986. *Writing against Neocolonialism*. Nairobi, Vita Books.

Wai, D.M., 2013. The Addis Ababa Agreement on the Problem of South Sudan. In *The Southern Sudan* (pp. 235–258). Routledge.

Woodhouse, T., Miall, H. and Ramsbotham, O.P., 2005. *Contemporary Conflict Resolution*. London, Frank Cass.

1 Ethnic Conflicts and Civil Wars

Introduction

The 1983–2005 Sudan second civil war and its peace deals suddenly launched the Comprehensive Peace Agreement (CPA) aiming to strike a peace deal acceptable to Sudan and South Sudan. Following the CPA guidelines on South Sudan self-determination, there was a renewed idea that South Sudan national peace processes be drawn from its diverse indigenous communities (Bedigen, 2017, 2020). However, to harmonise the varied and distinct indigenous peacebuilding practices of over 60 ethnic groups into a national peace plan would be complex. Apart from diversities, there was also hatred for the politically and militarily dominant Dinka and Nuer ethnic groups—seeing an increase in their direct clashes with minority ethnic groups. As we explore this chapter, we introduce the major ethnic group, Nilotic Lwo. Following, discussions incorporate interviewees' narratives on how inter-ethnic conflicts fed into civil wars, continued inter-ethnic (militia groups) conflicts during civil wars and their reunion under Sudan People's Liberation Army (SPLA) to fight the Khartoum government (Allen, 1994; Sawant, 1998).

The Nilotic Lwo, sometimes spelt Luo or Luwo, are an ethnic linguistic group commonly referred to as the Nilotics or Nilots (Allen, 1994; Kelly, 1985). They are located in an area that stretches from South Sudan, along the banks and rivers of the southwestern area of Ethiopia, through northeastern Uganda and eastern Democratic Republic of Congo (DRC) into western Kenya and ending in the upper tip of northern Tanzania (Evans-Pritchard, 1940; Reinton, 1971). They are said to have originated in Southern Sudan and occupied eastern Bahr el Ghazal, a vast swamp region of the Sudd region formed by the White Nile in the present-day South Sudan. This is a grassy, flat and virtually treeless region, flooded and swamped in rainy seasons, with various channels of deep water running through it. Mainly, the major Nilotic Lwo ethic groups, namely the Anuak, Nuer, Dinka, Acholi and many other minor Nilotic groups, currently occupy it (Collins, 1971; Kelly, 1985). These communities are largely egalitarian, organised under kingships, chieftaincies or clan systems, which are at times managed by

DOI: 10.4324/9781003133476-2

the indigenous institutions such as the Monyomiji (Bedigen, 2017; Evans-Pritchard, 1940; Reinton, 1971). Their main economic activities include pastoralism, cultivation, foraging, hunting and fishing (Evans-Pritchard, 1940; Reinton, 1971).

Although their indigenous political and economic set-up is intricately linked to their social lifestyles, only their social aspect, peacebuilding, will be explored for purposes of focus. Before exploring these indigenous peace approaches, a narrative that helps explain each ethnic group's involvement in the inter-ethnic and civil wars will be provided in the later chapters. Primarily, the narrative is related to their histories and how they have managed to co-exist for so long—thus the argument that their subtle ways could be utilised at national levels (Bedigen, 2017, 2020).

Context

Inter-ethnic Conflicts

> We, the Nilotic people, are fighters; we are resilient. Our women are resilient. We have always fought for both survival and for prestige. In those days, the war chief could not be respected if he did not capture the enemy chief and force him and his people to our cattle camp. We are brothers, you know! We can understand each other's language. Across the river can be another tribe, our brothers and enemies. We share water from the same river; this symbolises the blood bond that can never be broken even if we fight. We call ourselves brothers; this also depends on the discipline the other community reciprocates. During harvest, a chief would send word to invite the other community. Lots of food was cooked, alcohol was brewed, feasting, dancing to reconcile the communities. It means the crop growers could give some food to cattle keepers but it also helps in support, especially when another group came to interfere.
>
> (Mosa, 4 May 2013)

The above account shows that disagreements over resources caused inter-ethnic conflicts. Although the Dinka, Nuer, Anuak and Acholi ethnic groups have a common ancestry (Crazzolara, 1950; Collins, 1971; Kelly, 1985), they have often had disagreements (Johnson and Anderson, 1995; Reinton, 1971). In modern times, these disagreements spill over into other ethnic communities within South Sudan and neighbouring countries, furthering intra- and inter-ethnic conflicts (Johnson, 2003; Deng, 1995). Significantly, two of these ethnic groups, namely the Dinka and Nuer, are historically more influential in this region's inter-ethnic conflicts and civil wars. In contrast, others, such as Acholi, Anuak, Shilluk, Murle, and other minor groups, are less influential. Figure 1.1 shows the ethnic groups under the study.

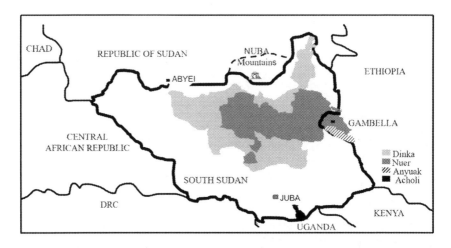

Figure 1.1 The Location of Ethnic Communities Under Study

As described by wa Thiongo (1986), most Western writers portray all these groups as hostile. Other authors indicate that all these groups are often involved in conflicts due to political greed and cultural reasons. For example, Deng (1995) and de Waal (2014) point to conflicts of identity as the root causes of conflicts in South Sudan. Some African writers, such as Nyerere (1968), Ngugi wa Thiongo (1986) and Jok et al. (2004), are of the view that there is no such thing as historical or tribal enmity among these groups. They argue that cultural erosion caused by colonial influence and imperialism has intensified conflicts, while others say their involvement in the conflict and civil wars was somewhat accidental. For, each ethnic community felt obliged to assert or defend cultural pride where these were threatened. Also, they fought for tangible reasons, survival and the protection of socio-economic and individual ethnic (tribal) socio-cultural existence (Ineba, 2000; wa Thiongo, 1986).

Before the civil wars and as far back as the 13th century, intermittent inter-ethnic conflicts existed between the various Nilotic Lwo ethnic groups (Crazzolara, 1950; Collins, 1971). Although these communities have interacted in economic, social and political spheres, it appears that they have continuously pursued incompatible goals. Arguably, each ethnic community interpreted inter-ethnic conflict causes and potential resolution through a lens of existing and/or perceived ethnic marginalisation (Schneckener and Wolff, 2004). In particular, the Dinka and Nuer are perceived by other ethnic communities to be aggressors due to their cattle raiding habits (Allen, 1994; Bedigen, 2017). Such traditional economic practices, without alternatives, exacerbate disagreements over resources, livelihoods or the individual community's actual needs. Nevertheless, marginalisation existed in cultural rights, recognition and property ownership and the lack of opportunities when it comes to sharing water and grazing land. Awareness of these kinds of marginalisation often led to economically and culturally justified aggressive actions that, at times, fuelled major conflicts (Bedigen, 2017; Ineba, 2000). Aggressions were further fuelled by revenge, hatred and substantial animosities (Evans-Pritchard, 1940; Collins, 1960; Reinton, 1971). Inter-ethnic conflicts, described as 'traditional minorities' type of conflicts, became more frequent and have fed into the numerous civil wars in South Sudan since 1983 (Schneckener and Wolff, 2004:1).

Despite these communities' socio-cultural linkages through inter-marriages and proximity (Reinton, 1971; Kok, 2011), their conflict encounters have escalated into the mass and brutal killing of the vulnerable (children, disabled, women and the elderly) since the 1970s. Historically in their cultural war ethics, these kinds of killings were abominable acts that could be punished severely (Ineba, 2000). In addition, their resolution would require a communal cleansing, compensation and other relevant indigenous peace-building processes. The complexity is that both kinsmen and others perpetrated these brutalities during the civil wars en masse. In addition, because of easy access to superior weapons, communities are more inclined to fight rather than seek peace (Leff and LeBrun, 2014; Nna and Pabon, 2012). This raises the question of whether indigenous methods of reconciliation still hold or can deliver sustainable peace. These sorts of questions will be dealt with in later chapters. For now, we turn our attention to the Dinka involvement in the inter-ethnic conflicts and civil wars.

Dinka Involvement in Inter-ethnic Conflicts and Civil Wars

> The older people's place is in the village where they are to assume family responsibilities and positions of authority. In the camp, there is a maximum of freedom and a minimum of obligations and authority; the elders, with their courts and social controls, remain in the villages.
> (Zanen and van den Hoek, 1987:182)

The Dinka are the largest Nilotic Lwo ethnic group (Kelly, 1985). Historically, the Dinka political and socio-economic activities are defined by pastoralism and cultivation (Kelly, 1985; Zanen and van den Hoek, 1987). These activities determine who lives where. The cattle camps are where youth live, and the villages are where elders live. The youth live in cattle camps to tend cattle and, once married, clear land and settle into family life in the village. Whereas the cattle camps are places of maximum freedom and leisure, the villages are places for obligations and authority. Thus, with their courts and social controls in peacebuilding, the elders remain in the villages (Zanen and van den Hoek, 1987:182). These economic activities do not only define Dinka settlement relations with their neighbours. The Dinka have engaged in conflicts due to cattle raids and land grabs. In the Upper

Nile region, the Panyikang Shilluk and the Bailet Dinka entered into conflict mainly over land in Malakal, Nakdier and Lul Payams (Kamwaria and Katola, 2012). The 2009 government attempt to resolve the land issue by calling on all neighbourhoods to participate in the resolution detrimentally led to Dinka–Shilluk inter-ethnic conflicts causing further killings within the two communities (Bedigen, 2017).

Further, following independence, the South Sudan government disarmament policy was repressive (Grawert, 2014; Johnson, 2003; de Waal, 2014). It was characterised by killings, rape, defilement, the occupation of Shilluk community spaces and other war crimes. Although crimes such as rape and defilement were unheard of in Nilotic Lwo early wars, they occasionally occurred in the Dinka, Nuer, Acholi and Anuak communities. They were resolved effectively through indigenous cleansing rituals such as *Nyono Tong Gweno*. Dinka aggression, coupled with the unexplained arrests of Shilluk Members of Parliament, prolonged the Dinka–Shilluk inter-ethnic conflicts (Bedigen, 2017).

Unlike the Dinka–Shilluk conflict, the Dinka–Nuer inter-ethnic conflicts were fuelled by political goals, particularly during the second civil war (Jok and Hutchinson, 1999). This war, in which most Dinka and Nuer participated, started when the then Sudanese president, Jaafar Mohamed Nimeiri, violated the Addis Ababa Agreement that had ended the first Sudan civil war (Kok, 2011). From the late 1970s to 1983, many more Dinka, Nuer and other South Sudanese youth were inspired to join the rebel military camp in Bilpam. Soon afterwards, the movement forces united under John Garang, a Dinka man (Rights, 1997). The collapse of the Addis Ababa Agreement did not only cause the second civil war. It deepened a rift between the Dinka and Nuer ethnic communities in that many of their high-ranking military officials and political leaders continued to target each other's community. For example, those who had previously been absorbed into Nimeri's armed forces (i.e. Abdallah Chuol Deng, Gordon Koang, Samuel Gai Tut, William Nyuon, John Garang and others) went back to fight a guerrilla war against the Khartoum government, as well as each other's communities.

Further, disagreement between the above key figures led to the group's split into two camps. One was Garang's group, which later became known as Sudan People Liberation Movement/Army (SPLM/A), with William Nyuon, Kerbino Kwanyin and others (Deng, 2013). This particular group comprised mainly the Dinka, with a few other ethnic communities, for example, the Acholi. These forces perpetrated violence against those who opposed Garang's leadership, accusing them of having tribalistic tendencies. The other group who opposed Garang was headed by Samuel Gai Tut and Abdallah Chuol. It later became known as Anyanya 11. These were predominantly Nuer ethnic groups. The SPLM/A, a much stronger force, drove off the Anyanya 11 from Bilpam, who fled and set up their own camp at Thiajak (Rights, 1997; Kok, 2011). In his effort to capture his deserters, Garang's attack on the Anyanya 11 led to the death of Anyanya

11's leader, Samuel Gai Tut. Following, Dinka–Nuer inter-ethnic conflict revenge attacks that included combat, cattle rustling and abductions continued, intensifying the second civil war.

From the above, it can be seen that complex inter-ethnic conflict situations developed and escalated from political platforms. It is apparent that various issues ranging from economic, social, cultural, political, personal and external factors such as the proliferation of weapons contributed to the pattern of conflicts (Leff and LeBrun, 2014; Nna and Pabon, 2012). The majority of these issues represent a wider spectrum of conflict ranging from traditional or historical to modern or contemporary and have been widely considered by other authors (de Waal, 2014; Flint and de Waal, 2005; Johnson, 2003; Laremont, 2002). The intention of this book is not to delve into conflicts, as doing so can divert attention from their resolution. However, we note that their complexity points to the difficulties that may occur during peacebuilding—particularly the effectiveness of indigenous methods in dealing with a civil war phenomenon.

Further to the conflict causes listed earlier, the SPLM/A officials, who were under John Garang's leadership in August 1991, split into Torit and Nasir factions. The Nasir faction formed a new group, the South Sudan Independent Movement/Army (SSIM/A), under the leadership of Riek Machar. The SSIM/A welcomed and incorporated the Anyanya 11 forces, who, as mentioned earlier, were the first group to split from the SPLM/A. The Anyanya 11 then mobilised and launched revenge attacks against the SPLM/A (Rights, 1997). When this happened, the conflict became clearly defined along Dinka–Nuer lines, though this may not have been their initial motive. These attacks led to massive destruction, raids and indiscriminate killings in the Dinka–Nuer areas of greater Bahr el Ghazal and the greater Upper Nile. Those who managed to escape took refuge in neighbouring countries, such as Kenya, Uganda and Congo.

On the surface, it was widely believed that differences in the political views of Garang (who wanted to liberate Sudan as a whole) and Riak Machar (who wanted to liberate only the South) caused the second split of the SPLM/A. Research by Jok et al. (2004) indicates that historical differences, hatred, anger and animosity fuelled this Dinka–Nuer conflict. This clearly demonstrates the difficulty in proposing a workable solution since these are characteristic of human nature cut across cultural and political differences (Blumberg et al., 2006). As such, this research will focus on the disputes or crimes and their resolution through Nilotic Lwo peacebuilding institutions, customs and practices. By examining the study context, research analysis will consider indigenous methods that prevent extreme violence, conflicts and post-conflict indigenous peacemaking and peacebuilding methods.

Although splinter groups reunited to fight a political course around 1987, from the onset of conflicts, there was no clear vision or leadership, as conceded by John Garang (Rights, 1997). Mbiti's (1970) study on Nilotic

Lwo ethnic communities shows that, historically, *Jodong Lweny* (the war chief) took the lead in war preparations. He explains that *Jodong Lweny* consulted with the ancestors and other community elders before engaging in conflicts and post-conflict reconciliation. Both the community and chiefs they elected were instrumental in times of war (Crazzolara, 1950; Reinton, 1971). In these conflicts, there was a split within the communities. The young and/or western educated took control of the war (Wunlit Peace and Reconciliation Conference, 1999) while the community leaders/elders became disengaged. For instance, recruitment into the forces took place without the chiefs' knowledge. This implies that the old traditional leaders lost their authority, were disempowered and could only watch the descent into chaos. As mentioned earlier, the youth who went to Bilpam with the motive to train and fight the Khartoum government (the common enemy to both Dinka and Nuer) resorted to fighting each other's villages and the chiefs could neither disarm nor control them. This highlights the challenge of integrating old and new systems in resolving modern societal problems. Considering Cashmore and Rojek's (1999:124–126) work on Douglas' concepts of 'preliterate and literate societies' or indigenous cultures can be utilised to tackle problems in 'literate' or modern societies. Such would include the *Gomo Tong* and *Akigath* rituals that some Nilotic Lwo have utilised in post-conflict inter-ethnic and civil war peacebuilding.

Acholi Involvement in Inter-ethnic Conflicts and Civil War

Historically, the Acholi/Acooli or Shuli community occupied the Eastern Equatoria in South Sudan, Northern Uganda and Northeastern Democratic Republic of Congo (DRC) (Atkinson, 1994; Ochola, 2009). They have faced marginalisation in these locations since colonial rule. Their sociopolitical organisation's culture is under chiefdoms (Atkinson, 1994). The Acholi are among the smallest ethnic communities in South Sudan but possess significant peacebuilding cultures. Historical migration accounts show that they experienced an intra-family conflict over land. It led to their split and conflicts with their neighbouring ethnic communities, namely the Madi and Didinga communities. Historically, inter-marriage between the Acholi and these neighbouring communities reduced tensions, so there were no major inter-ethnic conflicts. However, from 1983, the relatively easy formation of militia groups and the access to firearms furthered tensions between these neighbourhoods. Bedigen (2017) indicates that this community faced attacks from the Lord's Resistance Army (LRA). The LRA leadership and majority combatants are from the Uganda Acholi community. An interviewee indicates that some Acholi, Madi and Didinga army commanders recruited youth from within their communities into a militia group during the second civil war. According to the Acholi culture, groups such as these never gained community support and were disowned by the Acholi elders. Significantly, unlike in other communities (the Dinka, Nuer and Anuak) that experienced similar militia operations, the role of the elders and intermarriage effectively prevented both intra- and inter-ethnic conflicts and their outcome.

To begin with, Ochola (2009) narrates the story of 'The spear and the bead'. A traumatic tale about the Acholi ancestry showed how unforgiveness and revenge between the two ancestral leaders and brothers led to a young girl's death caused by an attempt to recover the bead and the brothers' eventual separation. Labongo, the elder brother, could not forgive Gipir, the younger brother, for losing the ancestral spear (a symbol of leadership) that was handed to him by their late father. Likewise, Gipir, after recovering the spear and in revenge, could not forgive Labongo's daughter for swallowing his bead. The tale ends with the two brothers separating and relocating, thus transforming a potentially violent situation into a culture of non-violence among the Acholi. I think such acts of war avoidance are fundamental in reducing hostility and promoting peaceful co-existence.

Before the first civil war (1955–1972), the Dinka had settled in Eastern Equatoria, a homeland to the Acholi. Dinka domination caused disgruntlement and ethnic tensions after the first civil war in which most Acholi participated. The Acholi asked President Nimeiri (then the president of Sudan) to fulfil his promise of economic development (Laremont, 2002). One possible way of implementing this was by sending the Dinka away from Eastern Equatoria, the Acholi land. The Acholi believed that the Dinka's corrupt administration and tribalistic tendencies had hampered economic development in their homeland. The Dinka, in the course of their departure, carried out atrocities on the Acholi and other ethnic communities. When the opportunity to recruit soldiers came to Owiny Ki Bull, where most of the Acholi live, most youth joined with the intention of revenge.

Moreover, the Acholi were not exempt from the Arab marginalisation that caused South Sudanese to engage in the first civil war (Rights, 1997). Therefore, when John Garang's idea of creating a new Sudan was presented to the Acholi, they welcomed it, put aside all their ethnic differences and joined the SPLA in the first Sudan civil war. One can argue the Acholi involvement in the civil war was not rooted in political claims but rather banditry and struggle against Dinka domination, marginalisation and aggression.

Nuer Involvement in Inter-ethnic Conflicts and Civil War

The Nuer are the second largest ethnic group in South Sudan. They occupy both South Sudan and Ethiopia, but the majority live in South Sudan (Evans-Pritchard, 1940; Kelly, 1985). Their expansionist nature has caused them to engage in inter-ethnic conflicts with their neighbours, namely the Murle, Anuak, Shilluk, Dinka and the Ethiopian ethnic groups (Evans-Pritchard, 1940; Kelly, 1985; Reinton, 1971). Nuer are mainly cattle keepers and crop growers, and their inter-ethnic conflicts arise due to competition for natural resources such as grazing land and water (Kelly, 1985). In the South Sudan Jonglei state, the Nuer clashed with the Shilluk over land in the Pigio area. These land conflicts were due to the fact that from 1955 to 2005, civil wars displaced the Shilluk from their homeland, Pigio area, which became occupied by the Nuer (Bedigen, 2017). This land grab made the majority Shilluk landless, so their youth joined the rebellion with the hope of regaining their lost land after the war. In addition, up to about 700 Jablin Shilluk were massacred at the peak of the civil war in 1990. With the promise that the 2005 Comprehensive Peace Agreement offered, some Shilluk sought to return to their homeland, which had been occupied by other ethnic communities, including the Nuer.

In August 1991, during the course of the second civil war, a split within the SPLA along ethnic divides led to the formation of two rebel groups under the Nuer and the Dinka, therefore fuelling Dinka–Nuer inter-ethnic conflicts (Jok and Hutchinson, 1999). Samuel Gai Tut's successor, Abdallah Chuol, moved deep into Nuer land, setting up new rebel camps and recruiting more Nuer youth to avenge Samuel Gai Tut's loss. They launched many attacks against the SPLM/A or Dinka. It was during one of these conflicts in 1985 that Abdallah Chuol was killed. Nevertheless, his successor continued fighting the SPLM/A (Dinka). With the initial motive of fighting their common enemy, the Arab Muslims, forgotten, both groups blamed and accused each other of tribalism (Rights, 1997). In addition, their involvement in numerous wars is linked to the collective nature of these communities (Jabs, 2014). Jabs explains that conflict between two people can become a community conflict due to individuals' responsibilities and duties to the group and vice versa. Based on historical accounts, the nature of the South Sudan civil war is rooted in the historical conflicts between the major two ethnic groups, i.e. Nuer and Dinka. Because their kinship/relationship and political ideas are deeply intertwined with conflict tendencies, finding a sustainable resolution has been a challenge. Thus, it creates a need to explore the role of kinship/relationship in indigenous peacebuilding—something that this book will deal with in later chapters.

Anuak Involvement in Inter-ethnic Conflicts and Civil War

Like the Nuer, the Anuak (Anywaa or Anyuak) people live in two countries: the South Sudan Jonglei region and the Gambella region in Ethiopia, where the majority live (Bacon, 1922; Evans-Pritchard, 1940; Kurimoto, 1996). At times referred to as riverine people, the Anuak settlements spread in between rivers and across both countries. This riverbank settlement has shaped their settlements, economic activities, political and social engagements with neighbours. This region is a lavish, productive, self-sustaining land. It is a hostile environment with very limited government investment. Historically, their socio-political organisation is under nobles (*nyieya*) and village headmen (*kwaaro*). Nobles and village headmen are also referred to as 'fathers of the land and river' (Kurimoto, 1996:47). It is believed its borderline nature has at times deterred Ethiopian and South Sudanese governments from maintaining direct authority over the region. While it is true that the majority of Anuak communities in South Sudan remain underdeveloped, this is not the case for Ethiopian (Gambella) Anuak. The 1974 social revolution in Ethiopia led to the general infrastructural development and education of the Gambella Anuak. For example, the introduction of cotton farms and the construction of a dam on the Aluoro River were developmental and exploitative. The reason being, other ethnic groups, the Tigre and Kambata, respectively, were resettled in Anuak land, along the Baro and Giilo Rivers (Kurimoto, 1996). Consequently, many Anuak traditional institutions and customs (nobles and village headmen) were abolished as they were deemed unprogressive.

Generally, with limited infrastructural development compared to the rest of South Sudan, the security status in Anuak communities remains precarious (Reinton, 1971). As such, the majority of Anuak have continued to survive on indigenous economic activities such as pastoralism, cultivation, fishing, hunting and foraging (Kurimoto, 1996; Jok et al., 2004). In South Sudan, their experiences of historical cattle raids, kidnapping and forced evacuation from their traditional land influenced their engagement in inter-ethnic conflicts (Lacey, 2013). Their settlements and cultivation along the rivers' inner curve (*Cwiay-gol*) has particular significance in the socio-cultural sustenance of the Anuak economy and peace values. *Cwiay-gol* is a combined word: cwiny (liver) and gol (another word for riverbank) (Kurimoto, 1996:46). Also, their existence along the borders appears to have shaped their peace cultures in two ways. First, the Anyuak prevented direct engagement in conflicts by crossing over and taking refuge in safer areas, either Ethiopia or South Sudan. However, the disadvantage of such existence is seen in how their neighbours perceive them. For example, in the Gambella region of Ethiopia, the indigenous ethnic communities continued to view Anuak as weak aliens. As such, they were continuously subjected to persecution and killings. Second, neighbourhood aggressions caused them to give up cattle keeping but maintained crop growing (Jok et al., 2004). Their decision to abandon livestock farming and cross over to safer borders whenever the need arises signifies conflict prevention for co-existence. This practice can be productive in indigenous peacebuilding.

During the civil war, both the Sudanese and Ethiopian government forces, including various rebel groups, camped in Anuak territory (Bedigen, 2017). The occupation of Gambella land by both refugees and the SPLA from South Sudan led to a formation of a political wing, the Gambella People's Liberation Movement (GPLF). They manipulated and armed Anuak youth as well as their neighbours (the Murle and Nuer) and encouraged ethnic groups to fight each other or join the rebel movements. The Anuak initially fought against the SPLA dominance but later joined them. While the Anuak did not have any political reason for joining the rebels, i.e. the SPLM/A, they did so much later with the hope of benefiting from security and defence for their homeland. According to the Anuak Justice Council report (2012), the Anuak joined the second Sudanese civil war (1983–2005) to fight for freedom.

Nyerere (1968:12) describes this situation as 'a philosophy of inevitable conflict between man and man.' Also, the Anuak fought the inter-ethnic conflicts with the Murle in 1973 and with the Nuer in 1983. During the 17-year long war, the first Sudan civil war, many Anuak lost their lives. When the war ended, the survivors did not have access to education or other social services. Neither did the community directly benefit from the regional political posts created. Significantly, to the Anuak, the success of this war and the signing of the CPA agreement, which stipulated a security protocol for all ethnic groups, were steps in the right direction. It raised their hope that the new South Sudanese government would protect the entire Anuak community.

In this section, I have highlighted inter-ethnic aggression and violence as well as co-existence. Issues of identity, politics, society and economics remain the main drivers of inter-ethnic conflicts that have fed into the numerous civil wars. In South Sudan, it was initially a Dinka–Nuer dominated inter-ethnic conflict and civil war. Sooner or later, other ethnic communities, such as the Acholi, the Anuak and other minority communities, joined the civil war, fought for and made demands based on both historical discontentment and perceived contemporary opportunities. This resulted in an ethnic claim for religious and cultural rights, equal economic and political opportunities, including self-determination. Although self-determination was gained in 2005 and political opportunity through independence in 2011, ethnic communities, mainly the Dinka and Nuer, continue to demand and fight each other for economic and political domination. These caused another Dinka–Nuer inter-ethnic conflict and the 2013 civil war (de Waal, 2014; Grawert, 2014; de Vries and Schomerus, 2017b).

Next, I explore the course of the civil war.

Civil War

> We the Nilotics have always fought each other for the same reasons you see today: mistreatment, exploitation, prejudice, grabbing land, cattle and now oil. We live in our communities under our kings' and/or chiefs' leadership. They are responsible for wars and peace.
>
> Particularly the Nuer and the Dinka are known as people with a very egalitarian social organization. The Nuer are the product of hard egalitarian upbringing, deeply democratic, and easily roused to violence. They live in an ordered anarchy. The social organization is well matched to the personal character they have developed, for, as he says:

'it is impossible to live among the Nuer and conceive of rulers ruling over them.'

(Reinton, 1971:241)

Since 1955 and before they gained independence from Sudan in 2011, the Southern Sudanese faced and participated in extended Sudan civil wars (Grawert, 2014). The causes of conflicts can be traced back to colonial influence, ethnicity, religions, oppression, discrimination, slavery, economic marginalisation and political dominance of the northern Arabs over the southern black Africans. Poku and Mdee (2014:12), in their book *Politics in Africa*, indicated that colonialism brought with it and legitimised 'the politics of dominance to be pursued against people of difference.' Reinton (1971:240) suggests that the colonial masters' 'vertical economy' was intended to exploit South Sudan. Minority Southern Sudanese ethnic groups still experience dominance by major ethnic groups such as the Dinka and Nuer. These major groups are well managed under indigenous institutions, even during the wars (Reinton, 1971). Adding, Wibo's account above raises a question that members do not seem to understand why the war is not given a local interpretation but referred to as a civil war. Bedigen (2017) indicates that a joint pastoral letter, aimed to coincide with the first anniversary of independence on 9 July 2012, identified four ongoing wars in South Sudan.

Conflicts that the *Sudan Tribune* (2012) refer to as 'the three civil wars' include:

i) Inter-ethnic conflicts in the Jonglei (fought between the Dinka, Nuer, Anuak and other minor ethnic groups). According to the United Nations (2005) and Human Rights Watch (2015) reports, these conflicts claimed up to 1.5 million fled their homes and up to 100,000 people sheltered by the United Nations.
ii) The Darfur conflicts since 2003.
iii) Wars in the South Kordofan (Nuba Mountains) and the Blue Nile took place from 2011.

The South Sudan civil war is infamous when examining contemporary conflicts; therefore, it deserves special attention in exploring its origins and interlinkages with ethnic conflicts. Although South Sudanese ethnic communities have fought in numerous conflicts, major wars include the first Sudanese civil war, which took place between 1956 and 1972; the second civil war from 1983 to 2005; the third 2010 civil war and the 2013 civil war. All these civil wars are linked to the first civil war that was settled through conventional approaches without addressing ethnic conflict causes. But this approach has never brought peace to South Sudan. Interpreting South Sudan's violence or conflict as a political conflict fails to acknowledge the less visible indigenous causes of violence and oppression that the majority of South Sudanese have historically experienced. Primarily, it is these less visible forms of indigenous causes that need to be addressed. The spotlight on the political differences and the need to rebuild peace between warring political parties excludes communities from being part of the solution. Also, the failure to recognise other types of localised peacebuilding approaches makes South Sudan a hostile environment to communities.

When South Sudanese failed to realise what the Sudanese (Khartoum) government had promised to deliver through the international-led Addis Ababa Agreement at the end of the first civil war, they could not think of any way forward other than fighting. Therefore, in 1983, the Sudanese People's Liberation Movement/Army (SPLM/A) constituted of defected South Sudanese army generals, commanders and officers from Sudanese forces. They initiated the Sudan second civil war. Their initial target was to destroy all forms of Khartoum/Arab/Muslim government representation in the Christian black African Southern Sudan. They did this by disabling government infrastructures and personnel. After that, the destruction of government structures, personnel and civilians became the trend. These targeted attacks are similar to the 2013 civil war, resulting in the majority of indigenous people losing trust in the government's ability to meet their needs (Branch and Mampilly, 2005; de Waal, 2014; De Vries and Schomerus, 2017). Therefore, as indicated by Bradbury et al. (2006), and in interviewees' account, communities continued to draw from their indigenous institutions, customs and practices to govern themselves.

Following the SPLM/A formation, de Waal and Flint (2005), various rebel groups such as the Sudan Liberation Movement (SLA/M), Justice and Equality Movement (JEM), South Sudan Independent Movement/Army (SSIM/A) and many others emerged to fight the Khartoum government over the marginalisation issues mentioned earlier. These rebel groups waged war on towns and government infrastructures such as police stations, killing hundreds of police officers. Such violent bandit activity makes the South Sudan situation fit well into the definition of civil war given by Wallensteen (2004:131), as a 'conflict concerning the control over government' but also characterised by 'armed conflict ..., short-lived rebellions, actions by militias, armed gangs, bands, ... and ... freedom movements.' Given these, John Garang, the SPLA founder himself, acknowledged this problem. He was quoted as having said that they, the SPLA, 'did not start as a movement in the classical way of Latin American liberation movements ... we started as a mob' (Rights, 1997:63; de Wall, 2014). In 1983, SPLA became the major rebel group fighting against the Khartoum government and the most internationally recognised group to engage in peace negotiations. However, such mob formations sparked a wave of localised conflicts, at times, under the umbrella of fighting for all South Sudanese freedom. This early story of ethnic survival and political ambitions demonstrates ethnic–civil war complexities, whose resolution continues to challenge efforts of conventional peacebuilding.

For instance, in the 2013 civil war, wrangles within the governing Sudan People's Liberation Movement (SPLM) and its army, the Sudan People's Liberation Army (SPLA), caused its split into political factions characterised by ethnic clashes (Branch and Mampilly, 2005; Deng, 2013). The major group, led by President Salva Kiir, remained in charge of the government and the national army. At the same time, Riek Machar, the former vice president, became the SPLM-in Opposition (SPLM/A-IO) leader. This party comprised a coalition of military commanders. Attempts to build peace between these two groups, nationally, included the signing of numerous unsuccessful ceasefires, which were mainly influenced by the international community (De Vries and Schomerus, 2017). In August 2005, warring parties were pressured to sign a power-sharing agreement on the Conflict Resolution in the Republic of South Sudan (ARCSS) (Richmond, 2001). Only two warring parties were recognised and engaged in the peace processes; thus, violence continued. While some scholars (de Waal, 2014; De Vries and Schomerus, 2017; Justin and De Vries, 2019) demonstrate that this was a politicised ethnic Dinka–Nuer conflict, peacebuilding along these lines proved unsustainable. The failure of the international community to recognise the existence of other minor warring groups, except the SPLM/A (Dinka-led) as the sovereign government and the SPLM/A-IO (Nuer-led) as the rebels, meant that indigenous institutions, customs and practices became excluded in the peacebuilding processes.

Interviewee, Gwort, in his narrative, describes his experience with the militias that fit into the civil war definitions given earlier.

> The militia groups claimed they would maintain law and order, get rid of witches, rustlers that came to the villages. However, they displayed a lot of violence, killings, raiding, rape, mutilation. They also made revenge killings. My Dad voluntarily provided them with food, and they often told him, 'ah, old man, we do not have any problem with you'. It was a messy situation; some of them came from Chad. Most of them died in the bush, including their commanders.
>
> (Gwort, 2 December 2013)

Gwort's account above reveals that rebel/militia groups caused losses to the Khartoum government, non-government institutions and civilians. These groups exhibited violence, as well as causing untold suffering and the destruction of property and civilian livelihoods (Jok and Hutchinson, 1999). Militia groups recruited by the government to suppress the rebellion committed similar atrocities. Wherever these groups showed up, they inflicted violence through vengeance, historical divisions and notoriety. The crimes they committed include (1) sexually related crimes such as rape, defilement, kidnap and abduction; (2) physical harm-related disputes, for example, indiscriminate killings, assault, beating and mutilation; (3) property-related disputes including raid, bandits or mafia; vandalism; theft and ownership of (land, cattle) rights. Civilians who could not face the horrors of war escaped to neighbouring countries; some returned after South Sudan gained its independence in 2011 (Grawert, 2014). Note that both the government and rebel groups committed war crimes, crimes against humanity and crimes against human rights. As such, the locals view both the government and the opposition as being opposed to peace (De Vries and Schomerus, 2017:336). The less known, however, is the significance of indigenous methods in preventing such crimes and rebuilding peace. The civil wars in total cost over 3 million lives due to famine, disease and fighting. It displaced over 2 million people to the neighbouring countries of Congo, Kenya, Uganda, Ethiopia, Central African Republic and Chad (Prunier, 2005; Iyob and Khadiagala, 2006). More recently, the 2013 civil war caused immense losses (oil production reduced to 30%, 100,000 malnourished, 1.9 million displaced and according to UN reports, left up to 6.4 million people in need of humanitarian assistance) (Rolandsen et al., 2015).

Moreover, some of these militia groups were not of South Sudanese origin but were from neighbouring countries and descended into South Sudan to take advantage of the chaotic situation (Hamilton, 2012). Schneckener and Wolff (2004:2) refer to this kind of group or conflicts as 'transnational minorities.' Such examples include the Lord's Resistance Army (LRA), which originates from Uganda. This particular group is significant here because, at times, it operates among the Acholi communities of South Sudan, and some of its ex-combatants have been re-integrated into the community through the Acholi indigenous peacebuilding system, the Mato Oput (Bedigen, 2017, 2019; Ochola, 2009).

Conflicts with transnational migrating groups, the influx of modern small arms, underdevelopment and marginalisation claims gave the rebels easy recruitment from within certain border tribes/clans. This is because, in the Nilotic cultures, blood relations must be supported, protected and maintained at all costs. In support of this, Shorter (1974) indicates that, in East African societies all members of traditional communities pay clan loyalties and that this would explain easy internal recruitment. De Waal and Flint (2005) adds to this argument by indicating that other factors such as drought, aridity and the support of rebel groups by neighbouring countries such as Eritrea, Uganda and Libya highly intensified the conflict. By the end of 2006, there were 12 rebel splinter groups in Darfur alone, most of whom were motivated to fight the Government (People–State) as well as other tribes (People–People) on self-interest motives rather than the common good, sovereignty. Further, by the end of the second Sudan civil war, there were over 30 such splinter rebel groups in South Sudan (Bedigen, 2017; de Waal and Flint, 2005).

African writers such as wa Thiongo expressed their views at around the time many African countries were fighting for independence from their colonisers. These writers' life experiences made them very critical of the western system and blamed every problem facing Africa, mostly conflicts, on colonialism. For instance, six decades since Sudan gained independence from its colonisers and Sudan's first civil war, scholars blame colonialism for conflict causes and failed resolution attempts. While colonialism is a historical burden, six decades since Sudan gained its independence is far too long a time to keep apportioning blame to colonisers. For example, the major ethnic communities (Dinka and Nuer) have continued to marginalise their minority counterparts. In the understanding of indigenous peacebuilding, this is contrary to the African concept of togetherness or brotherhood that encourages co-existence. It is acknowledged that ethnic conflicts and civil wars have affected generations and caused some changes in South Sudanese peace cultures. However, valuable indigenous peacebuilding practices remain effective at grassroots levels. Therefore, their usefulness at higher or national levels ought to be rediscovered.

Civilians who could not face the horrors of war escaped to neighbouring countries; some returned after South Sudan gained its independence in 2011 (Grawert, 2014;). Note that both the government and rebel groups committed war crimes against humanity and crimes against human rights. As such, the locals view both the government and the opposition as opposed to peace (De Vries and Schomerus, 2017:336). The less known, however, is the significance of indigenous methods in preventing such crimes and rebuilding peace. The civil wars in total cost over 3 million lives due to famine, disease and fighting. It displaced over 2 million people to Congo, Kenya, Uganda, Ethiopia, the Central African Republic and Chad (Prunier, 2005; Iyob and Khadiagala, 2006). More recently, the 2013 civil war caused immense losses (oil production reduced to 30%, 100,000 malnourished, 1.9 million displaced and according to UN reports, left up to 6.4 million people in need of humanitarian assistance) (Rolandsen et al., 2015).

Further, conflicts with transnational migrating groups, the influx of modern small arms, underdevelopment and marginalisation claims gave the rebels easy access to recruit from certain border tribes/clans. The reason is, in the Nilotic cultures, blood relations must be supported, protected and maintained at all costs. In support of this, Shorter (1974) indicates that, in East African societies, all members of traditional communities pay clan loyalties and that this would explain easy internal recruitment. Adding, de Waal and Flint (2005) argue that other factors such as drought, aridity and rebel groups supported by neighbouring countries such as Eritrea, Uganda and Libya highly intensified the conflict. By the end of 2006, there were 12 rebel splinter groups in Darfur alone. Most of them were motivated to fight the Government (People–State) as well as other tribes (People–People) on self-interest motives rather than the common good, sovereignty. Further, by the end of the second Sudan civil war, there were over 30 such splinter rebel groups in South Sudan (Bedigen, 2017; de Waal and Flint, 2005).

The arguments above highlight many contributors and dimensions to the civil wars—ranging from political, economic, social to cross-border (Poku and Mdee 2011). Wa Thiongo who attributes the inter-ethnic conflicts puts one other interesting argument forward and the civil war causes to the breakdown in culture through language. Indigenous peace values are communicated through cultures and languages. Scholars claim that, because the groups under analysis speak quite similar languages, they experienced communication breakdown at the introduction of the English language as the *lingua franca* (Bedigen, 2017; Reinton, 1971; wa Thiongo, 1986). Wa Thiongo explains that colonialism and imperialism instituted a breakdown in African cultures through western education, subsequently creating a negative attitude towards the traditional institutions, customs and practices. Thus, making them incapable of dealing with the new challenges communities face in the post-colonial era. Poku and Mdee (2011:13) add to this by indicating that throughout Africa, colonisers constructed education systems that served their own economic interests, not the continent's. In particular, wa Thiongo speaks of his school life experiences and writes that speaking his native language (Kiguyu at school) carried heavy punishment. He adds that those pupils who failed English by default failed their overall exams. He writes about his school friend who passed all his subjects with distinction but failed the written English language and therefore could not continue school education. He became a taxi driver, a poorly paid job, and this was because he could not be admitted to any higher institution.

Conclusion

While authors, such as Prunier (2005:76–80) and de Waal and Flint (2005:64), identify these conflicts as 'People–State' and 'People–People' conflicts, it is important to note that members of the ethnic communities under study were perpetrators or victims or both. It appears that the South Sudan civil war experiences are similar to the Rwandan genocide experience indicated in Mamdani's book *When Victims Become Killers* (Mamdani, 2001). Communities' involvement and conflict causes are best illustrated in Complexities of inter-ethnic conflicts and civil wars (Figure 1.2). In such a situation, the assumption is that indigenous methods, something that the communities understand and believe, are the most ideal.

In conclusion, then, drifting from Sudan (the origins of South Sudan's civil wars) and refocusing on South Sudan, three key issues emerge from this chapter. One, the ethnic and civil war causes are similar. Two, civil wars have been highly politicised, yet ethnic conflicts largely influence them. Three, the national peacebuilding processes have been majorly foreign or regional led. Of the many civil wars mentioned earlier, a minimal attempt has been made to distinguish between the conflicts and timelines

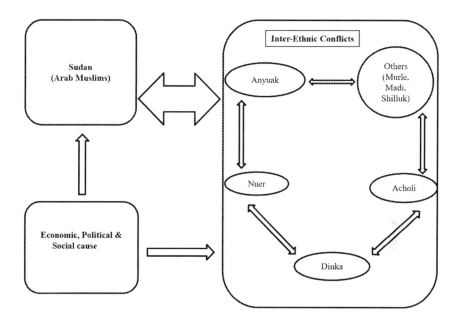

Figure 1.2 The Complexity of Sudan Inter-Ethnic Conflicts and Civil Wars 1983–2013

because (1) many conflicts and civil wars occurred concurrently (2) civil wars and other related conflicts exhibited similar criminal outcomes and (3) this investigation examines the Nilotic Lwo indigenous peacebuilding methods evidenced in institutional customs and practices of conflict prevention, peacemaking and peacebuilding. Any deviation from this core aim will widen the scope of the study. Therefore, this study focuses on the events from 1983, a time when conflicts became more intense, and several resolution attempts, including international, regional, NGO-led grassroots peace works and some indigenous processes, were not holistically implemented. The discussions will highlight these attempts. However, the next chapter provides us with the grounding into peace theories and indigenous peace approaches.

Bibliography

Allen, T., 1994. Ethnicity and tribalism on the Sudan-Uganda border. In K. Fukui and J. Markakis (Eds.), *Ethnicity and Conflict in the Horn of Africa* (pp. 112–139). London, James Currey.

Anuak Justice Council, 2012. *Anuak Justice Council Accuses Juba of 'Secrete Cooperation' with the Ethiopian Government; Urges President Kiir to Protect Anuaks*. Vancouver, BC, South Sudan News Agency.

Atkinson, R.R., 1994. *The Roots of Ethnicity: The Origins of the Acholi of Uganda before 1800.* Philadelphia, PA, University of Pennsylvania Press.
Bacon, C.R.K., 1922. The Anuak. *Sudan Notes and Records*, 5(3), pp. 113–129.
Bedigen, W., 2017. Traditional conflict resolution: The Nilotic Lwo of South Sudan (PhD thesis). Leeds, Leeds Beckett University.
Bedigen, W., 2020. Significance of societal customs in the South Sudan Civil War resolution. *Journal of Peacebuilding and Development*, 15(1), pp. 3–17.
Blumberg, H.H., Hare, A.P. and Costin, A., 2006. *Peace Psychology. A Comprehensive Introduction.* Cambridge, Cambridge University Press.
Bradbury, M., Ryle, J., Medley, M. and Sansculotte-Greenidge, K., 2006. *Local Peace Processes in Sudan: A Baseline Study.* London, Rift Valley Institute.
Branch, A. and Mampilly, Z.C., 2005. Winning the war, but losing the peace? The dilemma of SPLM/A civil administration and the tasks ahead. *The Journal of Modern African Studies*, 43(1), pp. 1–20.
Cashmore, E. and Rojek, C., 1999. *Dictionary of Cultural Theorists.* London, Hodder Arnold.
Collins, R.O., 1960. Patrols against the beirs. *Sudan Notes and Records*, XLI, pp. 35–59.
Collins, R.O., 1971. *Land Beyond the Rivers: The Southern Sudan, 1898–1918.* New Haven, CT, Yale University Press.
Crazzolara, J.P., 1950. *Lwoo Migrations.* Verona, Missioni Africane.
Crazzolara, J.P., 1951. *The Lwoo: Lwoo Traditions.* Verona, Missioni Africane.
de Vries, L. and Schomerus, M., 2017a. Fettered self-determination: South Sudan's narrowed path to secession. *Civil Wars*, 19(1), pp. 26–45.
de Vries, L. and Schomerus, M., 2017b. South Sudan's civil war will not end with a peace deal. *Peace Review*, 29(3), pp. 333–340.
de Waal, A., 2014. When kleptocracy becomes insolvent: Brute causes of the civil war in South Sudan. *African Affairs*, 113(452), pp. 347–369.
Deng, F.M., 1995. *War of Visions: Conflict of Identities in the Sudan.* Washington, DC, Brookings Institution.
Deng, L.A., 2013. *The Power of Creative Reasoning: The Ideas and Vision of John Garang.* Bloomington, IN, iUniverse.
Evans-Pritchard, E.E., 1940. The Nuer. Oxford. Hassoum, I. 1952: 'Western' migration and settlement in the Gezira. *Sudan Notes and Records*, XXXIII, pp. 60–113.
Flint, J. and De Waal, A., 2005. Darfur. In *A Short History of a Long War.* London, Zed Books.
Flint, J. and De Waal, A., 2008. *Darfur: A Short History of a Long War.* New York, Zed Books.
Grawert, E., 2014. *Forging Two Nations Insights on Sudan and South Sudan.* Addis Ababa, OSSREA.
Hamilton, A., 2012. *South Sudan-Sudan Relations in the Light of Current Conflicts and Border Disputes.*
Ineba, B.-M., 2000. *A Cultural Approach to Conflict Transformation: An African Traditional Experience.* Term Paper. Written for the Course: "Culture of Peace and Education" taught at the European Peace University. Austria, Stadtschlaining.
Iyob, R. and Khadiagala, G.M., 2006. *Sudan: The Elusive Quest for Peace.* Boulder, CO, Lynne Rienner Publishers.

Jabs, L.B., 2014. 'No monkey destroys his forest': A review of traditional African interpersonal conflict management. *Journal of Global Peace and Conflict*, 2(1), pp. 1–24.

Johnson, D.H. and Anderson, D.M., 1995. *The Prophet Ngundeng and the Battle of Pading. Revealing Prophets: Prophecy in Eastern African History.* Oxford, James Currey Publishers.

Johnson, D.H., 2003. *The Root Causes of Sudan's Civil Wars.* Oxford, James Currey Publishers.

Jok, J.M. and Hutchinson, S.E., 1999. Sudan's prolonged second civil war and the militarization of Nuer and Dinka ethnic identities. *African Studies Review*, 42(2), pp. 125–145.

Jok, A.A., Leitch, A.R. and Vandewint, C., 2004. *A Study of Customary Law in Contemporary Southern Sudan.* Rumbek, South Sudan, World Vision International.

Justin, P.H. and De Vries, L., 2019. Governing unclear lines: Local boundaries as a (re) source of conflict in south Sudan. *Journal of Borderlands Studies*, 34(1), pp. 31–46.

Kamwaria, A. and Katola, M., 2012. The role of African traditional religion, culture and world-view in the context of post-war healing among the Dinka community of Southern Sudan. *International Journal of Humanities and Social Science*, 2(21), pp. 49–55.

Kelly, R.C., 1985. *The Nuer Conquest: The Structure and Development of an Expansionist System.* Ann Arbor, MI, University of Michigan Press.

Kok, L.F., 2011, Nuer-Dinka animosity: Tension between Nuer and Dinka is nothing new. *South Sudan News*. Sudan.

Kurimoto, E., 1996. People of the river: Subsistence economy of the Anywaa (Anuak) of Western Ethiopia. *Senri Ethnological Studies*, 43, pp. 29–57.

Lacey, L., 2013. Women for cows: An analysis of abductions of women in South Sudan. *Agenda*, 27(4), pp. 91–108.

Laremont, R.R., 2002. *The Causes of War and the Consequences of Peacekeeping in Africa.* Portsmouth, N.H.: Heinemann.

Leff, J. and LeBrun, E., 2014. *Following the Thread: Arms and Ammunition Tracing in Sudan and South Sudan* Geneva, Switzerland, Small Arms Survey.

Mamdani, M., 2001. *When Victims Become Killers: Colonialism, Nativism, and the Genocide in Rwanda.* Princeton, NJ, Princeton University Press.

Mbiti, J.S., 1970. *Concepts of God in Africa.* London, SPCK.

Nna, D.N.J. and Pabon, B.G., 2012. Arms proliferation and conflicts in Africa: The Sudan experience. *Editorial Board*, 210, 233.

Nyerere, J.K., 1968. *Ujamaa–Essays on Socialism* (Vol. 359). Dar es Salaam, Oxford University Press.

Ochola, M., 2009.The spear and the bead in Luo history and culture. *Nile Journal*. Retrieved from http://nilejournal.net/culture/society/spear-bead-luo-history-culture.

Poku, N. and Mdee, A., 2014. *Politics in Africa: A New Introduction.* London, Zed Books.

Prunier, G., 2005. *Darfur: The Ambiguous Genocide.* London, Hurst & Company.

Reinton, P.O., 1971. Imperialism and the southern Sudan. *Journal of Peace Research*, 8(3–4), pp. 239–247.

Richmond, O., 2001. *Maintaining Order, Making Peace*. London, Palgrave Macmillan.
Rights, A., 1997. *Food and Power in Sudan: A Critique of Humanitarianism*. London, African Rights.
Rolandsen, Ø.H., Glomnes, H.M., Manoeli, S. and Nicolaisen, F., 2015. A year of South Sudan's third civil war. *International Area Studies Review*, 18(1), pp. 87–104.
Sawant, A.B., 1998. Ethnic conflict in Sudan in historical perspective. *International Studies*, 35(3), pp. 343–363.
Schneckener, U. and Wolff, S. (Eds.), 2004. *Managing and Settling Ethnic Conflicts: Perspectives on Success and Failures in Europe, Africa and Asia*. London, Hurst & Co.
Shorter, A., 1974. *East African Societies*. London, Routledge and Kegan Paul.
wa Thiong'o, N., 1986. *Writing against Neocolonialism*. Nairobi, Vita Books.
wa Thiong'o, N., 1993. *Moving the Center: The Struggle for Cultural Freedoms*. Suffolk, Boydell & Brewer.
Wallensteen, P., 2004. *Understanding Conflict Resolution: War, Peace and the Global System*. London, Sage.
Wolff, S., 2007. Ethnic conflict. In *A Global Perspective*. Oxford, Oxford University, p. 220.
Wunlit Peace and Reconciliation Conference, 1999. *Appendix: Wunlit Recommendations on Abductions*. From the Dinka Nuer West Bank Peace and Reconciliation Conference in Wunlit, March 1999. Retrieved from http://southsudanfriends.org/wunlit/index.html [Accessed: 2 March 2013].
Zanen, S.M. and van den Hoek, A.W., 1987. Dinka dualism and the Nilotic hierarchy of values. In R. de Ridder and J.A.J. Karremans (Eds.), *The Leiden Tradition in Structural Anthropology*. Leiden, Brill, pp. 170–196.

List of Interviews Cited in the Text

Interview with Wibo, 2012
Interview with Mosa, 4 May 2013
Interview with Gwort, 2 December 2013

2 Indigenous Peacebuilding, Peace Theories and the South Sudan Justice System

Introduction

This chapter aims to familiarise the reader with the indigenous approaches to peace. It begins by demonstrating the Nilotic Lwo understanding of peacebuilding which focuses on societal customs, beliefs and practices. It will argue that indigenous institutions and customary practices such as ceremonies and rituals are marginalised or under-represented concepts in conventional grassroots peace theories considered in this book. Exploration of indigenous institutions, customs and practices will contribute to knowledge in this area, suggesting a holistic approach.

Next, to help identify research gaps, it will review the literature on the current theories on grassroots peace approaches propounded by Lederach (1997), Galtung (1996) and Ramsbotham et al. (2005). Also, this chapter will utilise a cultural theory lens to give an understanding of the limitations of the above peace theories. It will argue that the pragmatic nature of Nilotic Lwo peace cultures, which is missing in the above theories, is significant in delivering sustainable peace. Further, the chapter will provide an overview of the South Sudan justice system that starts from customary law courts and will argue it demonstrates the potential for indigenous transitional justice systems relevant to the civil war situation.

Context

Understanding Indigenous Peacebuilding

In the introductory chapter of this book, we looked at why the need for indigenous peacebuilding in South Sudan. This section provides an understanding of what Nilotic indigenous peacebuilding constitutes. The word indigenous is applied to the native norms of cultural beliefs and practices indicated in Mbiti (1970), and the word traditional is applied to the native norms that have evolved over time (Jok et al., 2004; Bradbury et al., 2006). Indigenous peacebuilding begins with community norms and values (Shorter, 1974), and all concepts discussed in this book are indigenous or native cultural peace practices. This book conceptualises indigenous peacebuilding

DOI: 10.4324/9781003133476-3

situations in communities emerging from inter-ethnic conflicts and civil wars. It identifies and conceptualises the 'indigene-centric' or the core set of indigenous institutions, customs and practices that underpin the historical and foundational peace values in the Nilotic Lwo ethnic cultures and the South Sudan justice system. The argument is made that indigenous peacebuilding is mainly responsible for ethnic co-existence and sustainable peace that can apply to civil war situations and/or at national levels. Note that some of the concepts have been modernised by the locals to suit modern conflicts over the years. Thus, this book describes indigenous peacebuilding as a situation where the past–present knowledge, experiences, cultures and root causes of conflicts are considered when determining conciliation.

In agreement with Okot p'Bitek (1966), African and/or Nilotic Lwo traditional conflict resolution practices are deeply rooted in these communities' social-cultural, economic and political organs (see Figure 2.1). Historically, they have been utilised in grassroots peacemaking in and between communities that have lived in hostility and co-existence. Particularly in South Sudan, they are based on societal customs that include three main features: customary laws, beliefs and practices of a given ethnic community (Jok et al., 2004). An important factor revealed in the interviewees' stories is that the victim's customs, beliefs and practices are often applied in intra-ethnic and inter-ethnic conflict situations. Using the victim's societal customs demonstrates the uniqueness of the Nilotic (Lwo) traditional methods and offers satisfactory justice to the victim. In theoretical conceptualisation, this view agrees with the cultural theories that history, past experiences, cultures, beliefs, practices, values and consciousness are significant

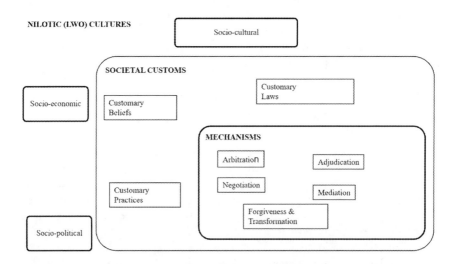

Figure 2.1 An Illustration of Nilotic Lwo Conflict Resolution Foundations

Indigenous Approaches to Peace 37

in resolving contemporary issues (Asante, 2003). This is contrary to a western-style justice system, where the most articulated argument wins, regardless of the truth. The victim's team is less articulate, which leads to further injustice.

While the Nilotic Lwo indigenous peacebuilding is foundational to the socio-economic, socio-political and socio-cultural organs, it is essential to note that the basic requirements for the process to commence are victim/offender, dispute/crime and family/community or representative.

This book considers indigenous peacebuilding as a process in which disputants narrate their stories and utilise their cultural norms (institutions, customs and practices) in resolving the root causes of their incompatibilities, giving the victim's culture precedence over the aggressor's in deadlock situations. More specifically, the process must adhere to the disputants' art of communication, ethics, interactions, networks, acknowledgement of wrong deeds and agreeable forms of justice. In the Nilotic Lwo, peace institutions and the nature of the dispute conform to an integrative bottom-up approach present within the indigenous structure itself. From bottom to top, it includes peer-to-peer, family head/elder, clan head/elder or village chief, sub-chief/inter-clan or inter-ethnic and up to executive chief or king level, the highest authority. Thus, peacebuilding mechanisms can be applied one at a time at the various court levels (see Figures 2.2 and 2.3).

Figure 2.2 The Basic Requirements for Indigenous Peacebuilding

38 Indigenous Approaches to Peace

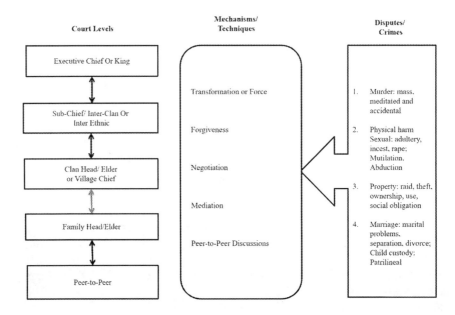

Figure 2.3 The Nilotic Lwo Indigenous Peacebuilding System

The Concept of Time in Indigenous Peacebuilding

Indigenous system embodies the past, present and future. In the Nilotic peace cultures, the past is believed to influence the present and the future; thus, the past must be central in any peace decisions (Nkyabonaki, 2019). For instance, Ogot (1999:180) elaborates that the Nilotic Lwo 'like any other people have always thought about the past as reflected in the present and as a basis for predicting the future.' Mbiti (1969:17) writes:

> *Actual time* is therefore what is present and what is past. It moves 'backward' rather than 'forward'; and people set their minds not on future things, but chiefly in what has taken place.

Whereas Kalumba (2005:11) refers to Mbiti's two-dimensional concepts of time—*Zamani* and *Saza*—as key in the African concept of time and that an indefinite past, present and infinite future are the three-dimensional western concepts of time, in indigenous peacebuilding, the past, present and future are interconnected. This implies that once a conflict occurs, a solution is sought in view of the community/clan/family/individual's history, laws, beliefs, practices and the incident. All these contribute to the Nilotic concept of time, an event rather than algorithmic. Unlike the linear and timed peace processes in conventional approaches (Darby and Mac, 2002), the connection between present-to-past and present-to-future (Figure 2.2) is significant

Indigenous Approaches to Peace 39

in indigenous processes but less understood in conventional peace processes (Bedigen, 2017).

Work by authors such as Mbiti (1969, 1970) and Ogot (1999) suggests the significance of time and reflection. Times off, during the indigenous conflict resolution process, give disputants space to reflect on their attitude and behaviour towards each other in relation to what is at stake—the future. Galtung considers attitude and behaviour key factors in peacebuilding, and Lederach (1996) supports the idea of separation. Allowing time and space to think is essential for spiritual healing in the Nilotic Lwo indigenous peace processes. It also implies that true justice can never be realised unless time has been taken to understand the history of the conflict and consideration of appropriate measures. Also, the African understanding of time as 'not to run anywhere' helps focus on problem-solving rather than solutions (Olupona and Nyang, 2013). Overall, time allows for reflection, consultation and involvement of the supernatural being in an indigenous peace process. The time frame of indigenous peacebuilding is packed with socialising events. In the Nilotic Lwo culture, it is not the actual time (algorithms) that matters most but the composition of events that happened, their effects and what must be accomplished, for example, ceremonies, rituals, dancing, wrestling and mock fights (Bedigen, 2021).

Diagne (2004:55–70) adds to this debate by indicating that,

> the acknowledgement that the true face of the African crisis is a crisis of meaning and signification within the context of time. Contemporary Africa is aware of its still contested-for past, the colonial interlude, and the slow disjunctive time of the present, making interpretations of the future problematic. The future is problematic because there is no clear sense of an African telos thereby making it possible almost by default for Western generated theories.

Whereas Diagne indicates that 'meaning and signification' in Africa are a crisis, such thinking is maintained by ideologies that persistently marginalise African concepts in all disciplines, including peacebuilding. With this view in mind, this work argues that timed processes render international involvement in local or civil wars unproductive in delivering a sustainable solution. The concept of time, as illustrated in Figure 2.4, is one of the significant contributions this work makes to peacebuilding literature.

Further, interviewee narratives reveal how severe cases, such as homicide, can take up to two years to resolve. The advantage of the indigenous process is that once a story is presented, time is taken off to examine both the story and the crime. By not setting time limits, decisions are not immediately concluded, which implies that no party is pressured into accepting unfair terms or making false promises. Significantly, these time-outs allow for healing to take place. It is suggested set deadlines are one of the main contributors to the failure of conventional methods. The Wunlit conference was conducted

40 Indigenous Approaches to Peace

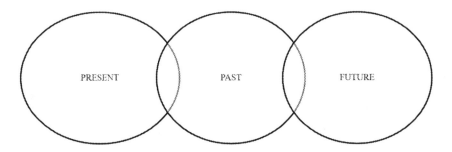

Figure 2.4 Present–Past, Past–Future Concept

within three days! Additionally, incorporating religious (Christian) and timed (western-style) stories meant that neither Dinka nor Nuer community members could express themselves at length. Self-expression is a necessary norm in the Nilotic Lwo peacebuilding culture because its process helps reveal facts. Therefore, for the many murders, rapes, abductions, forced marriages and atrocities that both Dinka and Nuer perpetrators had inflicted on each other's communities, it is highly likely that Wunlit 'traditional' justice was unsatisfactory.

During the Wunlit Dinka–Nuer inter-ethnic conference, the linear approach to time meant that a holistic indigenous process could not be achieved. Wunlit, in this book's view, was hardly an indigenous peace process. Moreover, the Wunlit conference was utilised as a framework for other grassroots peacebuilding processes (i.e. Liliir and Akobo). Such pseudo-indigenous inter-ethnic conferences lasted a much shorter time.

Peace Theories

Bottom-Up Theory

Firstly, I look at the bottom-up theory propounded by Lederach, one of today's most respected peace practitioners. He talks of how, in recent years, his peace approaches have concentrated on traditional approaches in Africa, for example, Ethiopia and Somalia. To him, this theory involves 'a process of first achieving discussions and agreements to end the fighting at local peace conferences' (Lederach, 1997:52–53). In his explanation, bottom-up theory is a comprehensive approach that integrates both short-term interventions to end violence and long-term conflict resolution. In his previous work, Lederach argues for an approach to peacebuilding that 'must be inclusive, embracing multiple facets, the interdependence of roles and activities, and a clear vision of the broader agenda peace-making and conflict resolution efforts undertake' (Lederach, 1996:12). Drawing examples from Somalia, he points out the significance of sub-clans and clan leaders' involvement in peacebuilding discussions, such as in the making of inter-clan peace agreements.

He further writes that the key characteristics of this bottom-up process, which include elders, storytelling, the creation of a forum of elders, negotiation and compensation, led to the Grand Borama Peace Conference (Lederach, 1996). While Lederach points out these key characteristics and acknowledges that they are similar to those in Nilotic Lwo traditional conflict resolution, this book's findings show that they fall short of Nilotic Lwo peacebuilding processes. This is because Lederach's work excludes what this book considers significant features of indigenous peacebuilding processes, for example, ceremonies and rituals, sharing food and drink, good manners or etiquette (see Chapters 4–6). It is these features that sustain peace. It is thus imperative to use cultural theory as a lens through which Nilotic Lwo cultures can be of significance to peacebuilding. Also, Lederach's work demonstrates the significance of elders and clan leaders; however, it does not explore the contributions that kinship, or blood relations, play in the sustenance of peace, specifically during court hearings, compensation or justice (see Chapter 4).

During data gathering, an interview with Samwiri, a Community-Based Organisation (CBO) worker who works with some Nilotic Lwo ethnic communities in matters of peace and conflict resolution, it became apparent that peace processes that ignore indigenous aspects of storytelling, etiquette, socialising, kinship and justice procedures are not embraced by communities. These are significant aspects of indigenous peacebuilding less known by international NGOs working in local communities. As such, they constitute relatively new concepts in the grassroots peacebuilding literature. South Sudan, Nilotic Lwo communities, are pretty distinctive in that although agreeing to any unifying peace conference, as indicated by Lederach, can be a challenge, these aspects of the indigenous peacebuilding process are unifying. Communities rely on their individual ethnic customary laws, beliefs and practices during peace processes. However, the victim's customs are utilised in deadlock situations (Bedigen, 2017). Lederach mentions compensation but does not clearly explain the indigenous justice process in his bottom-up approach. Moreover, interviews and literature findings show that, in most indigenous communities, reconciliation cannot happen without acceptable justice, typically demonstrated through compensation (Bedigen, 2020; Latigo, 2008).

Generally, and in line with Lederach's ideas, the current trend in conventional interventions focuses on concluding political agreements and promising security through negotiation. For instance, the IGAD Addis Ababa conference focussed on ceasefire, likewise the numerous agreements to resolve the December 2013 civil war (Johnson, 2013). In this book's view, signing agreements is a Eurocentric approach to indigenous peacebuilding. Thus, considering Asante's contextual approach (Asante, 1991,

2003) and Douglas' argument for less Eurocentric pre-occupation with others (Douglas, 1992), peace theories considered in this study are left wanting. Remarkably, Nilotic Lwo processes go beyond implementing ceasefire negotiations or agreements. They are focussed on the general well-being of the community. In doing so, they address other aspects, including psychosocial, economic and social issues. For example, the *Monyomiji* 'youth governance structure' plays a crucial role in the socio-economic aspects, including security roles within their respective communities (Simonse and Kurimoto, 2011). Lederach mentions negotiation as a critical method in the community peacebuilding process. However, other mediation methods are most effective during inter-ethnic or civil war breakouts. Intervening through indigenous mediation is very practical in that it helps ease animosities prior to face-to-face dialogue.

Further, although negotiation and mediation mechanisms are fundamental cornerstones to Nilotic Lwo indigenous peacebuilding processes, findings here show that they cannot be applied in isolation from the socialising aspects (see Chapter 4 for detail). These socialising aspects promote the successful practical application of indigenous negotiation and mediation. As Lederach indicates, they have been utilised in resolving murders and access to natural resources, which constitute sources of inter-ethnic conflicts that feed into civil wars. Similarly, indigenous mediation has been utilised in inter-clan intermittent conflicts. This is mainly due to other reasons such as raids, kidnap, theft, sexual crimes, revenge, and political and ethnic affiliation.

Peacebuilding from Below

While the bottom-up theory advocates for the involvement of local leaders, Peacebuilding from Below stresses the importance of involving all local sectors in the community. Ramsbotham et al. combine Levy's and Lederach's work (1996, 1997) to develop a framework for Peacebuilding from Below whereby 'solutions are derived and built from local resources' (Ramsbotham et al., 2005:216–218).

From the bottom to the top level, they categorise strategies suitable for peacebuilding into three main groups:

1) Bottom: local activists, leaders, social workers, entrepreneurs, ex-combatants and police;
2) Middle: parliamentarians, teachers, journalists, business investors, police chiefs and military officers;
3) Top: president, opposition leaders, religious authorities, central fiscal authorities and war time generals.

This book observes that this model leans towards a Eurocentric design of a community structure. Given cultural theory, hegemony and Afrocentric theories considered here exclude the indigenous institutions, customs, practices and the contribution of ordinary women and youth to peacebuilding. For example, South Sudan's justice system consists of customary laws facilitated by customary chiefs (Bedigen, 2017; Jok et al., 2004). Peacebuilding from Below theory is highly standardised and, in many respects, can be compared to some Nilotic Lwo indigenous institutions such as Monyomiji/ Honyomiji and the roles played by elders, women and youth in community peacebuilding. In a Nilotic Lwo indigenous peacebuilding system, duties and responsibilities at both individual and community levels matter. This implies that Peace from Below theory's specific and integrative nature could equate to duties and responsibilities.

This theory of Peacebuilding from Below brings together local people from bottom to top. It can work well in a society with organisational structure and state authority. This theory denotes that all individuals are experienced and are passionate about resolving conflict. While Peacebuilding from Below model can be applied to some Nilotic Lwo traditional democratic structures whose organisational structure consists of king/executive chiefs, chiefs, sub-chiefs, clan leaders and elders, such as the Nuer and Anyuak, it is inapplicable to other non-centralised or egalitarian communities such as the Dinka and Acholi (International African Institute, 2011; Reinton, 1971). Also, although it is a grassroots model, it appears pretty vague as there is no specific 'below' but a combination of different groups. The most suitable traditional structure this model can equate to is the Monyomiji system, practised in some Nilotic Lwo communities of South Sudan. As discussed in Chapter 5, this system involves men of ages 15–45 who rule for an average of 15 years. In their roles, they have authority over other community members and leaders, such as the rain chief and the war chief, ensuring that all those concerned perform their duties adequately. In addition, each Monyomiji member is accountable to peers, elders and the community. This is an aspect that Ramsbotham, Woodhouse and Miall's model is missing (Ramsbotham et al., 2005:223).

Further, they argue that Peacebuilding from Below must be a partnership of local and global actors' crossbreed partnership. A partnership is significant in peacebuilding because it can bridge the knowledge gap and attract resources, particularly the funding of peace processes. On the downside, crossbreed partnerships in peacebuilding can possess numerous disadvantages including:

1) Loss of autonomy when indigenous people become sidelined.
2) Psychological issues because sidelined individuals feel less valuable.
3) Future complications as terms of agreements are often foreign influenced.
4) Instabilities due to a weak foundation in peacebuilding.

In addition, it is argued that partnership can, at times, be overwhelming. For instance, at the height of the conflict in a small country like Rwanda, there were over 200 NGOs with foreign links. Moreover, a partnership may be effective only with only two disputing parties. In South Sudan, the situation is more challenging due to the prevalence of various inter-ethnic conflicts and militia groups. For instance, when the second South Sudan civil war reached its peak, there were up to 30 splinter militia groups (Bradbury et al., 2006). It appears that being a militia member or leader became the norm. Numerous militia groups in the Sudan and South Sudan civil wars reflect Julius Nyerere's argument that conflicts in African societies can be traced back to European socialism or the capitalist system. Nyerere suggests such systems make civil wars good and necessary. He states that capitalism

> planted the seeds of conflict within society ... apostles sanctified the conflict itself into a philosophy. Civil war was no longer looked upon as something evil, or something unfortunate, but as something good and necessary ... a means inseparable from the end.
> (Nyerere, 1968:11)

Adding to the above, during negotiations that ended the second Sudan civil war, other militia groups went on the offensive simply because the CPA recognised only the main political and military group, the SPLM/A (Bradbury et al., 2006). If a partnership is to be effective, as in most Nilotic Lwo indigenous structures, it must incorporate all community members and recognise their specific duties and responsibilities. Further, a question about the partnership level and whether it is an acceptable way forward for all partners can be raised. For example, some Nilotic Lwo communities are extremely conservative such that, when it comes to conflict resolution, they only implement what their tradition dictates (Mbiti, 1970). This narrows the possibilities of partnerships with outsiders.

Although this model may work in specific communities, this framework is based on the authors' peacebuilding experiences in Europe and South America. In view of Douglas' cultural and Asante's Afrocentric theories, Peacebuilding from Below is not pragmatic—thus, not contextual to the indigenous African institutions or Nilotic Lwo peace structures. Peacebuilding from Below model ignores the contribution an ordinary person can make to peacebuilding; moreover, local people (Nilotic Lwo) are the essence of culture. For example, in his book *The Moral Imagination*, Lederach gives examples of communities such as the Dagoma and Konkomba communities and the Wajir women in Kenya, where ordinary people transformed conflict situations into peace (Lederach, 2005). Other examples of the contribution made by ordinary people include the refusal of women to fulfil their conjugal rights until their men disarm. They all failed when national and international peacebuilding partners convened various peace talks during the 2013 South Sudan civil war. Thus, women called for a sex strike, a Nilotic Lwo indigenous practice aimed at forcing combatants to surrender (Red Pepper, 2014).

Indigenous Approaches to Peace   45

Another relevant example is the refusal to support husbands and sons in the planned invasion of another community, for example, in the Pokot women stories (Bedigen, 2017). Additionally, this may include the refusal of elders to bless their warriors. Although hybrid approaches, where a third party works with the locals and top government or international officials in peacebuilding processes, can be considered, this may only not work well within the conservative Nilotic communities (Mac Ginty, 2010a, 2011). Summarily, Peacebuilding from Below structure may create compromise, delusion, deviation, confusion and accountability issues.

Galtung Model

Galtung's model of conflict, violence and peace gives an illustration in three triangles. These include (1) contradiction, attitude and behaviour; (2) structural, cultural and direct violence; (3) peacebuilding, peacemaking and peacekeeping (Galtung, 1996). This theory differs from the above two because it considers conflicts and their resolution at personal and/or individual levels (see Figure 2.5).

Figure 2.5 is adopted from the Galtung model (Galtung, 1996). While attitude, behaviour and contradictions cause conflicts, sustainable peace can be achieved by changing them. In the Nilotic Lwo indigenous peacebuilding processes, ceremonies and rituals are utilised purposely to transform the parties' attitude, behaviour and conscience (Bedigen, 2017). Also, in Galtung's argument, peace culture embraces language, art, ideology, religion, empirical and formal science. He regards these as permanent and sustainable peacebuilding processes. Embracing these disciplines in grassroots or civil war peacebuilding places third parties at the centre of grassroots peacebuilding. For instance, in implementing this model, Galtung

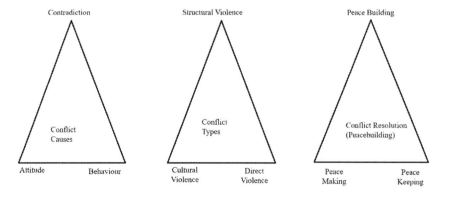

Figure 2.5 Conflict Cause, Types and Resolution

urges third parties to identify structural and cultural aspects to be included in peacebuilding processes. This idea is embraced by international peace and humanitarian NGOs. For example, Bedigen (2017) indicates that the International Crisis Group encourages the involvement of regional states and international governments in ending civil wars and rebuilding nations. However, placing third parties at the centre demonstrates Galtung's limited understanding of capable decision-makers within the indigenous system—the women and male elders. Despite contextual differences between Galtung's model and the indigenous system, it can be argued that placing third parties at the centre of conflict resolution, decision-making or implementation mirrors the Nilotic Lwo system, where customs, beliefs and practices are central to peacebuilding.

Central to Galtung's idea for grassroots peacebuilding is the significance of positive peace, which he expounds on to include empathy, solidarity and community. Galtung's ideas of negative peace (absence of direct violence) and positive peace (overcoming structural and cultural violence) are evident in the South Sudan situation. This book notes that cultural violence is the biggest contributor to conflicts (Jok et al., 2004; de Waal, 2014). Moreover, Galtung emphasises the significance of culture and religion in peacebuilding. This matches this book's understanding of indigenous peace processes among the Nilotic Lwo (Bradbury et al., 2006; Jok et al., 2004; Machar, 2015). For instance, what has fuelled and could resolve issues between Salva Kiir and Riek Machar in the 2013 South Sudan inter-ethnic and civil war is the one-time prophecy made by the greatest Nuer prophet, Ngundeng Bong, who lived more than a century ago. Johnson and Anderson (1995), in their book *Revealing Prophets: Prophecy in Eastern African History*, point to Ngundeng as one of the greatest Nuer prophets, possessed by a Dinka spirit commonly known by the Nuer as *Deng*. Dak (2009) and Bedigen (2017) indicate that some of Ngundeng's prophecies, claimed by his Nuer loyal followers today, have come to pass. It is claimed that his prophecies include (1) the independence of South Sudan from Sudan; (2) the anticipated surrender of a bearded man (believed to be the current president, Salva Kiir) to a left-handed man (believed to be Riek Machar—the current rebel leader); (3) Riek Machar, according to the prophecies, will lift up the flag or *Dang* of South Sudan (or retain Ngundeng's rod *dang*—see Figure 2.6) to become the president. However, Bedigen (2017) and Dinka interviewees are of the view that Riek Machar, supported by his Nuer followers and fighters (the white army), has politicised the *dang* prophecy. Such beliefs make them determined to fight, as Riek Machar is believed (by the Nuer ethnic group) to be the rightful leader of South Sudan (refer to Martino's narratives account). Moreover, some Nuer people, including Ngundeng's descendants, believe the prophet was a divine peaceful man who joined the battlefield only in community defence (Dak, 2009).

Galtung's view that culture and religion play a significant part in peacebuilding is laudable. This is manifest in indigenous religions, Islam and

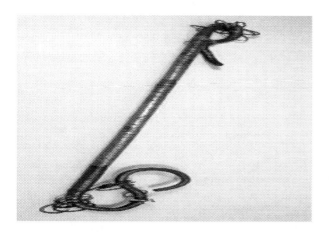

Figure 2.6 Prophet Ngungdeng's Rod

Christianity (Bedigen, 2017). For instance, the New Sudan Council of Churches (NSCC), a religious leaders' organisation, has represented South Sudanese at national levels of peace negotiations and mediation. The NSCC put forward a political argument that South Sudanese culture (African) and religion (Christian) justified their separation from Sudan, as the latter consists predominantly of Arabs and the main religion is Islam (Ahmed, 1988; Gurr, 1995; Malwal, 1981). From the onset of the civil war in 1983, NSCC worked tirelessly to bridge the gap between the SPLM/A, IGAD, the Sudan government and the international community. However, an IGAD-led peace deal was signed in Addis Ababa in January 2015, and fighting continued. Such furthered deaths, lootings, rapes, raids and displacement into the Internally Displaced Peoples' Camps (IDPCs) and neighbouring countries—exposing the ineffectiveness of third parties' involvement in peacebuilding. Cultural and religious beliefs play a significant role in indigenous peacebuilding in that it contributes to peaceful co-existence between hostile communities and has at times created unity of purpose at national levels. In the indigenous practice, before one goes for a fight or raid, they are obliged to consult spiritual leaders to seek their views (Mbiti, 1970; Schapera, 1970). In the case of South Sudan, there are three concerns: (1) Their practitioners can misrepresent and misinterpret the religious and cultural features; (2) foreign religions such as Christianity may not be effective; (3) indigenous people are not only Christians but also practitioners of African Traditional Religion (ATR). For instance, some Nuer Christian interviewees claim that Nyungdeng's rod represents witchcraft and idolatry, blurring its positive contribution to community unity and leadership.

Looking at the above peace theories has helped identify research gaps in grassroots peacebuilding approaches. Peace theories utilised here conceptualise post-civil war peacebuilding as a linear integrated approach. The approach starts with the international governments, followed by NGOs, regional governments, the state, local authorities and lastly the locals (Bedigen, 2017). These theories disregard the efficiency of indigenous institutions, customs and practices in resolving civil war and post-conflict peacebuilding. However, their utilisation through conventional structures and initiatives is often encouraged. In this book's view, it is apparent that undermining indigenous systems is a historical Eurocentric practice. That is, other non-European institutions, customs, and practices are informal and incapable of dealing with issues that affect the community (Mac Ginty, 2011). Thus, Douglas' argument for a non-Eurocentric perspective is utilised to situate this project within a relevant peacebuilding context or local cultures. Thus, the arguments will focus on the uniqueness of Nilotic Lwo peace cultures, which includes their institutions, customs, beliefs and practices. Discussions will identify and analyse Nilotic Lwo indigenous peace cultures that suit the South Sudan civil war resolution and post-conflict peacebuilding.

When civil wars happen, the external institutions' leadership and control have excluded local people, preventing the realisation of sustainable peace. As such, it is suggested that the knowledge of indigenous peacebuilding is illuminated, which brings us to ask some fundamental questions:

i) What indigenous peacebuilding approaches do the Nilotic Lwo (Dinka, Nuer, Acholi and Anuak) have to intra-ethnic and inter-ethnic disputes resolutions?
ii) How do people who have knowledge of and experience in both indigenous approaches to ethnic conflict resolution and the civil war understand them?
iii) How can these indigenous approaches be utilised in the civil war to deliver sustainable peace?

A theoretical framework developed from a combination of context-based theories such as Douglas' cultural theory, Gramsci's hegemony and Asante's Afrocentric theory is utilised to help us answer the above questions. Examples of the Nilotic Lwo indigenous peace approaches will be identified and analysed, followed by discussions of their contribution to delivering sustainable peace in South Sudan. Also, the gaps identified are analysed in the following chapters.

Thorny Issues in Conventional Indigenous Peacebuilding

Quality: The quality of indigenous peacebuilding, or ways of resolving disputes using native values, has generally attracted criticism from the west. Authors such as Mansell et al. (1995) argue that these mechanisms lack efficiency compared with western-style justice systems. The conventional or international law or legal peacebuilding methods have been instrumental

Indigenous Approaches to Peace 49

in handling international crimes such as war crimes, crimes against humanity and crimes of aggression through the International Criminal Court (Fassbender et al., 2012; Orentlicher, 1990). However, its origins from the Roman statutes (Koh, 1996) have widely remained incompatible with the indigenous institutions (Bedigen, 2017; Mac Ginty, 2011). The concept of international law/legal conflict resolution methods first appeared in 1783 and has evolved through history in classical writings, traditions, treaties and declarations of international courts. Examples of this include the International Court of Justice, International War Crimes Tribunal, World Court, The Law of War, The Hague Conventions and Nuremberg Principles (Bantekas and Nash, 2009; Barash, 2000; Barrash and Webel, 2002). Conventional peacebuilding strategies based on negotiation and mediation have been utilised in many post-conflict situations since the 1930s. It is thus wrong to overgeneralise or compare it to localised or community-based practices. Also, conventional peacebuilding is meant for conflicts between parties that do not practice or have access to a legitimised system of norms and systems. The assumption that certain communities or nation-states exist without norms or systems capable of dealing with their problems is quite patronising. As such, the majority of resolution attempts that have been applied in the South Sudan situation have remained wanting. Moreover, South Sudan has its own justice system that has been historically utilised in resolving crimes similar to the civil war crimes—making quality claim questionable.

Enforcement: There is a thin line between peacekeeping and peace enforcement in the conventional peace processes (Sarigiannidis, 2007). As such, there have been difficulties with the enforcement of conventional methods as some authors regard them as mere customs while others consider them contradictory (Ginty, 2011). For instance, Barash (2000:113) indicates that conventional methods contain 'some useful restraints in some cases, while being woefully inadequate in others.' While some states' legislations embody aspects of international laws within their own legislation, they are not necessarily obliged to comply with similar versions of the international law, such as Human Rights Laws—which have been significant issues in the South Sudan civil wars. Challenges in its enforcement imply that the universal claim for its effectiveness is difficult to substantiate (Richmond, 2001).

Moreover, authors such as Sandole (1993) argue that changes should be made to legal norms if they are inadequate in resolving conflicts. Remarkably, this book highlights that the indigenous peacebuilding systems are self-regulatory. An example of this is the Monyomiji institution, where members can remove chiefs who misbehave from office (Bedigen, 2019).

Perpetrators: When dealing with perpetrators, the conventional justice system focuses only on a court-based retributive system to apportion blame. In contrast, the indigenous system operates on public consensus. In the South Sudan civil war, conventional laws were applied in issuing the arrest warrants of the militia leaders, including President Bashir. An example is the involvement of the International Criminal Court in legitimising Ongwen's arrest and trial (Bedigen, 2017; Orentlicher, 1990; International African Institute, 2011). The ICC rejected the Acholi request to try Ongwen in the Acholi traditional process/courts known as Mato Oput (Mac Ginty, 2011). Ongwen's trial at The Hague illustrates the hegemony of conventional methods in peacebuilding whereby the ruling class exerts authority over the masses (Gramsci, 1992). The ICC's involvement in Ongwen's case contradicts Asante's arguments that problem-solving should be contextual (Asante, 2003). Bearing in mind Douglas' arguments for less pre-occupation with others, the Acholi people and their Mato Oput peace processes were capable of handling Ongwen's case. After all, it has handled similar cases before. The chiefs or local authorities are obliged to conduct an investigation, and members are expected to demonstrate belief, trust and respect in the chief's authority. The chief's neutral investigation, representation and final word are binding. These sorts of internal investigations are often regarded as one-sided in the western lens. Also, the absence of legal representation and lack of justice reviews in indigenous peace processes cast doubts over justice in conventional contexts (Jeong, 2005).

Mamdani (2001) writes about the Rwandan genocide in his book *When Victims Become Killers* and Schenkel (2015) in his article 'Uganda: The thin line between victim and perpetrator.' While there are clear distinctions between victims and perpetrators in some conflict situations, such are entirely blurred in this civil war. It is argued that the SPLA and other militia groups conscripted children who became perpetrators of violence (Bedigen, 2017). For example, Ongwen was one of the children abducted and forced to inflict suffering and pain on their victims, including family members, by the Lord's Resistance Army (LRA) militia group. Interview data showed that most Acholi regard the LRA combatants and ex-combatants as victims, not perpetrators (Latigo, 2008). Due to this blurriness, most Acholi in northern Uganda, including the victims, advocate for indigenous methods of peacebuilding that create conditions to end the war by reintegrating ex-combatants and victims into the community rather than retribution (Schenkel, 2015).

Further, the Nilotic Lwo indigenous peacebuilding is concerned with integrating social, economic and spiritual harmony, as opposed to conventional dominance of political and economic integration. In traditional systems, there are various peace mechanisms embedded in the institutional customs and practises that deal with disruptions to post-conflict integration. While the Nilotic Lwo descriptions of indigenous peacebuilding have strong resonance with the broad descriptions given by Lederach, the starting points for indigenous and conventional peacebuilding processes are generally different. For instance, in the conventional perspective, peacebuilding is linked to post-conflict intervention, whereas in the Nilotic perspective, peace is an entity that should always exist and be sustained. As such, peace values and skills are taught from childhood (Shorter, 1974). Indigenous peacebuilding begins with conflict prevention, peacemaking and then peacekeeping. Although both processes often take a long time, western writers such as Lederach attempt to set time on conflict resolution aspects of conflict prevention and peacebuilding. This may not be logical because this book reveals that peacebuilding is a process, not an outcome.

South Sudan Justice System

To strengthen the argument that the Nilotic Lwo indigenous peacebuilding methods are crucial in delivering peace in civil war contexts, it is crucial to gain knowledge of South Sudan's justice system. This is because it constitutes customary law courts (customary laws, beliefs and practices) aspects this book addresses. As demonstrated in Figure 2.5, the New Sudan or South Sudan Judiciary comprises a six-tier court system. However, this book will focus on the lower or customary law courts (refer to Figure 2.5). Although Figure 2.5 portrays smooth operation between traditional courts, government-run customary and statutory law courts are alien to the locals. They are confusing; the locals commonly withdraw their cases from the justice system and revert to traditional methods of conflict resolution outside the justice system, as indicated by Jok et al. (2004). Withdrawal from government law courts is also indicated in the work of Leonardi et al. (2010). There are many reasons why the traditional courts appeal to the South Sudanese. The main one is that they are free, unlike the government courts that require the payment of some fees that the majority cannot afford.

Further, in South Sudan's justice system, family members can attend government courts and be regarded as parties to conflicts. Regrettably, in their current operations, the government-run customary courts do not promote interaction, including socialising, visitation, feasting and rituals—to be elaborated further in the findings. Discussions show that government-run customary courts do not contribute to future inter-communal unity or conflict prevention. The government system takes away the African and Nilotic Lwo culture of socialising, a unique aspect that invisibly contributes to peace and conflict resolution.

Figure 2.7 shows the South Sudan Justice System Court Hierarchy (Jok et al., 2004). Like most countries previously colonised by the British, South Sudan's justice system embraces both statutory (state or government) law courts and customary or indigenous courts/methods (Jabs, 2014). These two law courts may operate separately, depending on the dispute. While the customary law courts operating under the government justice system can include chiefs from various communities, they can also be absorbed into the government system and become independent of these communities. Remarkably, most disputes/cases, including murder and sexual crimes, can be reported to or resolved at a family, clan or community level. However, for various reasons, similar cases could be reported and resolved at the government-run customary law courts or taken to the statutory and appeal

52 *Indigenous Approaches to Peace*

court. Leonardi et al. (2010:33), referring to the South Sudan justice system, indicate that it 'remains a predominantly oral culture; evidence in court cases largely takes the form of the word of witnesses.'

With the availability of these two options, victims choose which court to attend. Jabs (2014) indicates that conflicts within a family, plus conflicts relating to education or wealth, favour the government system, and the nature of the dispute leads people to choose between the indigenous system and government courts. Also, during data gathering, it was observed that other reasons that affect the choice of the court include religious and political factors (Bedigen, 2017). Interviewees' stories reveal that families who have received some western education tend to be cynical of indigenous methods or go to hybrid courts, a view supported by (Leonardi et al., 2010:35). Likewise, conservative Christian believers shun indigenous ceremonies or purification rituals, opting for the state justice system.

Further, victims or the victim's families may choose to take the case to government courts in the hope of more significant monetary gains or compensation. At times, government authorities intervene immediately in cases of homicide or massacre, giving the victim no choice but to report to government courts. Figure 2.6 illustrates the relationships between traditional court levels, disputes/crimes and South Sudan's justice system, and it shows that all disputes can be resolved in customary or indigenous settings.

Looking at both figures (2.7 and 2.8), it is evident that the South Sudan justice system, which incorporates indigenous institutional set-up, customs and practices, can cope well in the civil war resolution process and post-war

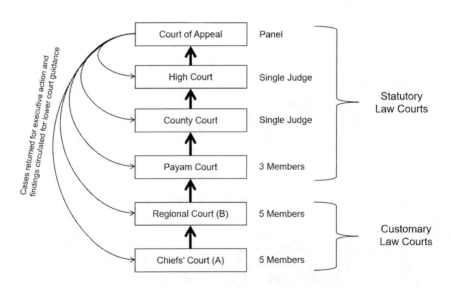

Figure 2.7 The New Sudan Judicial System—Court Hierarchy

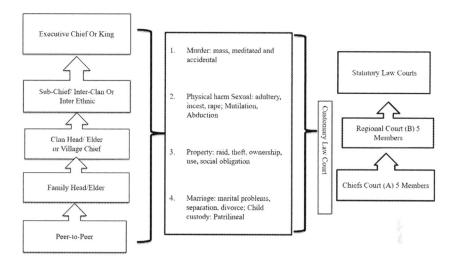

Figure 2.8 Indigenous Court Levels Disputes or Crimes and South Sudan Judicial Hierarchy

peacebuilding. However, as mentioned earlier, South Sudan's peace processes have been run by the international community. Under the humanitarian pretext, the international community, as in other conflict-stricken African countries, automatically assumes the right to intervene in South Sudan without considering what South Sudanese have or interests. Since the 2005 CPA, peace processes in South Sudan have been given African or 'indigenous faces' and avoided holistic indigenous peace norms—thus, their failures to deliver sustainable peace. For example, the African-led NGOs, such as African Union (AU) and regional governments through IGAD, predominantly implement conventional negotiations and mediation (Bedigen, 2017). Much as they may involve indigenous chiefs, they exclude indigenous knowledge and practices. It is essential to point out that AU and IGAD processes follow international peacebuilding models that do not fit within indigenous contexts.

Considering Lederach (1997), Galtung (1996) and Ramsbotham et al.'s (2005) views on grassroots approaches discussed earlier, what is being implemented in South Sudan does not fall within the grassroots or indigenous contexts of peacebuilding. According to these authors, grassroots peacebuilding should include the locals, NGOs, the government and the international community. However, this book argues for a focus on indigenous features that exclude direct involvement of international organisations and approaches. The reason is that the South Sudan justice system includes or begins with customary courts, which include indigenous features. It is a grave mistake for conventional peace institutions and actors to undermine the local social contexts and South Sudan's justice system, particularly customary courts.

54 Indigenous Approaches to Peace

Further, in support of the above, McGovern, an anthropologist, reviews an article, 'Writing about conflict in Africa: Stakes and strategies,' in the International African Institute journal (2011:324–325). He writes about how analysts of African conflicts often follow colonial and business-like rhetoric. Referring to Finnstrom and Coulter's work, he states that:

> Both authors make convincing cases for cultural critique of the international human rights regime. The underlying assumptions on which the logic of transitional justice is constructed are ethnocentric, and do not seem to fit easily with the local notions of justice... the international (really Euro-American) justice common sense is 'wrong' in these settings, ... It is clear that the international human rights and transitional supporting and legitimating their activities than poor Africans have ... justice institutions have vastly greater sums.

The above argument indicates that the biggest problem that surrounds and prevents the utilisation of indigenous methods in civil war situations is not their weaknesses but the low opinion of peace actors.

In Africa, the existence of indigenous systems supported by the government system (customary courts) is not isolated to South Sudan but others, such as the Rwandan *Gacaca* indigenous courts. Authors such as Roht-Arriza and Mariezurrena (2006), Venter (2007) and Clark (2010) have argued for *Gacaca*'s viability, as opposed to the western-style justice in the Rwandan post-civil war justice and reconciliation. However, other authors argue otherwise. In her article in the *Journal of the International African Institute* (2011), Thomson argues against the *Gacaca* system. She refers to it as a state-manipulated system that is instead furthering the political ambition of the ruling government. She says that

> international academics and journalists laud the outcomes of Gacaca ending impunity and promoting reconciliation as national policy accomplishments rather than recognising Gacaca as central to the state-run legal system that produces a particular version of justice and reconciliation that reinforces the power of the post-genocide government at the expense of the individual process of reconciliation.

Feeding into Thomson's argument, Wol, the head of the Sudanese People's Liberation Movement-in-Opposition (SPLM-IO), laments IGAD's non-neutral position as a negotiator in the 2013 South Sudan civil war. In his article, published in the *Sudan Tribune* newspaper, he writes that:

> I remember in April the warring parties agreed on Declaration of Principles (DoP) and it was ready to be signed but the mediators refused and asked the parties to go for a recess and the document will be signed

in the next session. When the parties reported back in May they got the DoP was abandoned and a new document called "Draft Agenda 1" was produced as a "leave or take it" document. The delegation consulted with its leadership and constituencies and accepted the "Draft Agenda 1" document but the government delegation refused and again it was abandoned by the IGAD, who formulated another document called "Draft Agenda 2" which accommodates the government position and asked all the stakeholders to respond to it.

(Wol, 2014:2)

In the above quote, Wol points out that the Sudanese People's Liberation Movement (SPLM), the then government of South Sudan, has time and again influenced IGAD and shifted positions, ultimately leading to delays in the signing of a peace deal. This book argues that a state justice system should holistically incorporate indigenous systems and regularly check on the state's motives. Also, the benefit of the indigenous system is that it possesses attributes such as neutrality and consensus that can be useful. Considering Thomson's and Wol's arguments, the traditional system can be trusted to handle the civil war peace process because it is popular among the locals. Indigenous peacebuilding systems are pro-community and are less likely to be exploited in political and economic aspects. Drawing arguments from theorists, authors and interviewees above, this book argues that indigenous processes must be recognised and placed at the core of peace processes.

The Government Court Functionality and Indigenous Peacebuilding

The indigenous court system resolves all kinds of crimes (Bedigen, 2017). It is incorporated into the South Sudan justice system, and it is this connection that this book argues has the potential in delivering sustainable peace in the region (refer to Figure 2.9). Figure 2.9 is a graphical representation of the Nilotic Lwo traditional court levels and the disputes/crimes it resolves. Remarkably, all disputes can be resolved at the peer-to-peer or family level, mainly if the offender is a kinsman.

In Figure 2.10, disputes 3 and 4 are resolved in the two lower courts. If a dispute cannot be resolved at these two lower levels, the case is forwarded to the next level, then the next, until it is resolved. It is important to note that these disputes at the peer-to-peer level do not generally progress to chiefs, but they do so when whole communities are affected. Further, clan heads and sub-chiefs often deal with disputes (i.e. 1, 2 and 3). These cases may be handled at the next (chief and executive chief) levels, where mechanisms that include mediation, forgiveness, transformation and force can be applied whenever suitable (see Figure 2.8). Force or retaliating raids can be applied as a last resort, commonly in situations of non-compliance.

56   Indigenous Approaches to Peace

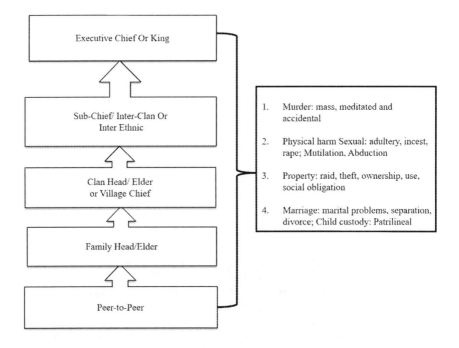

Figure 2.9 Nilotic Lwo Indigenous Court Levels and Types of Disputes or Crimes

The nature of the indigenous justice process is typically discussions and arbitration. Mansell et al. (1995), in their book *A Critical Introduction to Law*, indicate that the indigenous justice process does not necessarily have visible independent judges and a clear dispute resolution procedure, but rather a prolonged process, with no court buildings, no clear-cut laws and no enforceable decisions. This is contrary to interviewees' views, whose narratives demonstrate that there are obligatory laws developed from societal customs that members are obliged to follow. They further explain that indigenous courts are held under trees, market places and at times, in the arbitrator's house. Considering the grassroots theories reviewed and the conceptualisation of this study, it is the people—their past, present and relationships—that matter, not venues. Mbiti (1970) writes about how African religious beliefs and practices guide their lives, including peace and justice. The nature of indigenous court settings in these communities is less concerned with permanent structures for court venues that do not affect case rulings.

Further, in a culture that takes a holistic approach to reconciliation, customary beliefs and practices that lead to the reverence of ancestors and the environment are critical (Azibo, 1996; Mbiti, 1970). Therefore, since customary beliefs and practices dictate when, where and how a conflict should be resolved, it is common sense not to have a permanent court venue. Since

Indigenous Approaches to Peace 57

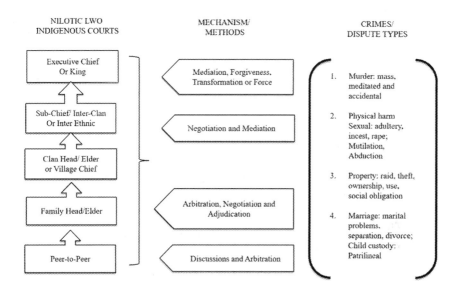

Figure 2.10 Indigenous Courts, Mechanisms and Crimes or Dispute Types

belief in supernatural beings and spirits is the norm, these two cannot be restricted to locations, so neither should conflict resolution.

Prolonged arbitration is legitimate in the Nilotic Lwo indigenous peace processes (Bedigen, 2020). However, it is vague to westerners and lacks fundamental attributes of conventionally acceptable arbitration (Mansell et al., 1995). It can be argued that this underlying assumption led the British colonialists, Arabs, modern international law and the government of South Sudan today not to include indigenous systems in justice processes. On the other hand, they have supplemented, introduced or utilised alternative systems unfamiliar to the locals. For instance, as seen in the justice system of South Sudan, statutory law courts are placed above customary law courts, and this asserts their superiority over customary law courts. Yet, as mentioned earlier, the majority of cases can be resolved in the indigenous court system.

It is also evident that the indigenous and state justice systems in South Sudan connect with one another; therefore, they offer a possibility of civil war resolution at national, not international, levels (Bedigen, 2017). For instance, Figure 2.11 illustrates the interface between the government and traditional courts in South Sudan. It shows two types of customary systems, government sponsored (which is run by state-appointed elders) and communal (commonly run by clan, chief or local elders), quite similar to the *Judiyya* system in Darfur and Kordofan regions (Bradbury et al., 2006). At times a few cases, such as mass murder, cattle raiding or land grab (all common in inter-ethnic conflicts), advance to the court of appeal. Moreover, as mentioned earlier, traditional judges (initially involved in the case) can be called

58 Indigenous Approaches to Peace

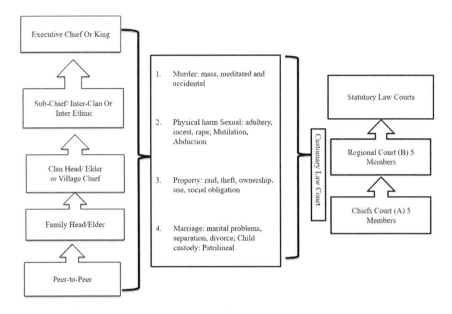

Figure 2.11 The Dual Justice System and Judicial Hierarchy

upon to deliberate at the high court of appeal (refer to Figure 2.11). While there are many reasons why some cases that could be resolved at the local level are presented at the higher court, this does not constitute a significant difference—the reason is customary judges or chiefs (who initially looked at the case) are called upon to continue in the higher court. Additionally, it may imply minimal changes in the final justice decision reached because the indigenous code of practice continues to be applied even at the court of appeal, a view supported by Leonardi et al. (2010).

Adopted from Jok et al. (2004), Figure 2.11 illustrates how cases previously referred to statutory law courts can be referred back to customary law courts. The above analysis demonstrates an interface between government and customary justice systems. It indicates that such a system can work at national levels of peacebuilding; however, there are some concerns in forwarding cases to the court of appeal. First, it helps to undermine indigenous justice by assuming it is inadequate in dealing with conflict and civil war crimes, which are similar to the historical crimes indigenous courts can resolve. Second, it theoretically helps deconstruct indigenous justice and makes it illegitimate in its homeland, further casting a shadow on the system's effectiveness to the outsiders. Subsequently, forwarding cases to the appeal court may help justify the use of foreign laws in South Sudanese local courts. When perceptions of civil war crimes become different from the long practised traditions, customs and beliefs, how they are dealt with changes.

Indigenous Approaches to Peace 59

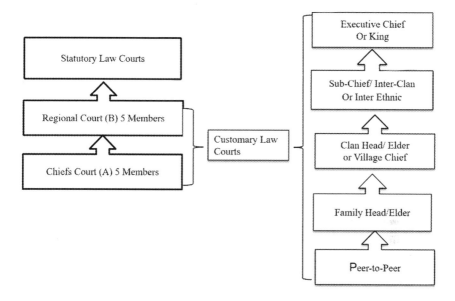

Figure 2.12 The South Sudan Judicial system and Nilotic Lwo Indigenous Courts

Perhaps this explains the ICC's dominance in South Sudan's post-war justice processes. For example, it ordered the arrest of perpetrators, including President al-Bashir, and then brought Ongwen, a former LRA commander, to trial (Bedigen, 2017; Schenkel, 2015). In comparison to the justice system that exists in western countries (the USA and Britain), ex-combatants are prosecuted (in their respective countries) for crimes of war and crimes against humanity they committed while in service (Bedigen, 2017). It can be argued that South Sudanese customary laws and practices are flexible in resolving civil war crimes without the state justice system's influences that infringe on their originality.

Conclusion

This chapter has reviewed the literature on grassroots peacebuilding theories. It has looked at the Nilotic Lwo descriptions of peacebuilding and the South Sudan justice system. The analysis demonstrates the existence of indigenous court systems within the state judiciary system—thus supports the argument for the usability of Nilotic Lwo peacebuilding methods in the current civil war situation. Also, this chapter has highlighted that the Nilotic Lwo indigenous institutions, customs and practices, such as ceremonies and rituals, are crucial in peacebuilding. Some indigenous concepts (beliefs, ceremonies and rituals) exist within the cultural theory framework. This renders it beneficial to utilise cultural theory as a lens to view and develop a contextual approach to peacebuilding. Thus, this book's theoretical contribution is that peacebuilding in post-conflict environments should be indigene-centred at local and national levels.

Bibliography

Asante, M.K., 1991. The Afrocentric idea in education. *The Journal of Negro Education*, 60(2), pp. 170–180.

Asante, M.K., 2003. *Afrocentricity: The Theory of Social Change*. Chicago, IL, African American Images.

Azibo, D. (Ed.), 1996. *African Psychology in Historical Perspective and Related Commentary*. Asmara, Eritrea, African World Press.

Bantekas, I. and Nash, S., 2009. *International Criminal Law*. New York, Routledge.

Barash, D.P., 2000. *Approaches to Peace: A Reader in Peace Studies*. Oxford, Oxford University Press.

Barash, D.P. and Webel, P.C., 2002. *Peace and Conflict Studies*. London, Sage.

Bedigen, W., 2017. Traditional conflict resolution: The Nilotic Lwo of South Sudan (PhD thesis). Leeds, Leeds Beckett University.

Bedigen, W., 2019. Youth (Monyomiji) and conflict resolution in the South Sudan Civil War. *Journal of African Cultural Heritage Studies*, 2(1), pp. 18–35.

Bedigen, W., 2020. Significance of societal customs in the South Sudan civil war resolution. *Journal of Peacebuilding and Development*, 15(1), pp. 3–17.

Bedigen, W., 2021. Honyomiji: the local women's peacebuilding institution in South Sudan. *Peacebuilding*, 9(4), pp. 457–476.

Bradbury, M., Ryle, J., Medley, M. and Sansculotte-Greenidge, K., 2006. *Local Peace Processes in Sudan: A Baseline Study*. London, Rift Valley Institute.

Branch, A. and Mampilly, Z.C., 2005. Winning the war, but losing the peace? The dilemma of SPLM/A civil administration and the tasks ahead. *The Journal of Modern African Studies*, 43(1), pp. 1–20.

Branch, A., 2011. Neither liberal nor peaceful? Practices of 'global justice' by the ICC. In C. Susanna, C. David, and S. Meera (Eds.), *A liberal peace? The problems and practices of peacebuilding*, London, Bloomsbury Publishing, pp. 121–138.

Bitek, O.P., 1966. *Song of Lawino and Song of Ocol*. Nairobi, East African Pub.

Dak, J.G., 2009. Rod of Nuer prophet to arrive Juba by mid-May. *Sudan Tribune*. South Sudan. https://sudantribune.com/article30989/.

Darby, J., and Mac Ginty, R. (Eds.), 2002. *Contemporary Peace Making: Conflict, Violence and Peace Processes*. London, Springer.

de Waal, A., 2014. When kleptocracy becomes insolvent: Brute causes of the civil war in South Sudan. *African Affairs*, 113(452), pp. 347–369.

Diagne, S.B., 2004. On prospective: Development and a political culture of time. *Africa Development-Senegal*, 29(1), pp. 55–70.

Douglas, M., 1992. *Risk and Blame: Essays in Cultural Theory*. London, Routledge.

Douglas, M., 2002. *Implicit Meanings: Selected Essays in Anthropology*. London, Routledge.

Evans-Pritchard, E.E., 1956. *Nuer Religion*. Oxford, Oxford University Press.
Fassbender, B., Peters, A., Peter, S. and Högger, D. (Eds.), 2012. *The Oxford Handbook of the History of International Law*. Oxford, Oxford University Press.
Galtung, J., 1996. *Peace by Peaceful Means*. London, Sage.
Gebre, Y.G. and Ohta, I., 2017. *African Virtues in the Pursuit of Conviviality: Exploring Local Solutions in Light of Ðlobal Prescriptions*. Langaa RPCIG, Cameroon, African Books Collective.
Gramsci, A., 1992. *Prison Notebooks (Vol. 2)*. New York, Columbia University Press.
Gurr, T. R., 1995. Transforming ethno-political conflicts: Exit, autonomy, or access? In K. Rupesinghe (Ed.), *Conflict Transformation* (pp. 1–30). London, St Martin's Press.
Jabs, L.B., 2014. 'No monkey destroys his forest': A review of traditional African interpersonal conflict management. *Journal of Global Peace and Conflict*, 2(1), pp. 1–24.
Jeong, H.-W., 2005. *Peacebuilding in Postconflict Societies*. London, Sage.
Johnson, D.H. and Anderson, D.M., 1995. *The Prophet Ngundeng and the Battle of Pading. Revealing Prophets: Prophecy in Eastern African History*. Oxford, James Currey Publishers.
Johnson, D.H., 2013. New Sudan or South Sudan? The multiple meanings of self-determination in Sudan's comprehensive peace agreement. *Civil Wars*, 15(2), pp. 141–156.
Jok, A.A., Leitch, A.R. and Vandewint, C., 2004. *A Study of Customary Law in Contemporary Southern Sudan*. Rumbek, South Sudan, World Vision International.
Kalumba, K.M., 2005. A new analysis of Mbiti's "the concept of time". *Philosophia Africana: Analysis of Philosophy and Issues in Africa and the Black Diaspora*, 8(1), pp. 11–20.
Koh, H.H., 1996. Why do nations obey international law. *Yale Law Journal*, 106, p. 2599.
Latigo, J., 2008. Northern Uganda: Tradition-based practices in the Acholi region. In L. Huyse and M. Salter (Eds.), *Traditional Justice and Reconciliation after Violent Conflict: Learning from African Experiences* (pp. 85–120). Stockholm, IDEA.
Lederach, J.P., 1996. *Preparing for Peace: Conflict Transformation across Cultures*. Syracuse, NY, Syracuse University Press.
Lederach, J.P., 2005. *The Moral Imagination: The Art and Soul of Building Peace*. Oxford, Oxford University Press.
Lederach, J.P., 1997. *Building Peace: Sustainable Reconciliation in Divided Societies*. Washington, DC, United States Institute of Peace Press.
Leonardi, C.,Moro, L.N., Santschi, M. and Isser, H.D., 2010. *Local Justice in South Sudan (Peaceworks Number 66)*. Washington, DC, United States Institute of Peace.
Mac Ginty, R., 2011. *International Peacebuilding and Local Resistance: Hybrid Forms of Peace*. London, Springer.
Machar, B., 2015. *Building a Culture of Peace through Dialogue in South Sudan*. Juba, South Sudan, The SUUD Institute.
McGovern, M., 2011. Writing about conflict in Africa: Stakes and strategies. *Africa*, 81(2), pp. 314–330.

Malwal, B., 1981. *People and Power in Sudan: The Struggle for National Stability*. London, Ithaca Press.
Mamdani, M., 2001. *When Victims Become Killers: Colonialism, Nativism, and the Genocide in Rwanda*. Princeton, NJ, Princeton University Press.
Mansell, W., Meteyard, B. and Thomson, A., 1995. *A Critical Introduction to Law*. London, Cavendish Publishing Limited.
Mazurana, D., Raven-Roberts, A. and Parpart, J. (Eds.), 2005. *Gender, Conflict and Peace Keeping*. Oxford, Rowman and Littlefield Publishers.
Mbiti, J.S., 1969. *African Religions and Philosophy*. Oxford, Heinemann.
Mbiti, J.S., 1970. *Concepts of God in Africa*. London, SPCK.
Nkyabonaki, J., 2019. The influence of indigenous administration on post-independence administration in Tanzania. in D. M. Bondarenko and M. L. Butovskaya (Eds.), *The Omnipresent Past: Historical Anthropology of Africa and African Diaspora* (pp. 183–195). Moscow, LRC Publishing House.
Nyerere, J.K., 1968. *Ujamaa: Essays on Socialism*. London, Oxford University Press.
Ogot, B.A., 1999. *Building on the Traditional: Selected Essays 1981–1998*. Nairobi, Anyange Press Ltd.
Olupona, J.K. and Nyang, S.S. (Eds.), 2013. *Religious Plurality in Africa: Essays in Honour of John S. Mbiti* (Vol. 32). Berlin, Walter de Gruyter.
Orentlicher, D.F., 1991. Settling accounts: The duty to prosecute human rights violations of a prior regime. *Yale Law Journal*, 100, pp. 2537–2615.
Ramsbotham, O., Woodhouse, T. and Miall, H., 2005. *Contemporary Conflict Resolution: The Prevention, Management and Transformation of Deadly Conflicts*, 2nd edition. Cambridge, Polity Press.
Reinton, P.O., 1971. Imperialism and the southern Sudan. *Journal of Peace Research*, 8(3–4), pp. 239–247.
Richmond, O., 2001. *Maintaining Order, Making Peace*. London, Springer.
Roht-Arriaza, N. and Mariezcurrena, J. (Eds.), 2006. *Transitional Justice in the Twenty-First Century: Beyond Truth versus Justice*. Cambridge, Cambridge University Press.
Sandole, D.J., 1993. Paradigm, Theories, and Metaphors in Conflict and Conflict Resolution'. *Conflict Resolution: Theory and Practice, Integration and Application*. Manchester, Manchester University Press (pp. 3–24).
Sarigiannidis, M., 2007. Legal discourses on peacemaking/peacekeeping/peacebuilding: International law as a new topos for human security. *International Journal*, 62(3), pp. 519–538.
Schapera, I., 1970. *A Handbook of Tswana Law and Custom*. London, Frank Cass & Co.
Schenkel, M., 2015. Uganda: The thin line between victim and perpetrator. *Mail and Guardian*, 16, 17.
Shorter, A., 1974. *East African Societies*. London, Routledge and Kegan Paul.
Simonse, S. and Kurimoto, E. (Eds.), 2011. Engaging 'Monyomiji', bridging the gap in East Bank Equatoria: Proceedings of the Conference 26–28 November 2009. Nairobi, Pax Christi Horn of Africa, pp. 2–129.
Wol, D.M.D., 2014. South Sudan conflict: IGAD fights, mediates and negotiates. *Sudan Tribune*. 10 September. Retrieved from http://www.sudantribune.com/spip.php?article52349 [Accessed: 15 January 2015].
Venter, C.M., 2007. Eliminating fear through recreating community in Rwanda: The role of the Gacaca courts. *Texas Wesleyan Law Review*, 13(2), pp. 577–597.

3 Narrative Inquiry

Introduction

This chapter takes us through the research process and highlights the significance of using qualitative narrative inquiry or stories in indigenous research. Through face-to-face focus groups and online interviews, interviewees told their stories and life experiences that confirmed data from the literature review and brought to light new information. Narratives revealed ethnographic aspects existent in the cultural theory framework (Douglas, 1966, 1970, 1973, 1992; Sedgwick and Edgar, 2002). They include narratives and observations of interviewees' everyday lives, practices, rituals, symbols, inter-connections or relationships, customs, values and beliefs (Lapan et al., 2012; Edmonds and Kennedy, 2013). Such data provided further comprehensive perspectives utilised to generalise concepts or themes (discussed in the following chapters).

In conducting a literature analysis, ethnographic data sources such as figures, photos, histories and newspapers are utilised (Lapan et al., 2012). The ethnographic aspect of cultural theory, a selection of knowledgeable and experienced participants who know the community's norms and culture well, has been used. They provided opportunities to identify comprehensive perspectives discussed in the chapters that follow.

Further, concerning cultural theory, anthropological aspects provided information on the Nilotic people's history and their communities/cultures' development in migratory and settlement years (Collins, 1971; Johnson and Anderson, 1995). This included, for instance, the development of indigenous peace cultures such as *Mato Oput*, *Gurtong* and *Nyono Tong Gweno* into suitable civil war resolution practices (Latigo, 2008).

Considering cultural theory, concepts that help explain how South Sudan civil wars can be resolved through traditional cultural practices were derived. Significant to note, the Nilotic Lwo narrative culture (p'Btek, 1966; Ogot, 1999; Wa Thiong, 1986) helped in bringing peace cultures that are also cultural theory concepts to light. These concepts are summarised into five main themes: spiritual authority, socialising, etiquette, traditional roles of youth, and women and mothers.

DOI: 10.4324/9781003133476-4

64 Narrative Inquiry

This chapter re-states the study aim and research objectives, methods considered, method of choice (narrative inquiry), research design, justification of the narrative method, data collection and analysis, methodological limitations, author's reflection on the methodological process and conclusion.

Context

Re-stating the Study Aim and Research Objectives

The introductory chapter states the purpose of this book. That is, to examine the indigenous peacebuilding approaches, i.e. the traditional institutions, customs and practices of the Nilotic Lwo in delivering sustainable peace in South Sudan. To achieve this, three questions were posed:

i)   What indigenous peacebuilding approaches do the Nilotic Lwo (Dinka, Nuer, Acholi and Anuak) have to intra-ethnic and inter-ethnic disputes resolutions?
ii) How do people who have knowledge of and experience in both indigenous approaches to ethnic conflict resolution and the civil war understand them?
iii) How can these indigenous approaches be utilised in delivering sustainable peace during conflict and in post-civil war situations?

To answer the above research questions, the following objectives were stated:

i)   To explore Nilotic Lwo (Dinka, Nuer, Acholi and Anuak) indigenous conflict resolution peace cultures.
ii) To explore inter-ethnic conflicts, Sudan and South Sudan civil war and analyse conflict resolution attempts.
iii) To examine interviewees' narratives on the Nilotic Lwo indigenous methods of addressing conflict.
iv) To examine the usefulness of these methods in delivering sustainable peace in South Sudan civil war situation.

Methods Considered

Ethnographic research (or method of the people) could be considered to be a useful method in this study due to the claim that it is 'the systematic study of a particular cultural group or phenomenon ... focus on real people and their everyday activities ... beliefs and practices from people's own point of view' (Lapan et al., 2012:163). For instance, Edmonds and Kennedy (2013:124) indicate that it is utilised in the study of cultural aspects of everyday lives, practices, rituals, inter-connections, customs, values and beliefs. It utilises data sources such as figures, histories and newspapers, which, according to

Lapan et al. (2012), aid the identification and articulation of cultural beliefs, norms and perceptions. Ethnographic research's traditional approach of chain sampling emphasises the selection of knowledgeable participants who know the community's norms and culture well. Additionally, it is one of the most in-depth research methods possible because it provides opportunities to identify comprehensive perspectives compared to other forms of qualitative research methods. This allows for the generalisation of indigenous methods, concepts and theories into other situations, such as civil war. Its form of analysis is not statistical but more narrative, which gives an added advantage to this kind of study.

However, ethnographic research, an in-depth research method, requires staying with the participants, observing and living with them for an extended period. This takes time, can be intrusive and requires consideration of more ethical issues, for instance, the privacy of the interviewees. In addition, as indicated by Edmonds and Kennedy (2013), presenting these facts objectively may not bring out a strong argument for indigenous methods. Further, ethnographic research has limited breadth compared to the narrative method. For instance, generalisations are almost non-existent since it observes a single phenomenon, leaving the study ambiguous. It is, therefore, unsuitable as the effective method to be utilised singly here.

Another way of conducting this study could be through phenomenological research. This method cuts across other qualitative approaches, such as ethnography. It involves data gathering techniques, such as observation, interviews and discussions. Edmonds and Kennedy (2013:136) indicate that it describes 'the self's knowledge of phenomena.' The strength of phenomenological research is that it provides rich, detailed data about experiences, composition and perspectives, which is impossible to obtain through surveys or structured questions. My role in conducting this research, through phenomenology, would be to describe and determine the meaning of interviewee responses to open-ended questions and reflect on interviewee stories. This generates large quantities of data suited for bigger studies so that it can cause problems with analysis. In addition, generated data may not neatly form categories; therefore, an unsuitable method to be utilised here.

Method of Choice—Narrative Inquiry Qualitative Research

Research Design

The research process follows the narrative inquiry descriptive design (see Figure 3.1) propounded by Edmonds and Kennedy (2013:131). While the research topic emerged from the literature because it showed the importance of Nilotic Lwo cultures in ethnic and inter-ethnic conflict resolution, Chapters 4–6 emerged from interviewee stories; they developed as the analysis of these stories continued. The composition of this study's phenomenon includes interviewees' stories and narratives on cultural knowledge, conflict

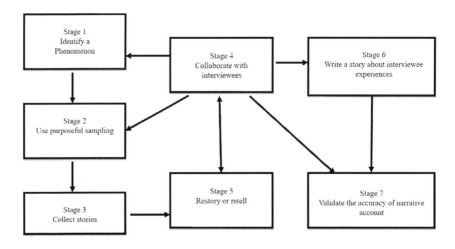

Figure 3.1 Narrative Inquiry Descriptive Design

and civil war experiences, including indigenous conflict resolution experiences. Selected interviewee narratives are quoted and briefly analysed within chapters. Significantly, concepts that contribute to knowledge are drawn from all interview responses.

The use of the narrative method to research Nilotic Lwo is not new. For instance, Johnson and Anderson's (1995) anthropological work on the Dinka and Nuer communities was based on historical narrative accounts. Therefore, in agreement with Andrews et al. (2008:4), the significance of using the narrative method here is that it is a 'route to understanding ... a social phenomenon.'

Definitions of Narrative Inquiry

Lapan et al. (2012:15) define narrative inquiry as 'a qualitative research method that seeks ways to understand and represent experiences through the stories that individuals live and tell.' Riessman (2008) and Andrews et al. (2008) view it as a process where interviewees tell stories based on their experiences and knowledge. Adding, Edmonds and Kennedy (2013:129) indicate that 'Humans are storytelling beings by nature; we lead storied lives, both individually and collectively.' Concerning this study, narrative culture is evident in the work of Nilotic Lwo writers (namely, p'Btek, 1966; Ogot, 1999; Ngugi Wa Thiong, 1986). Moreover, the majority of interviewees agree with the Nilotic Lwo oral culture as a means by which indigenous communities transmit norms and values. Thus, its application in exploring cultural stories to determine meaning is crucial, making it a preferred method to gather and analyse data instead of ethnographic and phenomenological research. More specifically, the narrative method suits this study's aims and research questions in that:

i) Nilotic Lwo people are culturally storytellers (Edmonds and Kennedy, 2013; Fulo, 3 April 2013).
ii) It brings to light common notions of stories that differ within the selected groups of study.
iii) It allows deeply hidden concepts to emerge (Lapan et al., 2012).
iv) It allows marginalised groups, unprivileged voices and indigenous knowledge to initiate change in these communities (Canagarajah, 1996; Lapan et al., 2012).

Given the indigenous context of this study and taking into consideration Connelly and Clandinin's (1990:2) definition of narrative inquiry qualitative research as 'the study of the ways humans experience the world,' this book's understanding of narratives is that they are data sources with rich cultures that are lived experiences. Narrative inquiry qualitative research is, therefore, a means through which data sources with rich (Nilotic Lwo) culture, including customs, stories, legends, riddles, proverbs, comedy, songs, symbols, names and nicknames, poetry, images or photos, and beliefs of a community, are passed on and learned through generations. A Nilotic Lwo writer, Ogot (1999), acknowledges the existence of these narrative sources in their cultures. He indicates that, in the Nilotic Lwo cultures, folklore includes a range of popular myths and beliefs that relate to people's places of origin, lifestyle, community and co-existence. In these cultures, everything has a story about itself. Symbols or incomplete stories can be made complete in a story transmitted for learning purposes (refer to Fulo's and Efo's stories). Adding, Ngugi wa Thiongo, in his account, validates this Nilotic Lwo or African narrative culture. He narrates personal childhood experiences and how they learned to retell the same stories to other children. He writes:

> I can vividly recall those evenings of storytelling around the fireside. It was mostly the grown-ups telling the children but everybody was interested and involved. We children would retell the stories the following day to other children who worked in the fields.
> (wa Thiongo, 1986 :10)

Justification of the Narrative Method

The Nilotic Lwo Narrative Culture

To justify the use of narrative inquiry, this section discusses that narrative culture exists among the Nilotic Lwo. A Nilotic Lwo interviewee, Fulo, explains that stories and narratives are a means through which they learn their culture.

68 *Narrative Inquiry*

> We don't provide a straight answer to a question but tell a story. This is because a story provides detailed information. Such stories are interpreted at the end. However, sometimes, a story is told halfway, and the narrator will say '*diel pe oyango naka iyiibe*', (loosely translates as – you never skin a goat up to the tip of its tail). This means the listener is to think about the story in relation to the situation and make his or her own interpretation/conclusion. In this way, we learn about our history, culture, animals and everything about humans and their environment.
>
> (Fulo, 3 April 2013)

Fulo's account of the Nilotic Lwo narrative culture is evident in the work of the majority of Nilotic Lwo writers such as p'Btek (1966), (Ogot, 1999) and wa Thiong (1986). Through the narrative method, stories about the civil war and Nilotic Lwo peace cultures that make up this book are recorded. Similar to Fulo's narrative is Efo's account below:

> When we were young, we were told and we learned to tell lots of stories from adults. In our culture, we tell stories throughout the day, during daily activities, work parties and at social gatherings. Such stories discourage bad habits or encourage good habits. We often joined our mothers, aunties, sisters in their daily activities. They told jokes, tales, sang songs and told us stories with cultural meaning and values. When something happens in the villages, they compose new songs and stories of the incident. In the evening, we sit around a fireplace waiting for supper, storyteller (*Obok lok)* told us children stories, to keep us awake. At the end, *Obok lok* interprets the story. Tales are often concluded with something like 'so that is why today, so and so are friends' or 'that is why the two do not meet', or 'that is what happens when the spirits are angered'. I don't even remember these stories anymore. I attempted to tell my son a story, he was keen but I could not complete it; because I have forgotten all the stories.
>
> (Efo, 10 May 2013)

In view of Efo's account, oral transmission, storytelling and narratives are a natural part of the Nilotic Lwo's lives—thus, its implementation in this study. In justifying the narrative method, Clandinin and Huber's work featured in Peterson and McGaw (2010) gives guidelines that include personal justification, social justification and practical justification of inquiries. In this case, inquiries will focus on the Nilotic Lwo indigenous peace methods, conflict and civil war resolution. Thus, within these contextual, theoretical, social and personal experiences are the indigenous peacebuilding guidelines justified (Peterson and McGaw, 2010).

Given traditional conflict resolution definitions and contexts, it is justifiable to utilise the narrative inquiry method in this study. For instance, El-Affendi (2005:79) defines indigenous conflict resolution as 'a lengthy process of traditional conflict resolution, through traditional traditions of airing grievances, storytelling and cleansing rituals' and Baines (2007:104) indicates that they are conflict resolution practices based on the 'principles of truth, accountability, compensation and restoration of relationships.' There has to be an oral account, storytelling or a narrative to establish the truth within the traditional conflict resolution process. In addition, restoration of relationships implies further conversations and interactions between disputants. Based on these definitions, it is evident that stories and narratives form a foundation for and are part of an indigenous peace process. Also, before a story is told about the incident, the indigenous peace process cannot commence or conclude, and a resolution cannot happen (see Figure 3.2).

Adding to Fulo and Efo's accounts, Martino, an Acholi interviewee from South Sudan, says:

> We the Acholi of South Sudan cannot start Mato-Oput reconciliation process with the LRA returnees or our brothers in Northern Uganda unless Kony comes back and tells us his side of the story. This is simply because no one can tell why he did what he did and if he instructed his soldiers to cause atrocities in our community as they claim. It is only him who can give us a clear picture of the invasion and atrocities committed in our village.
>
> (Martino, 2 September 2014)

Further, the reasons for utilising this method are that (1) it is complementary, and (2) the narratives themselves help reveal a broad, rich culture

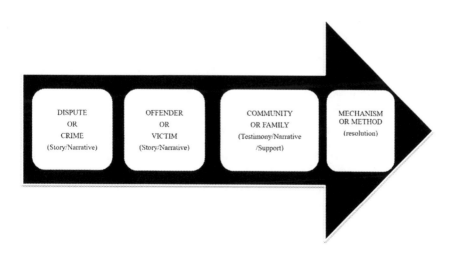

Figure 3.2 An Indigenous Conflict Resolution Process

of the Nilotic Lwo indigenous peacebuilding in both the present and past through legends, proverbs, riddles and stories. This is demonstrated through *Obok lok* 'storytellers' or *boko lok* 'storytelling' as seen in Efo's story illustrated earlier. Adding to these, the living are believed to connect with their ancestors, who reveal what ritual the medium should perform. The medium narrates this revelation to other community members for purposes of conflict resolution. Based on Efo's revelations, the Nilotic Lwo narrative culture contains data sources that provide a detailed picture of the narrative method. For instance, focus group interviews (2014) indicate that

> Stories, legends, riddles, and proverbs are an important part of Luo culture. Luo boys and girls gather there in the evenings to be taught the traditional norms. In the evenings, after people have returned from their gardens, they gather to tell and listen to stories.

Riessman (2008:4) contributes by listing narrative data sources as 'present in myth, legend, fable, tale, novella, epic, history, tragedy, drama, comedy, mime … conversations.' Riessman adds to this list by including memoirs, folk ballads, diaries, photographs and other works of art as sources of narratives. Also, p'Bitek (1966:67) corroborates this socialising and narrative culture among the Acholi in a poem that describes the daily lifestyle of youth and their mothers:

> At the *orak* dance
> A good girl
> Whose mother is blind
> Dances vigorously
> And glances at the sun,
> She returns home
> Before sunset
> A good daughter
> Releases her mother
> She sits around the evening fire
> And tells folk tales
> To her younger ones.

Most of the data sources mentioned here have been utilised in this study.

Additionally, the narrative inquiry method not only complements and reveals a rich, detailed picture of the Nilotic Lwo culture, but also the narratives/stories and all other data sources are lived experiences. For instance, Efo's earlier story demonstrates that stories can discourage bad habits or encourage good behaviour and that they are not only educative but entertaining. The Nilotic Lwo believe that narrating stories keeps people united because hidden grudges are brought to light. In support of this, Machar (2015:2) highlights a local Nilotic saying that 'what is not said is what divides.' The fact that the Nilotic Lwo learn their cultures through narratives supports the argument that their indigenous peacebuilding concepts can be better researched and understood through the narrative inquiry method.

Wa Thiongo (1986:10) supports this learning aspect of narratives by narrating his own story:

> Not that we neglected stories with human beings as the main characters. There were two types of narratives: the species of truly human beings with qualities of courage, kindness, mercy, hatred of evil, concern for others; and a man-eat-man two-mouthed species with qualities of greed, selfishness, individualism and hatred of what was good for the larger co-operative community.

Theoretically, the narrative inquiry qualitative method is justified here. This section argues that selected grassroots peacebuilding theories from which this study is conceptualised have utilised some narrative inquiry data sources mentioned earlier. For instance, Galtung (1996) indicates that peace culture embraces language, art, ideology, religion, as well as empirical and formal science disciplines. He further points out that these attributes of peace culture are permanent and sustainable peacebuilding processes. This book's analysis and discussions consider Galtung's suggestions as lived experiences. A contribution by Elliott (2005) indicates that narratives interconnect the usual boundaries of disciplines, such as history, anthropology, geography and psychology. In this regard, peacebuilding discipline falls within these boundaries.

Further, Ramsbotham et al. (2005) point to Lederach's (1996, 2012) bottom-up theory and explain that there exist three strategies suitable for peacebuilding: bottom, middle and top. Lederach further says that various ways of communication and interaction exist between these strategies. Considering data sources, these kinds of communication can include archival documents, diaries, field notes, discussions, negotiations and conversations (Riessman, 1993, 2008). Some aspects of grassroots peacebuilding theorists embrace narrative approaches—thus, which justifies the utilisation of the narrative method here (Lederach, 1996, 2012; Galtung, 1996, 2004; Ramsbotham et al., 2005; 2009; Woodhouse and Ramsbotham, 2005).

This book finds Lederach's bottom-up theory of peacebuilding particularly aligned with the narrative method. In his 1997 work, he views conflict resolution as 'a process of first achieving discussions and agreements to end the fighting at local peace conferences' (Lederach, 1997:53). In his book, *The Moral Imagination* (Lederach, 2005), he utilises various narrative sources in arguing for moral imagination as the heart and soul of peacebuilding. Drawing examples from Somalia, he indicates that elders' storytelling, forums, negotiation and compensation are critical characteristics of this bottom-up process. He indicates that such narratives contributed to the Somaliland Grand Boroma Peace Conference of 1993.

For example, the use of *Gacaca* traditional courts in Rwanda during the civil war post-conflict reconciliation supports Lederach's arguments (Jeong, 2005). Victims, their families and perpetrators told their stories to local chiefs to reach resolutions in this peacebuilding process. Additionally, Bradbury et al.'s (2006) work on local peace processes in South Sudan points to grassroots conferences. These include the Dinka–Nuer Wunlit peace conference of 1999 and the multi-ethnic Liliir East Bank conference of May 2000. They demonstrate that traditional processes utilised narrative sources, such as stories, conversations, discussions, meetings, oaths, negotiations and religion, to resolve inter-ethnic conflicts during the civil wars.

Lederach uses the artistic drawing of September 11 by Akmal, a Tarjik, to express his experience and knowledge, and find meaning and resolution to what he calls 'cycles of violence' (Lederach, 2005:5). Additionally, he uses speeches to illustrate how historical enmity between the Dagomba and Konkomba disputes over land, killings and denigration was finally resolved. Finally, he uses a story to illustrate how a few women stopped the war in Wajir, Kenya. This same story was mentioned in the focus group interviews. In this story, a woman was tired of dashing with her children to hide under her bed to dodge enemy bullets, during inter-ethnic disputes. She shares her concerns and the need to do something about the situation with her mother. Her mother tells her a similar story about how she had hid under the bed with her (the daughter) to dodge enemy bullets. It is a similar war experience, 'lived experiences' narrated by both daughter and mother. Examples such as these and the data sources mentioned earlier will be utilised throughout the study to justify the suitability of narrative inquiry as a method for conducting this study.

Further, this method is chosen because it offers a wide range of investigative techniques, flexibility and options commonly utilised in social science disciplines, such as peace studies. In particular, focus groups, in-depth interviews and personal stories are utilised. Such peacebuilding techniques embrace various data sources or narratives. To iterate, the narrative method utilises multiple data sources that include field notes, journals, diaries, interviews, storytelling, discussions, conversations, letter writing, autobiography, biography, newsletters, visual materials, audio recordings, emails and artistic paintings, as indicated by authors (Connelly and Clandinin, 1990; Elliott, 2005; Riessman, 2008; Andrews et al., 2008). These narrative data sources offer a more comprehensive range of options and a flexible framework to select concepts for analysis. In support of this argument, Andrews et al. (2013:1) indicate that 'narrative research offers no automatic starting or finishing points ..., offers no overall rules about suitable materials or modes of investigation, or the best level at which to study stories.' This aligns with the indigenous peacebuilding process—known to be flexible (Bradbury et al., 2006). Most of these data sources, for example, field notes, interviews, stories, discussions, conversations, newsletters, photos, symbols, audio recordings, symbols and emails, have been utilised in the discussion in Chapters 4–6.

Ethical Considerations

The university's ethical clearance was obtained prior to the commencement of data collection. Identified ethical issues included safety in South Sudan due to the ongoing war and revoking past painful memories or experiences in interviewees. To mitigate these, data (face-to-face interviews) were collected among refugees in Leeds. Questions asked focused on conflict resolution rather than causes and perpetrators. Further, my past professional training and experiences as an adviser on sensitive issues provided transferable skills to deal with such painful incidents if they were to occur. The data collection process was voluntary. There was no form of either direct or indirect coercion of interviewees. No monetary or non-monetary incentives were promised or given to gain access to research interviewees. The consent form was explained, and the interviewees were asked to sign and return it prior to data collection. Interviewees were made aware of their rights to withdraw at any stage of the interview and their entitlement to a copy of the results.

Sampling

The sampling procedure was guided by access and reason for selection. The samples, members of the Sudanese community in Leeds, were easily accessed due to their regular visits to the centre and its proximity to the university, where the researcher is based. Access was gained through the community manager. The researcher followed the university's research ethics and the centre's social rules to maintain access. Other than their rich culture, sampling was determined by the availability of the members of the groups under study. The sample group included Nilotic Lwo (who have had a civil war or traditional conflict resolution experiences), including some non-Nilotic people. All participants were over 18 years of age. Face-to-face samples were selected from the interviewees in Leeds but not from those in South Sudan. This choice was made primarily to minimise logistical complications.

Sample Size

The sample size was 35 people in total, 25 of whom were Nilotic Lwo people, 5 Nilotic-Other and 5 non-Nilotic people. From the 25 interviewee samples, five were distance or online (online data collection) interviewees. There were five focus groups from the sample of 20 based in Leeds. Each group consisted of two to four people, three groups were selected and eight people from this sample were selected for in-depth face-to-face interviews. Four were selected from the five Nilotic-Other. Two were selected from the five non-Nilotic people sample for face-to-face in-depth interviews. Of the five distance or online (online data collection) interviewees, three interviewees were selected; four were selected from lead interviews. Therefore, 30 interviews were conducted, from whom 3 focus groups, 18 in-depth face-to-face interviews and 3 online interviews were selected. The interview evidence can be made available on request. Almost all in-depth interviews were carried out, more than once, with each of the interviewees. According to the researcher, it bears similarities to Riessman's narrative study of infertility among South Indian women (Riessman, 2000). Those interviewed more than once possessed rich, detailed information related to the research aim, questions and objectives. Overall, the sample size was determined by the interviewees' knowledge and experiences. At a certain point, interviewees' information never showed any significant new ideas, as various vital concepts had already been revealed. Therefore, data collection ceased (O'Reilly and Parker, 2013).

Sampling Techniques

Purposive

Based on the knowledge of the sample group to be studied and the purpose of the study, purposive sampling was suitable. The sample group showed a willingness to participate, and they were readily available for further interviews. Sampling was based on the relevance of the research questions. Proportionality was not the researcher's concern, given that most Nilotic cultures bear similarities but with minor variance. The significance of purposive sampling here was that only the targeted group was approached, reducing logistical and time demands.

Snowball Sampling

Through the initial focus group samples, names and contacts of possible interviewees were obtained. Snowball sampling was significant because the research group, most of whom were employees, was challenging to locate. From these samples, in-depth interviews, i.e. face-to-face and online, were carried out. Through the snowballing technique, the researcher understood the research topic better and developed ideas, chapters and themes. As indicated in the sample section above, this process continued until the saturation level was reached. Eight months into the data collection process, no further significant information was gathered (Mason, 2010).

Data Collection

Data was collected from interviewees of different backgrounds, including lawyers, political activists, community workers, students and homemakers.

Interview questions were summarised or paraphrased depending on the interviewees' level of understanding and occupation. Interviewees' stories of customary codes of conduct, rituals or peacebuilding ceremonies are analysed in the following chapters. Not all the narratives were described at full length due to time limits. Nevertheless, more concepts cropped up as follow-ups continued.

The data collection process applied here fits into an experience-centred form of narrative research, and as Squire (2008) indicates, full written, oral and recordings of interviewee stories were included. At ties, the researcher prompted interviewees during discussions using open-ended questions. For instance, what, why, how, when, where and whom questions were asked about disputes or conflicts and their resolutions. This approach conforms to Riessman's (2008) description of narratives as having a range of ways to organise and tell stories. Generated from both literature and raw data, these disputes or conflicts whose narratives I asked for include:

i) Murder: mass, meditated or accidental.
ii) Physical harm sexual: adultery, incest, rape, mutilation, abduction.
iii) Property: raid, theft, ownership, use, social obligation.
iv) Marriage: marital problems, separation, divorce and child custody.

Some of these disputes or conflicts are not necessarily existent in the South Sudan civil war situation, but they give a general view of how these communities resolve a range of their conflicts.

Data Collection Tools

Electronic and manual tools were used in the data collection process to capture as much data as possible within the shortest time possible.

Open-Ended Interview Questions

The structured questions were designed and piloted when the data collection process commenced. It soon became apparent that this would not be effective because most Nilotic Lwo interviewees speak English as their second language, and some cannot read English. In addition, due to the interviewee's storytelling nature, it was better to prompt and let them continue.

These questions were then narrowed down into what, how, when, why and who open-ended questions. These were asked at the end of the story or some other time. Questionnaires were, therefore, not utilised. The researcher summarised and asked questions around three areas identified below.

Question: When an incident occurred in your community or between your communities, what, who, when, how and why was it resolved? Examples included:

i) Murder: mass, meditated or accidental.
ii) Physical harm sexual: adultery, incest, rape, mutilation, abduction.
iii) Property: raid, theft, ownership, use, social obligation.

To explain the above question further, *what* would refer to the dispute/crime, *who* to those involved, *when* to the time the incident/resolution took place, *how* to the circumstances under which it happened and any specific conflict resolution ceremonies and *why* to the reason for the choice of that particular method/technique/ceremony/ritual.

Field Notes

Because most interviews were informally carried out during noisy social events, gatherings or conversations, very little or no recording or writing could be achieved. In addition, the interviewees were often distracted, so they strayed away from their stories and, at times, made long pauses during discussions. At times, they joined in other conversations, so follow-up could only be possible if the beginning of the narrative was written. As a result, recording field notes became necessary. The use of field notes fits well within narrative research. For instance, Connelly and Clandinin's (1990) work on stories of experience and narrative inquiry stresses the significance of field notes as a primary tool of narrative research.

Electronic Devices

Electronic devices utilised in the data collection process were as follows:

i) Tape recorder to enable audio recordings to enhance data capture.
ii) Personal computer to send emails, skype text, calls as well as audio recordings of in-depth interviews.
iii) Phones, both mobile and landline. A mobile phone was specifically used to make skype calls and send skype texts, phone calls and texts. A landline phone was used to carry out lengthy conversations and/or interviews. The use of electronics at the later stage of data collection targeted the more knowledgeable interviewees. The process offered a reliable and creative exploration of ideas suitable for decision-making.

Data Collection Techniques

Desk-Top Research

Data collection started with literature desk-top research into Nilotic communities' cultural practices, traditional conflict resolution and the Sudan civil wars. This initial step was significant in informing the validity of the research topic, study aims and objectives. Nilotic communities were researched in depth. This led to identifying four suitable Nilotic ethnic groups (refer to the research aim). The reason for this selection is that these ethnic groups, at times referred to as 'Lwo ethnic groups', but which fall under a major ethnic group (Nilotic), occupy the South Sudan region, and they have got long historical inter- and intra-community disputes and relevant traditional conflict resolution techniques. These same groups have been enmeshed in numerous civil wars since Sudan gained its independence from British colonial rule in 1955. These inter-ethnic conflicts and civil wars have continued, even after South Sudan gained its independence from Sudan in 2011.

The information gathered, which included conflict and conflict resolution stories, and cultural stories and experiences, fitted well within the narrative research method (Elliott, 2005; Connelly and Clandinin, 1990; Tomboukou, 2003). It was noted that Nilotic cultures bear similarities. Interviewees often commented, 'we are all the same, we are one people.' Therefore, some examples from other Nilotic ethnic communities with practical traditional conflict resolution methods were incorporated. These include other Lwo ethnic groups: that were not selected in the study and the Kalengins/Maar and Ateker Nilotic groups that spread across East African countries. Sources of information included the internet, journals, textbooks and news articles, both published and unpublished. The data gathered was used to co-construct meaning and applied to the South Sudan civil war situation.

Focus Groups

After the desk-top research, the next step in data collection was to meet potential informants. A Sudanese Community Centre was identified in Leeds, and this became the first contact point. This technique was suitable at this stage because, at the start of the face-to-face interviews, it captures a broader range of informants and speeds up the research process. In conducting focus groups, a small number of two to four individuals were formed, and they were grouped into male and female, respectively. Grouping strictly adhered to the informants' cultural/religious beliefs and availability.

After that, the informants were brought together to discuss their cultural conflict resolution methods. The discussions immediately took off once the elder, Ludi, the community centre manager, introduced the researcher to the interviewees. The researcher facilitated the discussions and ensured that many aspects of the topic were explored. Due to the interviewees' busy and informal schedules, discussions were tape-recorded in bits to limit unnecessary recording (evidence can be available upon request).

These were then transcribed and analysed. Gaiser and Schreiner (2009) indicate that this method is a very useful qualitative method for developing a theory. This technique fits into the narrative method because personal narratives, conversational interaction through more intimate familiarity with the material, and social processes are embedded in the research process (Andrews et al., 2008).

By allowing collective discussion on one to two questions about traditional conflict resolution practices and the civil war, the focus groups provided a more comprehensive understanding of these communities' cultures of peace and peacebuilding (Wisker, 2001). Valuable data from these interviewees were incorporated into ongoing narrative records that helped shape the research progress regarding what ideas to follow, with whom and when. Applying this technique at the second stage of data collection was particularly important because interviewee experiences and knowledge were explored.

All 12 interviewees, at this stage, were Nilotic refugees from South Sudan, Leeds residents. Due to cultural and lifestyle routines, it was challenging to make prior arrangements for the focus group meetings, so the researcher's flexibility was necessary. Female interviewees attended their sewing classes at the Community Centre on Saturdays. Men joined in later for prayers or choir practice sessions. This allowed the opportunity to meet both women's and men's groups on the same day. I worked around their schedule. On Tuesday evenings, the youth were met before or after their computer skills training sessions.

Through this approach, a wide range of interviewees was involved. For instance, those who would generally decline to participate due to fear of the language barrier, if the appointment was requested or made, felt free to contribute to the discussions, conversations or narratives. At this stage, some interviewees gave new leads of those informants to be considered. These new leads, and some focus group members, became very significant in the following stages of in-depth interviews and to the successful completion of the data collection.

Snowballing Data Collection

The narrative method is not restrictive, so the snowballing technique fits well into narrative research because it involves interviewees retelling stories and takes advantage of social networks, leading to more potential contacts. Key informants often made book, article and journal recommendations. They sometimes offered information from their home book collections or made photocopies and posted them to the researcher.

Because this study is particular to Nilotic cultures and South Sudan, the importance of these recommendations was that they exposed the researcher to crucial information that would not otherwise be found in most library collections or on the internet. Data from these recommended sources was very significant, and some were used in identifying thesis chapters. Further, interviewees recommended individuals, their friends or people they knew, and other Nilotic ethnic cultures whose significance in conflict resolution they were aware of. In this book's view, snowballing in the narrative method is an experience-centred and culturally oriented approach to narrative inquiry (Squire, 2008).

As mentioned earlier, Nilotic cultures bear striking similarities. Some interviewees told vague stories of others' cultures. This information was vital as it furthered research on these vague issues. Scripts of the data collected can be made available upon request.

In-Depth Interviews

The total number of selected face-to-face in-depth interviews is 18. These interviewees are all based in the UK. They were interviewed individually, mostly in their homes, at the Leeds Sudanese Community Centre or public or university libraries. After this, due to some interviewees' limited time, some interviews with these significant informants continued through telephone conversations or texting. This vital follow-up of the face-to-face conversations was intended to expand upon vague issues.

During the in-depth interviews, open-ended questions were used, usually at the start of the interview (see Appendix B). Throughout the narrative, in-depth details were obtained. I ensured minimal intervention, except for occasional prompts to keep the interview on track. This technique was particularly useful, because it allowed the interviewees to answer from their own frame of reference rather than being restricted by the structure. It thereby permitted the informants to express their thoughts, experiences and knowledge freely, at length, on a wide range of issues (Wisker, 2001).

The interviewees were asked about their historical and traditional knowledge, experiences and perceptions of conflict and conflict resolution. Eight of these interviewees belong to the Dinka, Acholi, Anyuak and Nuer; one is Maasai. Some of them not only narrated their own cultural stories but those of other Nilotic ethnic communities. This number was to ensure that as many cultural narratives as possible were gathered to allow a deeper understanding of the Nilotic cultures. The other two (non-Nilotic) interviewees include a former NGO worker (an eastern European) and an academic (British).

These two were included to target non-Nilotic perspectives of indigenous methods. In agreement with Elliott (2005), narrative accounts of historical, cultural and work experiences helped provide meaning attached to interviewee experiences. These in-depth historical narratives further provided significance to this study, as seen in Lederach's (2005:135) references to Mbiti's views that 'in Africa time moves from the present towards the past.' These lengthy narratives were recorded in the form of memoirs.

Online Data Collection

From a sample of five, three were selected for in-depth online interviews. Considered experts, their opinions were gathered through the online data collection technique (Ward et al., 2014). They were asked open-ended qualitative questions via emails, skype calls or texts, a data collection technique indicated in the works of Wisker (2001) and Gaiser and Schreiner (2009). This technique fits into the narrative method, and Andrews et al. (2008:5) categorise the use of emails under 'a third form of narrative research.' These three interviewees are Nilotic. They included a South Sudanese local conflict resolution NGO worker, Samwiri (Acholi); Pete, a human rights lawyer (Nuer) and Opor (an Anyuak), also an Adventist Development and Relief Agency (ADRA) employee based in Geneva. All three have worked in South Sudan, so they were chosen based on their cultures, experience and knowledge. In addition, I wanted to know their views on the applicability of traditional mechanisms in modern-day conflicts. The data generated through this technique was analysed and fed back and forth to interviewees. Applying this technique in this research process was significant in that these interviewees, who possess vital insider knowledge, were hard to reach for face-to-face interviews.

Due to their busy schedules, email exchanges and skype telephone conversations consisted of disjointed short stories and extensive conversations on traditional methods (Andrews et al., 2013). Research interest at this stage was in their meaning and usefulness in resolving a modern conflict or civil war. This data was then used to produce co-constructed narratives that illustrated broad cultural narratives and conflict resolution concepts. Online data collection helped strengthen the validity of information from other sources (Gaiser and Schreiner, 2009). This technique was particularly suitable because non-interaction between informants, as occasionally witnessed during social gatherings at the Community Centre, was eliminated. The data gathered was printed and then filed in a folder to be grouped and discussed on a thematic basis (see broader themes in the next section).

Saturation and Data Analysis

The process of data collection was discontinued when saturation was achieved. Although this is a generally accepted concept in qualitative research (Heath and Cowley, 2004; Charmaz, 2006), some authors have criticised the claim of saturation. They argue that no data can be exhaustive and that the researcher is the determinant. In their view, there is no such thing as saturation (Morse, 1995; Dey, 1999). The saturation claim is made because the scope of the topic was reached when the research questions were answered. Therefore, there was no need for continued data collection.

Summary of Themes/Concepts

Overall, the data gathered generated broader themes below, some of which have been highlighted in the previous chapters. Others, which contribute to knowledge, will be discussed in detail in the findings (see Chapters 4–6). They include the traditional roles of:

- Women
- Motherhood and conflict resolution
- Youth and conflict resolution
- Storytelling
- Etiquette (dressing, expressions)
- Socialising (food, drinks, interactions, healing)
- Relations (offender, victim and family/community)
- Justice or compensation (offender, victim and family/community).

These are significant features in community and national peacebuilding. In support of this, Lapan et al. (2012:15) indicate that 'a critical event approach to narrative inquiry focuses on what the research participant identifies as important in the story.'

Methodological Limitations

As demonstrated above, the narrative inquiry qualitative method suits this study because it brings the advantages of contextual, theoretical, social and personal experiences. In support of this, Bell (2002:207) indicates that it allows 'researchers to present experience holistically in all its complexity and richness.' Despite this, certain methodological limitations must be highlighted. They include language barriers, the construction and reconstruction of stories, the data collection process and analysis.

Language and Perceptions

The majority of the interviewees are immigrants. Consequently, language barriers existed because some were limited in articulating their stories in the English language. This was experienced at the initial stages of the data collection process or focus group meetings. The services of an interpreter for the respective languages could have been enlisted, but this could have caused logistical or ethical challenges or unintended consequences. These very participants made recommendations of other names and contacts, which proved fruitful.

Further limitations, at the onset of the data collection, were the respondents' perceptions, commonly women, about the study. Their positive expectations hinged on the assumption that the outcome of this research would help address domestic issues, such as marital disputes or conflicts. A further explanation regarding the outcome was based on the emphasis that this study would produce concepts and recommendations for civil war resolution and the wider conflict.

Construction and Reconstruction

Bell (2002) points to the nature of narrative inquiry construction and reconstruction. For example, he indicates that interviewees can construct stories to enhance their self-image. In interviewing journey, self-praise and derogatory terms, the negativity of one group against the other was encountered commonly during in-depth interviews. Often, an interviewee belonging to a given ethnic community portrayed the other as the problem and took time to list their weaknesses and bad cultural practices that cause conflicts between communities living adjacent to each other. The 2013 civil war mainly caused these counter-accusations to flare up. To minimise this, the researcher politely guided interviewees to discuss possible resolutions, not the causes of conflicts. Construction and reconstruction are evident in the participants' responses and the researchers' narratives. Connelly and Clandinin (1990:2) support this argument by pointing out those narrative researchers engage in 'selecting stories to construct and reconstruct narrative plots.' In support of this argument, Ogot (1999) writes about how Nilotic Lwo communities with no professional storytellers had a few recognised individuals who learned about many different Nilotic traditions and utilised these narratives to reconstruct their own histories. Although this is a methodological limitation, the construction and reconstruction of narratives gradually contribute towards forming a narrative that aids learning about each individual's self and their world. Further, Bell (2002) indicates that all stories hold and provide people's beliefs and experiences. This is evident in the researcher's reflection on this research journey, beliefs and experiences.

Reflection on Methodological Process

This chapter draws on PhD ethnographic fieldwork data gathered between February 2012 and December 2014 with South Sudanese refugees who attended the Sudanese Community Centre, Leeds, United Kingdom, and later a post-doc research on similar issues in Juba, South Sudan. During this research period, the researcher conducted in-depth participant-observation fieldwork, documented in detailed daily field notes and attended community events organised by participants. Thirty in-depth narrative interviews with differently positioned women and men in Leeds and Juba were conducted. Among the participants in general, a thin line exists between family and community leadership, educational, religious, social support and peacebuilding roles. The research methodology, a narrative inquiry undertaken by the researcher as a Nilotic ethnographer, meant that the study was carried out in great detail. That is, the everyday conflict and peacebuilding experiences of the research participants could have been a challenge to a non-Nilotic ethnographer.

The researcher's ethnic identity and ability to understand key and similar words across the Nilotic Lwo languages were beneficial. The researcher participated in a range of community activities central to the social lives of the participants. These included participation in food preparations for events, attending religious functions, marriages, naming ceremonies, family/community peace meetings and other social gatherings. The idea and practice of 'peacebuilding food' such as sesame, honey and *Boo* were intriguing—their nutritional properties support the indigenous post-conflict healing process.

Also, it was time spent with individual women that the most valuable information about women's subtle ways and 'invisible' roles in peacebuilding were shared with the researcher. This narrative, ethnographic approach, coupled with the researcher's position as a Nilotic researcher, was enhanced by similarities in socio-cultural practices and civil war experiences. These permitted the researcher to become embedded in the participants' lives in a way that would not have been possible otherwise. Both women and men agree on the identified Honyomiji/Monyomiji roles and that, at times, women are obliged to keep a low profile and let men take the praise so as not to be seen to 'over-step' men's or husbands' headship. However, most, especially some older women, have designated peacebuilding roles at the family level.

Conclusion

This chapter re-states the study aim and research objectives, methods considered, method of choice (narrative inquiry), research design, justification of the narrative method, data collection and analysis, methodological limitations and author's reflection on the methodological process. Choosing a suitable method was not easy because conducting interviews based on people's painful past experiences required careful consideration. In addition, other obstacles included the willingness of those to be interviewed, their availability, my need to be flexible and, significantly, how to avoid discussions that might lead to the recollection of painful experiences. Using cultural theory ethnographic and anthropological aspects, conducting interviews gave very rich but 'under-represented' information, as identified earlier. At times, the interviewees gained a deeper understanding of the others' positive cultural experiences and how some of these cultural practices have been implemented in the civil war situation. The subsequent chapters (Chapters 4–6) will discuss the findings on 'under-represented' aspects of indigenous peacebuilding.

Bibliography

Andrews, M., Squire, C. and Tamboukou, M. (Eds.), 2008. *Doing Narrative Research*. London, Sage.

Andrews, M., Squire, C. and Tamboukou, M. (Eds.), 2013. *Doing Narrative Research*, 2nd edition. London, Sage.

Baines, E.K., 2007. The haunting of Alice: Local approaches to justice and reconciliation in Northern Uganda. *International Journal of Transitional Justice*, 1(1), 91–115.

Bazeley, P., 2007. *Qualitative Data Analysis with Nvivo*. London, Sage.

Bell, J.S., 2002. Narrative inquiry: More than just telling stories. TESOL Quarterly, 36(2), pp. 207–213.

Bradbury, M., Ryle, J., Medley, M. and Sansculotte-Greenidge, K., 2006. *Local Peace Processes in Sudan: A Baseline Study*. London, Rift Valley Institute.

Canagarajah, A.S., 1996. From critical research practice to critical reporting. *TESOL Quarterly*, 30(2), pp. 321–331.

Charmaz, K., 2005. Grounded theory in the 21st century: A qualitative method for advancing social justice research. In N. Denzin and Y. Lincoln (Eds.), *Handbook of Qualitative Research*, 3rd edition. Thousand Oaks, CA, Sage, pp. 507–540.

Charmaz, K., 2006. *Constructing Grounded Theory: A Practical Guide Through Qualitative Analysis*. London, Sage, pp. 3–101.

Collins, R.O., 1971. *Land Beyond the Rivers: The Southern Sudan, 1898–1918*. New Haven, CT, Yale University Press.

Connelly, M. and Jean, C.D., 1990. Stories of experience and narrative inquiry. *Educational Researcher*, 19(5), 2–14. http://www.tc.umn.edu/~dillon/CI%208148%20Qual%20Research/Session%2012/Narrative-Clandinin%20ER%20article.pdf [Accessed: 29 September 2014].

Dey, I., 1999. *Grounding Grounded Theory. Guidelines for Qualitative Research*. Bingley, Emerald Group Publishing Limited.

Douglas, M., 1966. *Purity and Danger: An Analysis of Concepts of Pollution and Taboo*. London, Routledge and Keegan Paul.

Douglas, M. 1970. *Natural Symbols. Explorations in Cosmology*. New York, Routledge.

Douglas, M., 1973. *Natural Symbols: Explorations in Cosmology*. London, Barrie & Rockliff.

Douglas, M., 1992. *Risk and Blame: Essays in Cultural Theory*. London, Routledge.

Edmonds Alex, W. and Tom, K.D., 2013. *An Applied Reference Guide to Research Designs: Quantitative, Qualitative, and Mixed Methods*. London, Sage.

El-Affendi, A., 2005. *Facing IGAD's triple challenges: New prospects for regional cooperation in the Horn of Africa*. Khartoum Conference to launch the IGAD strategy for Peace and Security, 1–3 October.

Elliott, J., 2005. *Using Narrative in Social Research: Qualitative and Quantitative Approaches*. London, Sage Publications.

Gaiser, J.T. and Schreiner, E.A., 2009. *A Guide to Conducting Online Research*. London, Sage, pp. 118–121.

Galtung, J., 1996. *Peace by Peaceful Means*. London, Sage.

Galtung, J., 2004. *Transcend and Transform: An Introduction to Conflict Work*. London, Pluto Press.

Heath, H. and Cowley, S., 2004. Developing a grounded theory approach: a comparison of Glaser and Strauss. *International Journal of Nursing Studies*, 41(2), pp.141–150.

Jeong, H-W., 2005. *Peacebuilding in Postconflict Societies*. London, Sage.

Johnson, D.H. and Anderson, D.M., 1995. *The Prophet Ngundeng and the Battle of Pading. Revealing Prophets: Prophecy in Eastern African History*. Oxford, James Currey Publishers.

Jupp, V., 2006. *The Sage Dictionary of Social Research Methods*. London, Sage.
Labov, W., 1972. *Language in the Inner City: Studies in the Black English Vernacular*. Oxford, Basil Blackwell, p. 360.
Lapan, D.S., Quartaroli, T.M. and Riemer, J.F. (Eds.), 2012. *Qualitative Research: An Introduction to Methods and Designs*. San Francisco, CA, Jossey-Bass.
Latigo, J.O., 2008. *Northern Uganda: Tradition-Based Practices in the Acholi Region*. Stockholm, International Institute for Democracy and Electoral Assistance.
Lederach, J.P., 1996. *Preparing for Peace: Conflict Transformation across Cultures*. Syracuse, NY, Syracuse University Press.
Lederach, J.P., 1997. *Sustainable Reconciliation in Divided Societies*. Washington, DC, USIP.
Lederach, J.P., 2005. *The Moral Imagination: The Art and Soul of Building Peace*. New York, Oxford University Press.
Lederach, J.P., 2012. The origins and evolution of infrastructures for peace: A personal reflection. *Journal of Peacebuilding and Development*, 7(3), 8–13.
Machar, B., 2015. *Building a Culture of Peace through Dialogue in South Sudan*. Juba, South Sudan, The SUUD Institute.
Mason, M., 2010. Sample size and saturation in PhD studies using qualitative interviews [63 paragraphs]. *Forum: Qualitative Social Research*, 11(3), Art. 8. http://nbn-resolving.de/urn:nbn:de:0114-fqs100387.
Mishler, E.G., 1986. The analysis of interview-narratives. In T.R. Sarbin (Ed.), *Narrative Psychology: The Storeyed Nature of Human Conduct* (pp. 233–255). New York, Praeger.
Morse, J.M., 1995. The significance of saturation. Qualitative Health Research, 5(2), pp. 147–149.
Morse, J.M., 2000. Determining sample size. *Qualitative Health Research*, 10(1), pp. 3–5.
O'Reilly, M. and Parker, N., 2013. 'Unsatisfactory saturation': A critical exploration of the notion of saturated sample sizes in qualitative research. *Qualitative Research*, 13(2), pp. 190–197.
Ogot, B.A., 1999. *Building on the Traditional: Selected Essays 1981–1998*. Nairobi, Kenya, Anyange Press.
p'Bitek, O., 1966. *Song of Lawino and Song of Ocol*. Oxford, Heinemann Educational Books.
Peterson, P., Baker, E. and McGaw, B., 2010. *International Encyclopedia of Education*. Amsterdam, Elsevier Science.
Ramsbotham, O. and Woodhouse, T., 2009. Peace operations. In The Routledge Handbook of Security Studies (pp. 431–443). London, Routledge.
Ramsbotham, O., Woodhouse, T. and Miall, H., 2005. *Contemporary Conflict Resolution: The Prevention, Management and Transformation of Deadly Conflicts*, 2nd edition. Cambridge, Polity Press.
Riessman, C.K., 1993. *Narrative Analysis: Qualitative Research Methods. 30.* Newbury Park, CA, Sage.
Riessman, C.K., 2000. Even if we don't have children [we] can live': Stigma and infertility in South India. In C. Mattingly and L. Garro (Eds.), *Narrative and the Cultural Construction of Illness and Healing* (pp.128–152). Berkeley, CA, University of California Press.
Riessman, C.K., 2008. *Narrative Methods for the Human Sciences*. London, Sage Publications.

Saunders, M., Lewis, P. and Thornill, A., 2003. *Research Methods for Business*. London, Routledge.

Sedgwick, P.R. and Edgar, A. (Eds.), 2002. *Cultural Theory: The Key Concepts*. London, Routledge.

Squire, C. 2008. Experience-centred and culturally-oriented approaches to narrative. In M. Andrews, C. Squire, and M. Taboukou (Eds.), *Doing Narrative Research* (pp. 42e63). Thousand Oaks, Sage.

Strauss, A. and Corbin, J., 1990. *Basics of Qualitative Research*. Newbury Park, CA, Prentice Hall, Financial Times.

Tomboukou, M., 2003. *Women, Education, the Self: A Foucauldian Perspective*. Basingtoke, Palgrave Macmillan.

wa Thiong'o, N., 1986. *Writing against Neocolonialism*. Nairobi, Vita Books.

Ward, P., Clark, T., Zabriskie, R. and Morris, T., 2014. Paper/pencil versus online data collection: An exploratory study. *Journal of Leisure Research*, 46(1), pp.84–105.

Warren, C. and Karner, T., 2005. The interview. Discovering qualitative methods: field research, interviews and analysis. *Los Angeles: Roxbury*, 115, p.35.

Wisker, G., 2001. *The Postgraduate Research Handbook*. London, Palgrave.

Woodhouse, T. and Ramsbotham, O., 2005. *Peacekeeping and Conflict Resolution*. London, Frank Cass.

List of Interviews Cited in the Text

1) Interview with Efo, 10 May 2013
2) Interview with Fulo, 3 April 2013
3) Interview with Martino, 2 September 2014
4) Focus group interviews, 2014

4 Socialising through Food and Etiquette in Peacebuilding

Introduction

The purpose of this book is to examine the indigenous peacebuilding approaches. That is the traditional institutions, customs and practices of the Nilotic Lwo in delivering sustainable peace in South Sudan. The previous chapter demonstrated that the investigation was conducted through narrative inquiry ethnographic methods such as in-depth interviews, focus groups and online interviews. The sample includes the Nilotic Lwo migrant community in the UK and Africa. They narrated their experiences and views. The researcher explored with experts who possess knowledge of and have experience in inter-ethnic conflicts, civil war, indigenous peacebuilding or peace studies. In their narratives, it became more apparent that socialising through food, food sharing and following the communities' code of conduct is significant in indigenous peace processes. Peacebuilding foods are symbolic and possess nutritional healing values. The purpose of this chapter is thus to discuss socialising through food, food sharing and associated rituals and ceremonies.

As seen earlier, societal customs utilised in traditional conflict resolution include customary laws, beliefs and practices, and concepts embedded in cultural and Afrocentric theories. Figure 4.1 shows the linkage of these features to societal customs.

Socialising refers to inter-linkages and interactions of social features in an indigenous peace process. Examples of peacebuilding features include offender or victim, dispute or crime, institution (i.e. family, community, youth, women, elders, representation), and method or mechanism (i.e. ceremony and ritual). Socialising requirements and activities accompany the above features. These include storytelling, etiquette, food and drink sharing, kinship/relations, networks, spirits, gods and justice (Bedigen, 2017). Whereas this chapter will discuss food, food sharing and etiquette, other socialising features will be discussed in the following chapters, i.e. Chapters 5–7.

In doing so, this chapter and the following three are to answer research questions 2 and 3 as well as accomplish research objectives 3 and 4. The

DOI: 10.4324/9781003133476-5

88 Socialising through Food and Etiquette

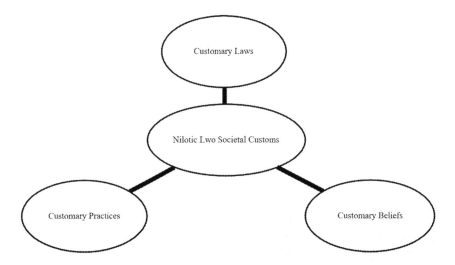

Figure 4.1 Features of Nilotic Lwo Societal Customs

first research question was achieved in Chapters 1–3. Four objectives were set out, and two were accomplished in Chapters 1–3.

To remind ourselves, research questions 2 and 3 are as follows:

i) What indigenous peacebuilding approaches do the Nilotic Lwo (Dinka, Nuer, Acholi and Anuak) have to intra-ethnic and inter-ethnic disputes resolutions?
ii) How do people who have knowledge of and experience in both indigenous approaches to ethnic conflict resolution and the civil war understand them?
iii) How can these indigenous approaches be utilised in delivering sustainable peace during conflict and in post-civil war situations?

Therefore, in answering the designed research questions and research objectives mentioned above, indigenous issues/practices discussed in this chapter include food, food sharing, good manners (etiquette), ceremonies and rituals (the liver-eating ritual; the use of plants, herbs, seeds, roots and wild honey in ceremony). Peace theories analysed in previous chapters do not give meaning to these practices, yet they are significant in indigenous peacebuilding. Therefore, these areas are this book's contribution to knowledge. Also, this book utilises cultural theory in viewing these under-represented indigenous practices.

A brief description of the interviewees is provided in discussing the under-represented indigenous practices. Their narratives will be utilised in analysing and discussing the usefulness of the under-represented customs in achieving sustainable peace. Direct quoting and paraphrasing of narratives from these sources will support the discussions. Some contrasting highlights will be made to the conventional perspectives and practices. In some cases, this analysis will include information from other interpretive data, for example, life history information.

Context

This chapter utilises Douglas and Lederach's theories as a framework to conceptualise socialising through food and rituals in indigenous peacebuilding. Douglas' cultural theory, for instance, provides a lens through which Nilotic Lwo indigenous peacebuilding methods can be understood because it makes meanings of symbols, rituals, blood and sacrifice. The utilisation of features listed is more organic than external peace actors' initiatives. Moreover, these indigenous practices that Lederach (1997:95) refers to are 'cultural and contextual resources for peace and conflict resolution'—thus, their consideration is crucial in community and national peacebuilding.

Unlike other peace theories that promote external intervention in conflicts and hybrid peacebuilding, some authors argue that local community elders should lead peacebuilding (Leonardi et al., 2010; Njeri, 2019; Lederach, 1997). Douglas adds to this by indicating that religious and cultural practices bring together people of different levels and that every culture naturalises a particular view of the human body, such as bones, blood, breath or excrement (Douglas, 1970, 1973, 2004). The findings show that the Nilotic Lwo make tiny cuts on disputants' bodies and drink/smear animal blood on human bodies during peacebuilding to unite and re-establish broken relationships. Moreover, other natural features such as animal skin, bird feathers and beads are given peaceful meanings. For example, white or blue colours are historically naturalised and socialised in peoples' beliefs and practices. These colours represent peace and are worn in clothes or beads utilised in day-to-day conflict resolution. Asante (2003) adds to this by indicating that these customs are essential in transforming a community. They are context based or communo-centred and make up a Nilotic-centred approach to peacebuilding—thus, they are sustainable (Bedigen, 2019; Gebre and Ohta, 2017:161; Mac Ginty, 2010:348; Millar et al., 2013).

Socialising Features

Figure 4.1 shows features or concepts in the Nilotic Lwo indigenous peacebuilding process drawn from empirical data. First, discussions indicate that food is a feature in socialising in the indigenous peacebuilding process, see Figure 4.2. In light of Douglas (1973) and Cashmore and Rojek's (1999) argument that cultural theory concepts organise people, I argue that food sharing and a focus on the re-establishment of relationships unite conflicting

90 *Socialising through Food and Etiquette*

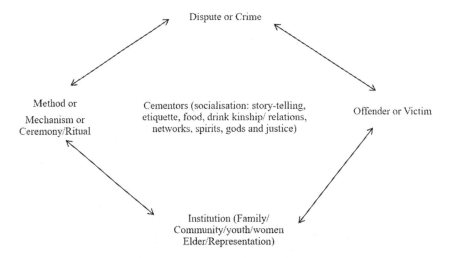

Figure 4.2 The Nilotic Lwo Indigenous Peacebuilding Features in Socialising

parties with the common purpose to reach a resolution—thus encouraging socialising in the process.

Food

Broadly, peacebuilding food is conceptualised within food security in conventional ideologies, and it is majorly constituted within economic recovery in post-conflict situations (Goetz and Jenkins, 2016). Peacebuilding food is understood as a humanitarian intervention by agencies like CARE, Oxfam and World Vision (Sullivan, 1970). Relevant to Nilotic Lwo conceptualisations are Holleman et al.'s (2017) arguments that demonstrate that 'conflict impacts on food insecurity and malnutrition, and how improvements in food security, nutrition and rural livelihoods' prevent conflicts and deliver sustainable peace. While conventional conceptualisation of peacebuilding food is useful in relieving humanitarian crises, it remains limited to resolving hunger and malnutrition. In the indigenous conceptualisations, the use of food is inbuilt within the peacebuilding process and beyond. For instance, the concept includes food availability, food types, properties and spiritual significance. That is, peacebuilding food should be shared, sacred and pleasing to the spirits (Bedigen, 2017). Significantly, the indigenous peacebuilding food conceptualisations require homegrown foods—thus promoting ownership. As Sellie narrates:

> There are set times for ceremonies; the primary determinant is food, except for emergencies – for example, lack of rain, calamities and

Socialising through Food and Etiquette 91

unending conflicts. One can tell when a community is not on good terms with its ancestors and gods. There is always suffering and no peace because we believe they want to be involved in our lives, and this is what we do historically. We solve all our problems through the revelation of traditional medicine men by sacrificing animals and offering certain seeds/plants. Most commonly, food such as chicken, goats, sheep, cows and plants like Boo are utilised. These sacrifices/offerings can help remove curses or illnesses caused by broken social rules or spirit possession of murder and general protection. These things do not make sense to the outsiders, but to us, they are a matter of life and death.

(Sellie, 12 January 2013)

Sellie's account demonstrates the significance of food, for it determines when an indigenous conflict resolution ceremony/ritual occurs. She points to the need to involve ancestral spirits and the gods. In her story, she explains that when a murder occurs in famine seasons, compensation is paid, but cleansing ceremonies or rituals are suspended until the harvest season when food is available. Other narratives demonstrate that socialising can only be possible when food and drink are shared during and after ceremonies and rituals. Food means much more than just a substance, 'it defines traditions and customs in Nilotic Lwo peace culture and intertwines with societal laws, customary beliefs and practices' (Sellie, 12 January 2013). Considering Douglas' view on sacredness and cleanliness (Sedgwick and Edgar, 2002), food in the Nilotic Lwo cultures is accorded meaning in that it determines when/how/when socialising (cleansing ceremonies/rituals and reconciliation celebrations) can take place, thus making Nilotic Lwo practices contextual in peacebuilding. Also, to maintain society's sacredness (Douglas, 1970), the kind of food to be shared is selected carefully. For example, white chicken, goat or heifer rather than black or red is preferred in cleansing rituals.

Adding, Sellie's narrative points out that food, in the Nilotic culture, defines cosmic relationships or relationships with the spirits. This view is reflected in Fulo's story. Interviewee narratives reveal that sacrificed animals, or chicken, are eaten during an indigenous peacebuilding process. Some animal body parts, such as the liver, front/right leg bone, skull and animal skin, are significant for specific use. Similarly, various plants and herbs, such as *Oput* 'bitter herbs' root, *Boo* 'black-eyed bean leaves,' sesame seeds and Kaal 'millet,' are of significance in peacebuilding. Nilotic Lwo interviewee narratives reveal that an after-ceremony meal, shared by others, including witnesses to the peacebuilding process, is not restricted to ceremonial observation.

An example of food sharing for peacebuilding purposes during the civil war is indicated in Sadrak's narratives. He narrates a story of how during the South Sudan conflict and the civil war, a militia leader used sharing to resolve Dinka–Nuer's inter-ethnic conflicts. He says that a buffalo was hunted and killed and that Riek Machar (a Nuer militia leader) shared this buffalo meat with his rivals to resolve inter-ethnic conflicts that had caused significant losses in their communities. Both sides reflected on their actions, and fights ceased for a while. Although cultural theory concepts of cultures, beliefs, history and practices exist in the peace theories considered in this book, the act of hunting an animal and sharing its meat for peacebuilding is excluded. Viewing these practices through the lenses of cultural and Afrocentric theories adds to knowledge in that it provides meaning to community peace cultures that are reasonably contextual and beneficial to national peacebuilding.

Sadrak, an interviewee, supports the above idea by indicating that 'sharing food reduces tension, demonstrates hospitality and is a Nilotic gesture of friendship' (Sadrak, 13 January 2013). He continues to explain that the disputants offer food and drinks to each other and are obliged to accept. Likewise, either party must not withhold food and drinks. Refusing food/drink offers is an outward demonstration of bitterness, selfishness and uncompromising behaviour, so it is often discouraged. During or after ceremonial meals, comedians, singers or storytellers can be invited to encourage relaxation, healing and forgiveness further. These may also involve jokes, songs, stories, name-calling (animals, pets and people) and renaming places/venues, such as markets and trading centres. While this book argues that all these efforts aim to ensure sustainable peace, it recognises that they have exacerbated conflicts in other communities. For example, some authors highlight that name-calling and derogatory jokes contributed to the Rwandan genocide (Bedigen, 2017; Longman, 2006).

Next, the book discusses the types of food utilised in indigenous peacebuilding ceremonies and rituals. These include animal and crop sacrifices to encourage socialisation and limit revert to conflicts. Generally, food utilisation is less discussed in the literature and conventional methods. Here, interviewee narratives will be utilised in discussing the Nilotic Lwo food for peacebuilding ceremonies and rituals, thus making this analysis a significant contribution to indigenous peacebuilding.

Food for Peacebuilding Ceremonies and Rituals

First is the liver-eating ritual narrative by Fulo and Kurimoto's anthropological study of the Anuak (Anywaa). In this book's view, Fulo's narrative and Kurimoto's study contribute to knowledge as they provide a complete understanding of how food and animal organs can be utilised in holistic peacebuilding to achieve sustainable peace.

Liver and the Liver-Eating Ritual

Kurimoto demonstrates:

> Cwiay-gol is a combined word: cwiny (liver) and gol (another word for riverbank). Cwiay means liver, but cwi alone means fertile. For the

Anywaa, the liver as well as the stomach is an organ of special significance. It is the location of sentiments. Anger, happiness and other feelings are generated in the liver. I may translate cwiny-gol as 'the heart of the riverbank.' This terminology, I suppose, suggests its importance in Anywaa thought and subsistence.

(Kurimoto, 1996:46)

Kurimoto's study corroborates Fulo's narrative on the significance of the liver. While Fulo's narrative demonstrates the significance of liver in peacebuilding, Kurimoto's study highlights its linkages to Anuak and their environment. In this book's argument, the community's settlement along the meandering river, economic activities and sustenance contribute to sustainable peace. Fulo, an ex-nun, qualified lawyer and an Acholi, in her narratives, indicates that:

> The liver is a major organ. In our tradition, it is customary for disputants to eat hoofed animals or chicken animals or chicken liver, to prevent subsequent fights and revenge. We call it Cwiny (heart). The hoofed animal or chicken is ceremoniously slaughtered, and its liver roasted and eaten by disputants. In inter-ethnic conflicts, the elders eat it. It purifies, links people ... it means you are one. It helps keep the disputing parties interacting, and the community will function normally, even after serious disputes, like adultery or murder, have taken place. Chicken/red meat for the ceremony is boiled without salt.
>
> (Fulo, 21 May 2014)

Historically among the Nilotic, an animal liver is vital in dispute resolution and reunion. Fulo explains that an animal is slaughtered in resolving sexual and, at times, murder cases. The liver is cooked or roasted, and then given to the disputing parties to share. In resolving inter-clan or inter-ethnic conflicts, the elders, or war chiefs, ceremoniously eat the liver. The Acholi believe that such severe cases cannot be resolved without a liver. When asked why particularly the liver, not any other organ, Fulo says the Acholi believe this organ is the most important in the body, as it coordinates body functions.

Similarly, other authors indicate that the liver performs many functions within the body, including metabolism, immunological, vascular, secretory, excretory and storage of nutrients (Gajda and Storch, 2015; Kim et al., 2020; Mitra and Metcalf, 2012). Also, the above authors highlight the liver's great function in that it regenerates damaged or dead tissues in the body. Without a liver, the body tissues can die immediately due to a lack of energy and nutrients.

In this book's argument, this regeneration function is what the Nilotic Lwo ancestors wisely attributed to peacebuilding and the re-establishment of damaged or non-existing relationships between disputing parties. Symbolically, sharing the liver represents the importance of continued existence as a community or body. In addition, it symbolises the need for disputants to resume normal relationships and function as both independent and interdependent community members. While the liver-eating ritual appears symbolic in indigenous peace processes, its philosophy is highly applicable to war-torn communities in South Sudan. If applied in national peacebuilding, it can kickstart a new approach to repairing broken relationships that intermittent conflicts have damaged over the years. In addition, the liver-eating ritual initiates a healing process that subsequently leads to functionality within and between disputants, something that is missing in the national peacebuilding efforts (Bedigen, 2017).

Further, the philosophy behind liver eating affirms these institutions as physical structures that must be kept in good condition, purified or cleansed through rituals. In this book, these institutions, i.e. family or community/communities, represent a body that must find ways to function, irrespective of its troubles (Bedigen, 2017). As with a physical body, these indigenous institutions must have the capability of continuously renewing various parts of their structures. For example, the socio-political and socio-economic segments must function efficiently for communities to co-exist.

While this book argues for a philosophical investigation of Nilotic indigenous peace cultures, it recognises that intermittent conflicts have highly exposed these communities to global challenges that may not be addressed by indigenous processes alone. The challenge these indigenous practices face today is the continued marginalisation of their values in national systems. Also, interviewee stories reveal that indigenous settings have been destabilised by the proliferation of weapons, disrespect for indigenous authority and the broader assumption that the international community must intervene in conflict situations. Nevertheless, this book reveals that indigenous practices work well in addressing conflicts in family, community and inter-ethnic situations. It is observed that these institutions, through their indigenous peace treaties, must remain as live entities for meaningful peace to be realised at the national level.

Overall, the centralities of family and community institutions are not only depicted in liver eating but one of the tenets of African culture—togetherness or collectiveness. Acknowledging that conflicts are a part of human life, an individual (represented by the liver) must recognise their potential as part of the community (body), so they must prepare for continuous renovation, rebuilding, purification, resilience and commitment to relationships. In this regard, peace values are expected to permeate all features of a person's life and community's cultural heritage. This enables the society to achieve social harmony and co-existence. A community member, who possesses the spirit of togetherness or *Cieng*, does not rest well knowing another is not at peace (Deal, 2009; Bedigen, 2019). Thus, the liver-eating practice empowers individuals and the community to work together to achieve sustainable peace. This is contrary to conventional methods, where third parties dominate peacebuilding processes, which denies disputants or the community a chance to participate fully, receive healing and reunite to ensure sustainable peace.

Next, the significance of other foods, vegetable plants, herbs, seeds and roots, in peacebuilding is discussed.

Plants, Herbs, Seeds, Roots

> Plants like Boo (black-eyed bean leaves) and Kaal (millet) are utilised in reconciliation ceremonies; likewise, Nyim (sesame). In a family dispute, after the day of quarrel, the older woman wakes up early in the morning and gets raw Nyim in a calabash. She calls the two – they must not get to start their daily activities before this ritual is performed. She instructs them to kneel, facing each other, in front of a hut. She tells them, 'This is a new day; let yesterday's bitterness end; do not carry it into the new day'. She asks each of them to take back their words through an apology. She then scoops some Nyim into her palm, puts it in her mouth and chews it until well ground. She spits this out and smears it on each disputant's 'heart' or (left chest). It is believed to cool their hearts and relieve the bitterness and stress of dispute/conflict.
>
> (Martino, 25 May 2014)

Martino, in his account, indicates that in Nilotic Lwo indigenous peace processes, *Boo* 'black-eyed bean leaves' and *Kaal* 'millet' are utilised as offerings to the gods, followed by feasting (food and local brew). In his narratives, Martino indicates that *Boo* and *Kaal* are the kinds of food always available in Nilotic crop-growing communities. *Boo*, in particular, is a common vegetable in the diet, eaten either fresh or dried. It grows fast—takes only three weeks for the leaves to be picked and cooked. 'It is a vegetable the community always survives on,' says Fulo.

Nyim 'sesame' seeds (see Figure 4.4), a crop commonly grown by the Nilotic Lwo communities, is a significant food in peacebuilding (see Martino's narrative earlier), as it is believed to cure bitterness or hypertension. Also, Muratori (1950:135) indicates that war songs are associated with Nyim, and Nyim is associated with community leadership. A Lotuko war song, '*Tali Lanyim*'? Where is Lanyim? '(Sesame—a leader).' This statement emphasises sesame's significance in spearheading peacebuilding in indigenous settings. The interviewee's responses indicated that conflict or peace originates in a person's heart. Symbolically, the expression '*Tali Lanyim*' calls for a heart for peacebuilding in those who seek to lead peacebuilding (Bedigen, 2020). Moreover, research indicates sesame's nutritional (preventive and curative) (Bedigen, 2017; Martinchik, 2011; Namiki, 1995). In this book's view, the linkage between its nutritional properties and peacebuilding remains fascinating and contributes to knowledge.

Interviewees reveal no other plants or crops known to be periodical except *Boo*, *Kaal* and *Nyim*. They are what the Nilotic Lwo people feed on throughout the year. The communities' reliance on them demonstrates the need for reliable peace methods. Once again, this demonstrates that sustainability is an essential factor in peace. Like liver, sesame seeds nutritionally possess regeneration elements symbolically significant in indigenous peacebuilding. Whereas utilisation of food, particularly the examples provided

Figure 4.3 Boo Plants

Figure 4.4 Kaal Seeds

here, has been grossly undermined in conventional methods, findings here illuminate their significance in family and community peace processes and argue they can be adopted at national levels of peacebuilding.

Further, these narratives demonstrate many benefits associated with subtle ways of peacebuilding. First, the utilisation of *Boo* and *Kaal* (see Figures 4.3 and 4.4), crops that are easily accessible foods for peacebuilding

Figure 4.5 Sesame Seeds

rituals, signifies the need for the prevalence of peace and anything that helps cultivate it. Second, it demonstrates readiness in dealing with conflict situations and third, the communities' open-mindedness in embracing available resources in local peacebuilding. These attributes are vital in ensuring that conflicts do not escalate and limit delays in sourcing resources for peacebuilding.

Wild Honey

> In our culture, wild honey is used in dispute resolution when it is inter-ethnic conflict. The youth are sent to the forest to collect wild honey. First, mediation takes place, and then both communities are summoned for a reconciliation ceremony. During the ceremony, honey is brought, and Odonge (elders) eat it ceremoniously. It is believed to heal relationships. I think the Odonge are clever; they never share this sweet thing.
> (Mosa, 6 April 2013)

Like sesame, wild honey has physical healing properties (Devasvaran and Yong, 2016; Khalil et al., 2010). These choices are well informed because interviewees confirm that these particular food choices, among others, have historically been utilised in resolving disputes and peacebuilding. While debates on African epistemology and philosophy remain contentious and under-represented in almost all disciplines, peace studies inclusive, this research has shown that utilising these particular foods (sesame seeds and honey) aligns with biological and nutritional benefits to a human body.

Likewise, the symbolic significance of liver and liver-eating rituals for peace purposes is commendable.

These findings challenge the conventional or western notions of what should be regarded as crucial in peacebuilding, be it at local or national levels. In contrast, indigenous methods have always been found to be of little importance to outsiders (Jeong, 2005). This work highlights the need to rethink and reshape interventions into local or civil wars by external agencies. These findings show a sharp contrast with conventional peace efforts, which include, for example, the signing of peace agreements, which, when compared to indigenous practices, appear impractical to locals and their disputants. Peace agreements may stop violence and protracted conflicts but do not heal hearts and establish genuine relationships between those communities that have historically hurt each other. Perhaps this explains why many conventional peace deals have failed in South Sudan and other conflict-prone zones in sub-Saharan Africa. Further, these findings highlight that indigenous practices are symbolically well informed by scientific evidence, for they are curative, regenerative and rebuild brokenness.

Next, we discuss elders' food in peacebuilding.

Elders, Food and Peacebuilding Rituals

Being an elder is an honour. Elders' role is to authenticate peace processes; thus, food and rituals are an essential aspect. In some Nilotic cultures, such as the Jabwor, being referred to as an elder implies one has to be over 40 years and should belong to an age-set. Up to three age-sets exist, and one has to graduate into each stage that is recognised with celebrations. Mosa's account indicates such celebrations are referred to as *Tedo Kidi* 'honouring of elders' in the Jabwor language. He explains that, during the celebration, political, social and economic issues affecting the community are addressed (Mosa, 6 April 2013). Other issues addressed include unruly youth and drunken women, and past unresolved conflicts are discussed, resolved and compensation is ordered. The age-set graduation celebrations utilise peacebuilding foods and rituals. Also, elders are regarded as those who should act and lead peace (Bradbury et al., 2006; Leornardi et al., 2010).

Tedo kidi is not just a celebration of elders; it includes discussions of agricultural-related activities. Such include the availability of land and its allocation to members—specifically those who may have joined the community in the past few months or those who have returned after a long time; or those whose land may have been taken over by others in their absence. Also, the annual crop harvest is discussed, including the growth of essential crops in bulk is encouraged. Such crops include staple and peacebuilding black-eyed beans, millet, sesame and domestic animals (cows, goats, sheep and chicken). If less has been harvested, the elders advise members to manage food carefully to prevent famine. As indicated by Holleman et al.

(2017), lack of food has, at times, led to family, intra-ethnic and inter-ethnic conflicts.

Following Tedo Kidi, *Aruko Jwi* initiation into an age-grade system ceremony is held. Mosa's story is interesting in that this progression, from *Tedo Kidi to Aruko Jwi*, is particularly significant because an elder, who becomes an *Aruko Jwi*, can become a negotiator, or arbitrator and mediator in peacebuilding. This event can also mark the passage from an ordinary community member to a more responsible community member or leader.

The next age-set ceremony is *Bonyo*, where elders are fed in a feast, and they are not required to contribute or do anything. However, youth are expected to join—marking their initiation into an apprenticeship in community leadership (Bedigen, 2019). According to Mosa's account, *Bonyo* celebrations formally introduce boys aged 13–15 to the leadership structure. During Bonyo celebrations, cultural leadership skills are introduced to the boys. Boys are expected to learn from elders as well as peers. Each boy in a family is required to bring five chickens. The boys get introduced to the food-sharing culture and men as the providers (Bedigen, 2019). All food is shared, and women take leftovers home.

Next, the code of conduct that the youth and elders are obliged to exercise is discussed.

Good Manners (Etiquette)

Next, this section discusses the Nilotic Lwo perspective on peacebuilding praxis regarding etiquette in indigenous processes. Etiquette here implies customary or cultural behaviour, the manner in which individuals (both local and foreign actors) dress, talk, sit and generally present and conduct themselves during an indigenous peace process (Bedigen, 2017, 2020). Large amounts of literature are available mainly in technical aspects of peacebuilding, such as customary arbitration, negotiation, mediation and elders' role (Belay, 2015; Bradbury et al., 2006; Leonardi et al., 2010; Simonse and Kurimoto, 2011). However, Nilotic Lwo literature on individuals' manners or etiquette during peacebuilding is scarce. There are debates about context-based approaches to peacebuilding (Adebayo et al., 2014, 2015). This book highlights that strict adherence to indigenous etiquette contextualises peacebuilding and prevents cultural domination by conventional code of conduct (Asante, 2003).

While the international actors and some Africans do not understand or value indigenous/cultural behavioural codes in peacebuilding, this book emphasises that their ability to influence the success or failure of a peace process is worth noting. The indigenous institutions are the perfectors, enforcers of cultural values and design cultural, behavioural codes. The general lack of awareness of the crucial role etiquette plays can be attributed to the 'breakdown of traditional structures of power and authority' and this can be traced back to colonialism when cultural values and practices became outlawed (Poku and Mdee, 2013:13). During the data collection, some interviewees, notably the western-educated Nilotic Lwo people, demonstrated indifference towards their own or others' customary etiquette, values and practices. Such individuals involved in peacebuilding did not advocate for the inclusion of cultural peace rituals or codes of behaviour. As such, they have continually been undermined, particularly during national peace processes. This is a grave problem because Nilotic Lwo traditions of peace are closely linked to daily life, morality and religion (Mbiti, 1970). It is assumed that illuminating the significance of these practices in this book will minimise doubts about their usefulness in modern conflicts.

For instance, Efo, an interviewee, tells of how some local Acholi communities got offended by how foreign NGO workers presented themselves at indigenous peacebuilding ceremonies. He remarks that

> if they (NGO workers) want to be part of the ceremony, they should dress up accordingly. Funding ceremonies do not give them automatic right to join and conduct themselves in a disrespectful to locals.

In his explanation, female NGO workers who come to facilitate or witness Mato Oput re-integration rituals dress up inappropriately in trousers. At times, they join locals in the after-ceremony dance celebrations. Such acts are disrespectful and criticised by the locals. This book argues that how NGOs operate is as significant as what they do; a practice/preached division enfeebles their credibility among the locals.

Further, Samwiri, an interviewee, talks about how his locally founded peacebuilding Community-Based Organisation (CBO), Bids Foundation, has strictly followed the communities' etiquette and has registered progress in inter-ethnic peacebuilding. This CBO organises and facilitates inter-ethnic peacebuilding workshops and seminars along the Kenya–Uganda–South Sudan borders. He points out that, before his team introduces any peace projects to these communities, they must find a person who speaks the local dialect fluently. He explains that the entire team must wear approved host's cultural outfits when visiting these communities. Only specific traditional dress codes, the locals' costumes, are acceptable. For example, skin hide and Shuka (sheet wrap) is an authentic ceremonial Nilotic Lwo outfit for men and women to wear Kikoyi, Leso and Khanga.

Other costumes worn by particularly peacebuilding leadership include headdresses, beads and other adornments worn during ceremonies (Bedigen, 2019). For example, the *Monyomiji* wear a tribal headdress of feathers. The Dinka, Nuer, Anyuak, Acholi, Masai, Pokot and Samburu wear beaded costumes. Non-compliance can lead to being unwelcomed or not listened to by the locals. Also, how NGO workers sit or present themselves during meetings with locals is watched closely. All individuals who do not hold any leadership positions are expected to sit on the floor or stand facing the elder, who is usually seated on a chair, acknowledging his status. In support of this, Edelstein (2011) suggests that ignoring or violating cultural customs can subsequently result in the rejection of vital information. For example, inter-ethnic conflicts have persisted among pastoralists communities such as the Karamojong, Jie and Pokot because the external interventions have often ignored the communities' code of conduct. Thus, locals do not respect NGO workers' suggestions or peace initiatives (Bedigen, 2019).

Another conduct that can influence peace works in local communities in South Sudan is the religious dress code. For example, interviewees reveal that non-Muslim NGO workers, when conducting work among Muslim communities, do not cover their elbows and legs or wear veils, believing that doing so affirms Muslim dominance or slavery that they (as Christians) suffered in the past. From the perspective of these Christian NGO workers, continuing to wear Muslim religious clothing is a symbol of oppression that overshadows the vision for freedom and liberation they want to spread among their Muslim neighbours. Such 'alien' behaviour generates distrust and disrespect—thus undermining NGO workers' credibility as peace workers. Closely related to the above perception is the Monyomiji indigenous institution members' dress code. While Monyomiji members' authority is believed to be reinforced by the feathered headdress costume worn and a spear held in the hand (see Figure 6.2), the government or NGO youth conflict resolution workers (of the same heritage) ignore Monyomiji dress code and adapt to the western style of dressing—thus preventing sustainable peace from happening.

The dress code does not only apply to peacebuilding but also to outsiders who engage in women empowerment and development projects. NGO community peace and reconciliation members working on Dinka–Nuer community dialogue initiatives were overlooked due to some staff's non-native dress code (observations of the Dinka–Nuer Cieng dialogue by the author). Dogra (2011:345) argues that western-style dressing by local women and NGO workers 'connotes development and modernity brought by the NGO ... through the vehicle of the NGO local staff, whose dress symbolises her status as being closer to Western women, thereby giving her legitimacy' to empower others through western-initiated development and empowerment programmes. Moreover, a strict dress code may not be an issue in urban settings where western types of dressing, particularly trousers, are perceived as expressions of empowerment and traditional dresses repressive (Dogra, 2011:342). In adhering to the community's strict dress code, individuals submit to a culture from which cultural norms are used to inform societal rules that empower them. In many respects, this dual submission enables women to voice their opinions and be heard—thus, including the significance of self-representation in contextualising peacebuilding and empowerment in the region.

An interviewee, Grace, a Dinka youth and university graduate peace educationist in Juba, tells of her work experience. She has worked with fellow Dinka communities, but the NGO (anonymised) she worked for experienced some hostilities in her first year of engagement. As in most Nilotic traditions, greetings take a long time in the Dinka culture, For instance, a greeting does not simply consist of 'hello' or 'good morning,' as is practised in western cultures, but is a long process. One is culturally obliged to ask about the well-being and wellness of the other person's family, animals and their productivity, rains, crops, harvests, the village, village/clan, etc. Admittedly, she attributes her team's failure to greet culturally to her reluctance to adhere to the community's etiquette. She explains that their team's western education exposure, and timed work schedules, caused this lack of attention to detail. She continues to say that when her team visited Dinka communities, the team greeted briefly but never revealed their 'bull names,' nor asked their hosts about their or their family's well-being or welfare. From Grace's and colleagues' perspectives, lengthy greetings would distract their jobs because they had daily targets to meet. This negatively impacted NGO work, because the locals continuously referred to them as 'alien peace workers.' Examples such as these show that ignoring locals' etiquette negatively influences peacebuilding efforts in the region.

Adding to this, Rosie, a Ukrainian former humanitarian worker currently living in Leeds, did some work with the humanitarian department in Albania. She talks of how they, as NGO workers, created clear boundaries between themselves and the local people by not considering locals' behavioural code of conduct that allows mixing. In her story, she indicates this attitude led refugees to question the motive of the 'helpers,' NGO workers. As an individual, she did not condone her team's discriminatory behaviour, and it was not before long that the locals branded NGO workers as arrogant. In her narratives, she says that:

> I did some work for the human resource department, I got disillusioned! Well, it was because of the way they operated. They were serving the people, but they did not want to interact with them. There was a clear sign on the door, 'STAFF MEMBERS ONLY'. The refugees were not allowed in our office area. It was the whole system; the management was judgemental. I think most of these people have their personal opinions they bring into operational policies. I never want to work with them again; it is all fake! Yes, they are big organisations, but I do not think they are very effective. No, I could not stomach it; I had to resign! As these people need outside help, they can think, they should not be treated as ignorant or outsiders in these processes.
>
> (Rosie, 20 March 2014)

Rosie's story demonstrates that one of the least understood aspects of intervention in local settings by western NGOs is the approach to engaging those being helped. International agencies' work conveys indirect ethical messages that can positively or negatively influence peacebuilding processes. For instance, when the locals are interacted with at arm's length, this is social exclusion, and a lack of recognition of the resilience and experiences of locals could inform NGO workers—manifesting western hegemony. For instance, Gramsci (1955, 1995), quoted in Bedigen (2017), argues for cultural hegemony and domination of society by the ruling class to cause a positive change. The model legitimises manipulation of the societal cultures (such as beliefs, perceptions, norms, values and procedures) by the minority or, at worst, foreigners. In view of Gramsci's perspective, this book maintains the argument that the whole community should institute hegemony. That is, hegemony should consist of the local people, structures, laws, beliefs, values, practices and etiquette—thus positively influencing changes in undesirable or conflict situations (Bedigen, 2017).

Earlier discussions on etiquette demonstrate that indigenous peacebuilding is primarily about respect, and less attention is paid to techniques. Etiquette validates indigenous institutions and, subsequently, their peace processes and outcome. Placing etiquette at the periphery, or relegating it during grassroots interventions and engagements, is highly likely the reason for the unfruitful work of external NGO peace works in South Sudan and sub-Saharan Africa.

Conclusion

Discussions in this chapter are drawn from research findings. It has introduced a concept of socialising, which will be referred to frequently in the following chapters. Interviewees' stories are utilised to demonstrate the significance of plants, herbs, seeds, roots, food, food sharing, food for peacebuilding rituals, ceremonies and etiquette in peacebuilding. It is suggested that they can influence indigenous peacebuilding processes. It's also highlighted the hegemonic position foreign NGOs seem to take and the role of elders in authenticating peace through food and food rituals.

To emphasise, food, food sharing, ceremonies and rituals embedded in socialising are crucial in peacebuilding (Bedigen, 2017). Moreover, significant to traditional conflict resolution philosophy is the purging of unhealthy habits in individuals and relationships through the ceremonies/rituals demonstrated in the utilisation of carefully selected foods and animal body parts. Further, these findings indicate that sustainable peace is not something that is 'planted,' as is common in conventional systems, but a conscience matter, a spiritual and lived experience. Acknowledging the difficulty in sustaining 'planted' peace in a deeply cultural nation such as South Sudan, the application of indigenous systems at all levels of peacebuilding is recommended. This is because, in this book's view, indigenous systems have historically withstood both internal and external pressures to some extent. Most importantly, sustainable peace can be realised only when all aspects of ceremonies, rituals and socialising are included.

Bibliography

Adebayo, A.G., Jesse, J.B. and Brandon, D.L. (Eds.), 2014. *Indigenous Conflict Management Strategies: Global Perspectives*. Lanham, MD, Lexington Books. Retrieved from https://rowman.com/ISBN/9780739188040.

Adebayo, A.G., Abdallah, M., Adesina, O.C., Adéyẹmí, O., Agena, J.E., Agbor, S.O., & Danso, S.O. (Eds.), 2015. *Indigenous Conflict Management Strategies in West Africa: Beyond Right and Wrong*. Lanham, MD, Lexington Books.

Asante, M.K., 2003. *Afrocentricity: The Theory of Social Change*. Chicago, IL, African American Images.

Bedigen, W., 2017. Traditional conflict resolution: The Nilotic Lwo of South Sudan (PhD thesis). Leeds, Leeds Beckett University.

Bedigen, W., 2019. Youth (Monyomiji) and conflict resolution in the south Sudan civil war. *Journal of African Cultural Heritage Studies*, 2(1), pp. 18–35.

Bedigen, W., 2020. Significance of societal customs in the south Sudan civil war resolution. *Journal of Peacebuilding & Development*, 15(1), pp. 3–17.

Belay, T., 2015. Conflicts, conflict resolution practices and impacts of the war in South Sudan. *International Journal of School and Cognitive Psychology*, S2, p. 013. doi: 10.4172/ijscp.S2-013.

Bradbury, M., Ryle, J., Medley, M., & Sansculotte-Greenidge, K., 2006. *Local Peace Processes in Sudan: A Baseline Study*. London, Rift Valley Institute.

Cashmore, E. and Rojek, C., 1999. *Dictionary of Cultural Theorists*. London, Hodder Arnold.

Deal, J.L., 2009. *Torture by Cieng: Ethical Theory Meets Social Practice among the Dinka Ciec of South Sudan* (Doctoral dissertation). University of South Carolina.

De Waal, A., 2014. When kleptocracy becomes insolvent: Brute causes of the civil war in South Sudan. *African Affairs*, 113(452), pp. 347–369.

Devasvaran, K. and Yong, Y.K., 2016. Anti-inflammatory and wound healing properties of Malaysia Tualang honey. *Current Science*, 110, pp. 47–51.

Dogra, N., 2011. The mixed metaphor of 'third world woman': Gendered representations by international development NGOs. *Third World Quarterly*, 32(2), pp. 333–348. doi: 10.1080/01436597.2011.560472.

Douglas, M., 1970. *Natural Symbols. Explorations in Cosmology*, New York, Routledge.

Douglas, M., 1973. *Natural Symbols: Explorations in Cosmology*. London, Barrie & Rockliff.

Douglas, M., 1999. *Leviticus as Literature*. Oxford, Oxford University Press.

Douglas, M., 2004. *Natural Symbols: Explorations in Cosmology*. London, Routledge.

Edelstein, S., 2011. *Food, Cuisine and Cultural Competency for Culinary, Hospitality and Nutrition Professionals*. Mississauga, ON, Jones and Bartlett Publishers.

Gajda, A.M. and Storch, J., 2015. Enterocyte fatty acid-binding proteins (FABPs): Different functions of liver and intestinal FABPs in the intestine. *Prostaglandins, Leukotrienes, and Essential Fatty Acids*, 93, pp. 9–16.

Galtung, J., 1990. Cultural violence. *Journal of Peace Research*, 27(3), pp. 291–305.

Galtung, J., 1996. *Peace by Peaceful Means*. London, Sage.

Gebre, Y.G. and Ohta, I., 2017. *African Virtues in the Pursuit of Conviviality: Exploring Local Solutions in Light of Global Prescriptions*. African Books Collective.

Goetz, A.M. and Jenkins, R., 2016. Agency and accountability: Promoting women's participation in peacebuilding. *Feminist Economics*, 22(1), pp. 211–236.

Gramsci, A., 1992. *Prison Notebooks (Vol. 2)*. New York, Columbia University Press.

Gramsci, A., 1994. *Letters from Prison (Vol. 2)*. New York, Columbia University Press.

Gramsci, A., 1995. *The Intellectuals and the Organization of Culture*. Turin, Giulio Einaudi.

Grawert, E., 2014. *Forging Two Nations Insights on Sudan and South Sudan*. Addis Ababa, OSSREA.

Holleman, C., Jackson, J., Sánchez, M.V. and Vos, R., 2017. *Sowing the Seeds of Peace for Food Security: Disentangling the Nexus between Conflict, Food Security and Peace* (No. 2143-2019-4789).

Jeong, H.W., 2005. *Peacebuilding in Postconflict Societies*. London, Sage.

Khalil, M.I., Sulaiman, S.A. and Boukraa, L., 2010. Antioxidant properties of honey and its role in preventing health disorder. *The Open Nutraceuticals Journal*, 8(1), pp. 6–16.

Kim, J.H., Han, J.W., Choi, Y.J., Rha, M.S., Koh, J.Y., Kim, K.H., Kim, C.G., Lee, Y.J., Kim, A.R., Park, J. and Kim, H.K., 2020. Functions of human liver CD69+ CD103-CD8+ T cells depend on HIF-2α activity in healthy and pathologic livers. *Journal of Hepatology*, 72(6), pp.1170–1181.

Kurimoto, E., 1996. People of the river: Subsistence economy of the Anywaa (Anuak) of Western Ethiopia. *Senri Ethnological Studies*, 43, pp. 29–57.

Lederach, J.P., 1997. *Building Peace: Sustainable Reconciliation in Divided Societies*. Washington, DC, United States Institute of Peace Press.

Lederach, J.P., 1996. *Preparing for Peace: Conflict Transformation across Cultures*. New York, Syracuse University Press.

Lederach, J.P., 2012. The origins and evolution of infrastructures for peace: A personal reflection. *Journal of Peacebuilding and Development*, 7(3), pp. 8–13.

Leonardi, C., Moro, L.N., Santschi, M. and Isser, H.D., 2010. *Local Justice in South Sudan (Peaceworks Number 66)*. Washington, DC, United States Institute of Peace.

Longman, T., 2006. Justice at the Grassroots? In N. Roht-Arriaza and J. Mariezcurrena (Eds.), *Gacaca Trials in Rwanda*, pp. 206–228. New York, Cambridge University Press.

Ginty, R.M., 2010. Gilding the lily? International support for indigenous and traditional peacebuilding. In O.P. Richmond (Ed.), Palgrave Advances in Peacebuilding, pp. 347–366. London, Palgrave Advances, Palgrave Macmillan. https://doi.org/10.1057/9780230282681_19.

Martinchik, A.N., 2011. Nutritional value of sesame seeds. *Voprosy Pitaniia*, 80(3), pp. 41–43.

Mbiti, J.S., 1970. *Concepts of God in Africa*. London, SPCK.

Millar, G., Van Der Lijn, J. and Verkoren, W., 2013. Peacebuilding plans and local reconfigurations: Frictions between imported processes and indigenous practices. *International Peacekeeping*, 20(2), pp. 137–143.

Mitra, V. and Metcalf, J., 2012. Metabolic functions of the liver. *Anaesthesia and Intensive Care Medicine*, 13(2), pp. 54–55.

Muratori, C., 1950. A case of magical poisoning in a Lotuko village. *Sudan Notes and Records*, 31(1), pp. 133–136.

Namiki, M., 1995. The chemistry and physiological functions of sesame. *Food Reviews International*, 11(2), pp. 281–329.

Njeri, S., 2019. Somaliland; the viability of a liberal peacebuilding critique beyond state building, state formation and hybridity. *Peacebuilding*, 7(1), pp. 37–50.

Poku, N. and Mdee, D.A., 2013. *Politics in Africa: A New Introduction*. London, Zed Books Ltd.

Ramsbotham, O., 2005. The analysis of protracted social conflict: A tribute to Edward Azar. *Review of International Studies*, 31, pp. 109–126.

Sedgwick, P.R. and Edgar, A. (Eds.), 2002. *Cultural Theory: The Key Concepts*. London, Routledge.

Simonse, S. and Kurimoto, E. (Eds.), 2011. Engaging Monyomiji: (Bridging the governance gap in East Bank Equatoria). Torit, South Sudan. Proceedings of the Conference, Nairobi, Pax Christi Horn of Africa, 26–28 November 2009.

Sullivan, R.R., 1970. The politics of altruism: an introduction to the food-for-peace partnership between the United States government and voluntary relief agencies. *Western Political Quarterly*, 23(4), pp. 762–768.

List of Interviews Cited in the Text

1) Interview with Fulo, 21 May 2014
2) Interview with Martino, 25 May 2014
3) Interview with Mosa, 6 April 2013
4) Interview with Rosie, 20 March 2014
5) Interview with Sadrak, 13 January 2013
6) Interview with Sedgwick and Edgar (2002)
7) Interview with Sellie, 12 January 2013
8) Observations by the author, Dinka Nuer Cieng Dialogue, Juba (2016)

5 Indigenous Communities, Institutions and Peacebuilding Methods

Introduction

This chapter discusses indigenous communities, institutions and methods of peacebuilding. Discussions demonstrate the distinctiveness of indigenous processes from conventional institutions. The chapter highlights the crucial contribution of indigenous principles such as unity, brotherhood, togetherness, humanity, cooperation and co-existence in delivering sustainable peace.

This chapter and the following two are intended to answer research questions 2 and 3 and accomplish research objectives 3 and 4. The first research question was achieved in Chapters 1–3. Four objectives were set out, and two were accomplished in Chapters 1–3.

To remind ourselves, research questions 2 and 3 are as follows:

i) What indigenous peacebuilding approaches do the Nilotic Lwo (Dinka, Nuer, Acholi and Anuak) have to intra-ethnic and inter-ethnic disputes resolutions?
ii) How do people who have knowledge of and experience in both indigenous approaches to ethnic conflict resolution and the civil war understand them?
iii) How can these indigenous approaches be utilised in delivering sustainable peace during conflict and in post-civil war situations?

Context

The Community/Locals

The majority of peace scholars agree with the need for communities to be involved in peacebuilding. For instance, peace theories by Lederach (1997), Galtung (1990, 1996) and Ramsbotham (2005) analysed in the previous chapters unanimously point to the significance of local people, community or grassroots involvement in indigenous peacebuilding. These authors point to the need for conventional peace actors to form partnerships with the locals, represent their voices and further advocate establishing a relationship

DOI: 10.4324/9781003133476-6

108 *Indigenous Communities, Institutions, and Methods*

between the community and the government. There is evidence that peacebuilding attempts in South Sudan have followed these guidelines to some extent (Bedigen, 2019). For instance, the Intergovernmental Authority on Development (IGAD), which includes the governments of Eritrea, Djibouti, Ethiopia, Kenya, Somalia and Sudan, and the IGAD-partner forum (the United States, the European Union and the United Nations), has led peace processes at national levels and included a selected community representative (Grawert, 2014).

However, most of the Nilotic Lwo interviewees disagree with this line of understanding of the community. The Nilotic are of the view that any interaction with the outsiders benefits only those selected individuals involved and the South Sudan government (refer to Opor's narrative; Bedigen, 2020). Moreover, the Nilotic people believe their communities are culturally sufficient in peacebuilding values and do not need any other. Author and peace activist Diana Francis (2004) supports this view by indicating that peace can only be realised if those communities in conflict are involved in peacebuilding. Thus, this book emphasises that the concept of community includes the people, their cultural practices and interests (Bedigen, 2017, 2020).

In support of the above, an interviewee, Kilo, in his narratives, states that:

> Our culture is everything, rich, and it lacks nothing. They (cultures) help organise and keep us at peace with each other. I do not think we need anybody to educate us on peace for one moment. The community cares for one another and neighbours. We live together, share the little we have and keep together. Our peace culture is so rich that external communities have nothing to add; all they should do is come and learn from us. However, they may help economically.
>
> (Kilo, 11 March 2014)

Kilo, who lives in the UK, is a Nilotic mixed tribe of Nuer and Masai. He is a hotelier and heads a group in the UK that promotes traditional cultures through talk shows, dances, drama and songs. He proudly and passionately speaks of his treasured memories as a child growing up in South Sudan and Kenya. He left his original community over a decade ago; he is aware of the difficulties (intermittent conflicts/civil wars) his communities are experiencing. He believes that communities require economic help from external peace actors, not their involvement in peacebuilding negotiations and justice. He reveals that indigenous peacebuilding methods can be applied to current conflicts, regardless of the high crime levels. His childhood experiences of inter-ethnic conflicts and their resolution shaped his understanding of what indigenous peacebuilding constitutes and its suitability in modern contexts. Considering the current complexities of these conflicts, he is optimistic that solutions are embedded in the culture of those in conflict. Kilo's narrative testifies to Asante's argument that solutions to problems must

Indigenous Communities, Institutions, and Methods 109

be contextualised to achieve the desired outcome (Asante, 2003). To Kilo, this culture implies communities' peaceful living, sharing and good relationships. The need for each other keeps them united and prevents future involvement in violence.

In this book's view, there is a disparity between locals' and international agencies' views on a suitable peacebuilding approach. Whereas the Nilotic Lwo is of the view that a resolution can be achieved only within the community and by the communities' members through their cultural practices, writers such as Lederach (1996, 1997, 2012), Galtung (1990, 1996, 2004) and Ramsbotham (2005) argue for comprehensive and holistic approaches that incorporate internal organisations and external communities. In the previous chapters, the involvement of the New Sudan Council of Churches (NSCC) and the Sudan government was highlighted. Conventional actors often view local organisations such as the NSCC as representative of all locals, but this work indicates otherwise. For instance, de Waal (2014) applauds the high-level reconciliation work undertaken by the South Sudan's church leaders through the NSCC.

Further, based on his field experience, Lederach offers a conceptual framework for indigenous peacebuilding (Lederach, 1996, 2003). Lederach sees the potential in community representatives'/elders' seminars or training. This book emphasises a bigger advantage in involving whole communities rather than a few selected community leaders. The challenge is whether this disparity can be narrowed by listening to one another and merging conventional and indigenous peacebuilding methods and practices. When considering this disparity, utilising cultural, hegemony and Afrocentric analytical, theoretical frameworks becomes significant. Moreover, Gramsci's hegemony (Gramsci, 1992) condones domination of the locals by other influential or non-local organisations. This book argues that sustainable peace is majorly possible by locals' hegemony in peacebuilding.

Further, Kilo describes his communities as caring and united. This principle of looking out for one another is fundamental. At times, it is referred to as brotherhood. It is embedded in the concept of Ujamaa (Swahili language, Kenya), *Ubuntu* or *Botho* or *Cieng*, the Dinka (spirit of togetherness) or Nywak, an Anyuak word for (sharing). The concept encourages members' mutual trust in dealing with community matters. The attitude of togetherness or brotherhood determines the extent to which Nilotic Lwo communities thrive or fail. To put this concept into perspective, Nilotic Lwo people refer to non-blood relationships as brothers or sisters—so do other ethnic African people (personal experience). Therefore, in resolving murder cases, both the deceased and victim's communities will refer to the deceased and offender as 'our brother.' The advantage of this cultural perspective is that it offers a degree of community closeness that can influence the course of peacebuilding. It can influence a negative or bitter situation and transform the peacebuilding process into a friendly protective process. Therefore, togetherness or brotherhood transcends legal techniques utilised in conventional post-conflict judiciary processes to provide a true sense of community.

On the other hand, the togetherness or brotherhood concept can be damaging because kinsmen can condone violent cultural practices, such as cattle raiding and bride stealing, due to the unwillingness to disclose a brother's fault. Kilo, an interviewee, hints that intra-ethnic and inter-ethnic conflicts (associated with such bad cultural practices) downplay the fact that these can lead to major conflicts (Bedigen, 2017). He explains that these practices are not alien to these cultures and that the communities' rich cultures can deal with such bad habits. Kilo's argument is appealing because the community and its cultures should be at the core of peacebuilding.

A story told by Martino serves as an example of where the Cieng concept can hinder peacebuilding. Martino, an Acholi interviewee from South Sudan, says that when a Dinka person gets into a fight with somebody from another ethnic group, other Dinka people will join the fight to defend their Dinka brother irrespective of what, why or who caused the fight. For instance, when the militia groups formed during the civil war, most groups were recruited from their ethnic communities (Bedigen, 2017). These forces remained loyal to their ethnic/political leaders, who committed, encouraged or forced them to commit war crimes and crimes against humanity or property (de Wall, 2014).

Further, most indigenous peacebuilding and management methods or concepts of Cieng, Diel and Nyuak are rooted in unifying principles of common humanity (Mbiti, 1970). This principle of unity is evident in cultural theory. For instance, Douglas (1973) and Cashmore and Rojek (1999) state that cultures organise people at all levels—so do the above principles. Unity brings together ordinary people, victims, perpetrators and community leaders during a peace process—all parties to conflict work towards addressing the cause for the common good. The unity principle revolves around a belief that all human beings are equal, despite cultural or ethnic differences. Thus, the communal way of life, kinship and access to basic needs such as natural resources and food are fundamental human rights in all communities. Therefore, his belief and value form a foundation for an indigenous peace negotiation of conflicts over land or livestock grazing grounds.

Adding, Ludi, an interviewee, says that 'all community members, including children, mothers, elderly people and youth, must be present because such issues affect everybody.' During such gatherings, each person is at liberty to narrate how they are affected and what works. In support of this, Ngugi Wa Thiongo (1986:10) indicates that, 'Cooperation as the ultimate good in a community was a constant theme' in society's situations. Mosa's narratives highlight similar principles that uphold humanity, fundamental rights and co-existence. He narrates that indigenous peacebuilding features revolve around the ultimate goal of co-existence rather than obliteration or isolation. In his narratives, he says that in the Nilotic communities, the primary purpose of solving the problem is co-existence because we historically share water sources, forests, sacred places, etc. When someone is killed, kasurube 'fine or compensation' is paid, but there is no amount of compensation that can ever bring that life back. In resolving it, the outcome should be the continued co-existence of both families/communities. If it happens within a family or community as it did to ours; when a child is abducted and brought back to kill his parents, who do you hate or make him pay? For example, Dominic Ongwen was ordered to hurt his family. His Acholi community wants him to undergo the cultural cleansing process, not be isolated or locked up in prison-like ICC desires. What matters is unity, brotherhood and co-existence, not retribution. The focus of our peace culture is the wellness/well-being of people and their property (i.e. animals and crops).

(Mosa, 5 February 2015)

The LRA rebels, with whom he lived for two weeks, once abducted Mosa, a professional accountant and an Acholi from South Sudan. He managed to escape. He attributes his survival and luck to customary beliefs and practices. Given the ordeal he endured in captivity, such as physical and psychological torture (hunger, exhaustion and suffering), he maintains the view that ex-combatants should be handled through a cultural process rather than through international institutions such as the ICC. For someone who has had first-hand experience with the militia, his views are fascinating. Perhaps his responses to challenges have been shaped by the peace values he learned when growing up. In this book's understanding, his views reflect a genuine spirit and meaning of what values a Nilotic Lwo community stands for. To iterate, they include unity, brotherhood, togetherness, humanity, cooperation and co-existence. Additionally, Mosa's account reveals that indigenous methods are helpful in post-conflict re-integration. Particularly child abductees were ordered by their commanders to harm their family members and others.

Relationships

From the discussions above, this book argues that relationships are maintained to benefit sustainable peace through socialising (i.e. post-conflict interactions). This book focuses on the significance of blood relationships in indigenous peacebuilding. An important point to note is some overlap and ambiguity regarding indigenous perspectives of what a community and relationships are. Among the Nilotic Lwo people, belonging to a family unit is essential, i.e. to be linked to, or in close association with, one. Interviewees revealed that this kind of relationship extends to the spirit world. The relationship with ancestral spirits has to be good and maintained to ensure peace, prosperity or sustainable peace. In support of this, Fulo says, 'we bury our own at home, in a family compound, because they watch over us.' It is a family's duty and responsibility to support their relative (offender or victim) throughout the reconciliation processes when it comes to peacebuilding.

While indigenous peacebuilding involves the offender and victim and their blood relations, this may not apply to specific disputes, such as stealing or sexual crimes (Bedigen, 2017). A family head is the first to be made aware of the situation, and he then informs the entire family and the victim's family. Once the offender has identified himself/herself, for instance, in cases of murder, he/she is not ostracised as such, but the chief or elder contacts the victim's family to commence a peace process. The findings demonstrate those blood relations empathically 'own' the crime by referring to it as 'the wrong we have committed.' Such a reference gives reassurance to the offended community. It is significant to point out that a community's acknowledgement and acceptance of apologies set apart the Nilotic Lwo indigenous peacebuilding methods from conventional methods. An interviewee indicates that everyone in the neighbourhood attends the customary court sexual or murder case hearing due to the belief that all are a unit.

While the above discussions demonstrate the significance of blood relationships in peacebuilding, blood (haemoglobin) is symbolic and is given meaning from cultural perspectives (Douglas, 1970, 1973, 2004). For instance, in Nilotic peace cultures, sacrificial animal blood signifies people's life, health and well-being (Mbiti, 1970). In the Mato Oput ceremony, the sacrificed animal blood is mixed with Oput bitter plant roots (Bedigen, 2017). This mixture, drunk by parties to the conflict, is believed to cleanse, rehabilitate and re-establish relationships. Also, in the context of this research, blood relations are significant in determining how the indigenous peace process is conducted or concluded.

Further, blood relations offer security in times of tragedy. If the offender does not have any blood relations, their closest friends or neighbours will act as their family if he/she wishes. In cases of accidental killing, family support is only given to the non-blood relation, well known by the offender's neighbours/adopted family. In addition, leniency occurs when a non-blood-related offender has some sort of link to the mother community, for example, if he/she has married from this community. Other premeditated crimes, such as theft, sexual assault, witchcraft or property destruction, are dealt with heavy-handedly. Often, the offender is driven away or killed, and their property confiscated.

In support of the above, Fulo tells a story of a tribe (Karamojong) who seasonally migrated to her neighbouring communities (Pokot, Teso, Acholi and Jabwor) to seek employment as cattle herdsmen. While this is often a temporary arrangement, each migrant employee is linked to their employer/host and lives with them. However, if both the host and migrant get on well, the stay continues for many years or generations. At times, these migrant employees adopt the host culture or even name their children after the host or hostess. However, the inter-ethnic continues. For instance, the

Karamojong, who remained in their homeland, invaded and raided cattle from the neighbouring communities (the migrant Karamojong communities lived). Distrust developed between the hosts and the migrants because they suspected pre-arranging cattle raids with their kinsmen. As a result, migrant employees were driven away or killed by their angry hosts and property confiscated. Fulo says her mother secretly sent their migrant employee away to safety. She concluded that if it were another tribe that raided these villages, the migrant employees would have been obliged to defend both the host's property and community. Significantly, migrant employees can participate in the hosts' cultural peacebuilding processes.

Further, in murder cases, where both the offender and victim are blood related, a meeting to discuss the incident takes place after burial and arrangements for compensation payment are made. According to an interviewee's story, a driver, a distant relation, ran over a five-year-old child. Leniency was shown when it came to justice or compensation because the child's family asked for two cows only, and she stresses that compensation would have been more significant (ten or more heads of cattle) if it were a non-relative. This kind of leniency applies to most cases of accidental killings. These practices contrast to the conventional processes, where there is no consideration of blood relations and individual human rights override public rights (Adebayo et al., 2014). Thus, this book argues that the conventional or the western approach to peacebuilding destroys relationships or the natural state of human-to-human relationships. Also, it disregards soul-searching and empathy but promotes a mechanical process, where rules have to be applied, irrespective of their effects on the persons or community concerned.

A typical example is Dominic Ongwen's case. The LRA rebels abducted Ongwen as a child, and he was forced to commit atrocities against his blood relations. He rose to the rank of commander, committed civil war crimes and ordered his forces to do likewise. Drawing from *Rupiny* newspaper, Bedigen (2017) explains that when he was captured years later, the Acholi community (from which Ongwen comes) wanted him to go through the indigenous justice system (see newspaper caption in Figure 5.1). For instance, the *Nyono Tong Gweno* ritual deals with crimes that are caused due to coercion. The international community declined the Acholi request. This reflects distrust and disregard of indigenous systems by conventional systems. Also, it is a lost opportunity for rehabilitation and re-integration of the ex-combatant.

Indigenous Institutions

Whenever conflicts erupt in Africa, the international community institutions are looked to for resolutions (de Wall, 2005), not indigenous/traditional institutions. However, interviewee narratives reveal the effectiveness of traditional institutions through which ethnic and inter-ethnic conflicts can be resolved. This view is supported by Machar (2015:2–3), who argues that

Figure 5.1 Acholi Community—Ongwen for Traditional Justice

to 'propagate a culture of peace, it ought to be pursued through structured social systems.' Lederach's work adds to this by drawing attention to the importance of traditional institutions in peacebuilding. This section discusses the significance of Nilotic peacebuilding institutions and mechanisms being applied in the current processes (Lederach (1996, 1997, 2012). In this respect, the interviewees' views are highlighted below.

To begin, Pete, a Nilotic Lwo human rights lawyer, points to the significance of customary laws in traditional institutions and leadership. He says that:

> Customary law can certainly work as an alternative justice system in grave systems ... There must be established community mechanisms to do this ... They work well, with a traditional cultural/leadership system in place.
>
> (Pete, 4 May 2013)

Kojo, a South Sudanese community elder in Leeds, makes reference to the indigenous peacebuilding system by saying that:

Indigenous Communities, Institutions, and Methods 115

We have this system ... people believe in it, so it works. The system here in the west is to punish, but our system is different; it restores.

(Kojo, 4 May 2013)

Further, Charlie, an English man and academic who has worked on various programmes in the Horn of Africa, including conflict monitoring and evaluation, argues that:

The structure and nature of traditional institutions in the Horn and other parts of Africa are essential in conflict resolution and peacebuilding. These mechanisms or techniques, for example, mediation and negotiation, can be beneficial. A good example one can draw on is the Wunlit Dinka-Nuer peace conference of 1999.

(Charlie, 2 May 2012)

Charlie points to the significance of indigenous peacebuilding institutions' mechanisms, methods or approaches to resolving conflicts. For instance, traditional negotiation and mediation led to the Wunlit conference, which took place in 1999 (Bedigen, 2017). Wunlit was organised by a western peace activist, William Lawrey, who had worked on grassroots peace initiatives in South Sudan for years. At the peak of the second Sudan civil war, this conference brought together Dinka and Nuer, who had turned to fight each other's communities. Although it embraced Nilotic Lwo peacebuilding practices of storytelling, etiquette, beliefs, sharing and justice to a great extent, it was compromised with western-style and Christian practices. For example, conference participants' narratives were timed, stage-managed, paper-based (signatures) and prayers led by priests. Traditional chiefs narrated stories of their communities' experiences of the inter-ethnic conflicts, civil wars and their impact.

Meanwhile, part of the armed forces and the perpetrators attended the conference as 'freedom fighters' under political parties. By doing so, they presented themselves as not 'wholly' accountable for the atrocities. Victims, on the other hand, primarily women, youth and children (most of whom were abductees), attended as 'supporters' and 'wives.' Such an 'indigenous' peacebuilding meeting highlights many problems:

i) The perpetrators never confessed their crimes.
ii) Victims did not testify against their abductors.
iii) Chiefs were not in charge but NGOs and militia groups.
iv) Women and youth were partially involved.
v) Peace-making (by means of signing an agreement) was the focus, not peacebuilding.

Moreover, interviewee narratives demonstrate that peacebuilding and conflict prevention are complementary aspects of the traditional peacemaking process. As such, their features, which include storytelling, etiquette, beliefs, sharing and justice implemented through socialising, must be included. Whereas both the indigenous and western systems aim for peacebuilding, it is clear that Wunlit only focussed on the peacemaking aspect of peacebuilding.

Charlie says: 'Wunlit peace agreements held for nearly a decade.' The conference was hailed for its successes. Similar conferences were implemented throughout South Sudan. Examples include the Liliir and Akobo inter-ethnic conferences, according to Charlie and Wibo's narratives. Whereas the Wunlit conference served as a reference point to a dozen other grassroots peacebuilding initiatives, it was not holistically indigenous; it collapsed (Bedigen, 2017). In this book's view, this was inevitable, given its pseudo-indigenous nature. For instance, stories were explicitly neither told nor heard, as is the custom in the Nilotic indigenous practices—refer to the concept of time, Chapter 2.

Fred, a politician and Dinka elder in Leeds, claims that locals trust the church and traditional leaders or institutions. He further supports the argument that Nilotic Lwo peacebuilding institutions, and their leaders/elders, can play a significant part in achieving peacebuilding in the current South Sudan situation. He narrates that insecurity caused most communities to form their own security forces. Similar observations are made by Gebre and Ohta (2017:124–134) in their discussions on 'Negotiating Statehood with Other Non-state Armed Groups.' By analysing the role of Arrow Boys (Home Guards) in expelling the Lord's Resistance Army (LRA) from South Sudan, Gebre and Ohta point to their contribution as a local security group. While the Arrow Boys expected rewards from a newly formed and economically fragile State, the authors indicate the government did not recognise their contribution—confirming that local institutions are less regarded in national peacebuilding efforts. Other indigenous groups/institutions, such as the Monyomiji, provide security and post-conflict peacebuilding through negotiation, mediation, ceremonies and rituals to their communities voluntarily at conflict intensities. Yet, their contributions are disregarded at national levels (Bedigen, 2019).

Problems of Indigenous Institutions

One possible explanation for their disregard is that these security forces, at times, acted as militia groups that attacked neighbouring communities. For example, Fred points out that the Dinka community of Abyei formed a militia or political group known as the South Sudan Liberation Movement—North (SSLM/N). He attributes the formation of militia groups to the ruling government's political failures, and his narratives suggest inter-ethnic conflicts at government levels. In Fred's view, the government's incapability to provide peace and security to its citizens has led to continued inter-ethnic conflicts and civil wars in South Sudan, despite recently gaining its independence from Sudan (Bedigen, 2017).

Indigenous Communities, Institutions, and Methods 117

Fred narrates:

> You know, we left here (the UK) a few years ago, went home intending to teach our people the new things we had learnt ... When the community came together, I tell you ... the elders talked, the women talked, even the youth. We wondered. We thought we would educate them about the new values, but we ended up not saying a thing. Instead, we sat, listened and learnt a lot.
>
> (Fred, 12 January 2013)

As seen above, Fred passionately speaks about his traditional roots and the significance of traditional institutions. He affirms the traditional system as a source of knowledge. However, his loyalty to the traditional system was questionable, as he had launched his political party. This could imply that he does not believe in the traditional institution, after all, or thinks the communities' or country's peace can be achieved through political rather than traditional means. In this book's view, he could work with the community's elders to create a better traditional system rather than initiate a political party with familiar western rhetoric. Perhaps Fred can emulate Julius Nyerere, who tried to transform Tanzania's post-colonial government into African democracy embedded in the Ujamaa concept. Ujamaa was a political socialist movement that embraced the traditional African principle of collectiveness. For someone like Fred, who embraces both traditional and modern cultures, it is a concept that he can harness to salvage South Sudanese unity and peace. On the other hand, Fred's views and contradictory actions highlight the limitations of traditional institutions, a view Charlie expresses in his narratives:

> these traditional institutions ought to be strengthened to better cope with the modern-day challenges.
>
> (Charlie, 3 November 2012)

Similar to Charlie's view above, Pete adds that

> traditional institutions are inadequate in a way ..., not because they have lost relevance, but the times demand that they adapt.
>
> (Pete, 5 December 2012)

Pete is a Nilotic Lwo man whose profession (human rights lawyer), whose views widely reflect the international perception of traditional methods. He highlights that indigenous methods have lost relevance. This is, perhaps, why the ICC rejected the Acholi community's demand that their son, Ongwen, be brought back to face traditional justice rather than be taken to The Hague. The ICC's decision ruled. He was taken to The Hague (see newspaper caption in Figure 5.2). This story demonstrates how peacebuilding and

118 *Indigenous Communities, Institutions, and Methods*

Figure 5.2 Why Ongwen Is Facing Trial at The Hague

justice differ in Nilotic communities and the western world. Significant to note, Nilotic Lwo cultural ethics create values that influence the implementation of justice, although both Nilotic and western justice may bear some similarities, for instance, compensation and punishment. These examples are inadequate in creating a universally accepted justice, particularly in civil war situations. Therefore, in view of hegemony, Afrocentric and cultural theories, this book argues that civil war resolution and the justice procedure should be rooted in an 'indigene-centric' approach, for it embraces restorative culture.

Sadrak, an NGO worker in South Sudan, is not optimistic about using indigenous peacebuilding mechanisms. He believes South Sudan does not have the commonality to resolve the conflict as it happened in South Africa. The previous chapters highlight the distinctiveness of Nilotic Lwo or South Sudanese cultures. For instance, Avruch (2004) indicates that culture is not uniformly distributed or ideally shared within a given ethnic community. Sadrak suggests that indigenous methods such as Ekisil should be used as a stepping stone to peacebuilding. Fred's actions and Charlie's, Pete's and Sadrak's views point to limitations of the Nilotic Lwo peacebuilding methods. These limitations were summarised in Chapter 2.

Community Peacebuilding Methods

Further, Charlie's narratives point to the essential aspect indigenous institutions play in peacebuilding. He highlights their use of mechanisms such as negotiation, mediation and arbitration. He continues that indigenous peacebuilding institutions incorporate methods that include ceremonies and rituals that the whole community should unitedly engage in. In-depth interviews and literature revealed that the Nilotic Lwo indigenous institutions currently utilised in some civil war situations include the Monyomiji, Mato Oput and Gurtong (Simonse and Kurimoto, 2011). It is worth noting that there are other indigenous institutions not named here because they are not significant to the conflict or civil war but, at times, may be referred to during the discussions. Some have occasionally been applied in inter-ethnic or similar peacebuilding situations by other Nilotic communities in neighbouring countries. Charlie's 30 years of experience working with international organisations on various programmes in the Horn, including conflict and economics, gives a more balanced view of the gap indigenous institutions and their methods bridge in ensuring peacebuilding. Charlie continues to describe what he understands by indigenous peacebuilding:

> in many cases, the process is between the two groups representing the two parties ... of course, some traditional mechanisms and methods do not need third parties.
>
> (Charlie, 11 June 2013)

Charlie's statement above refers to lower-level conflicts and their resolution by arbitration in this book's view. His mention of representation of disputing parties implies that family, or community elders, can represent their members in issues that concern all. Significant to note, the Nilotic Lwo indigenous institutions and methods include all local people, which is crucial because it allows consensus in decision-making. Peacebuilding methods enacted through ceremonies and rituals seek to demonstrate the African concept or spirit of unity, togetherness or brotherhood. Examples of these concepts include the Cieng or Diel or Nyuak or Kacoke Madit or Ubuntu, and the Ujamaa concept, evidenced in the work of authors such as Nyerere (1968) and Kamwara and Katola (2012). This concept was introduced previously in Chapter 2. While the indigenous peacebuilding methods through the concept of togetherness dictate that no individual is left to deal with their problems, such a communal concept contrasts with the western-style process that isolates wrongdoers. This is well elaborated in Sonia's narratives on her work experiences.

Sonia, a freelance journalist and radio presenter in South Sudan, talks of her work experience at the Mato Oput institution and indigenous peacebuilding methods among the Acholi in post-conflict rehabilitation. In her narratives, she states that:

> The ICC came in ... lots of money was poured into peacebuilding, and lots of international people turned up, people who were not even there in the beginning. Among them were some black people, but they did not speak like us. They spoke ... I think London accent. Some communities organised fake ceremonies or participated in attracting funding. Some genuine elders I spoke to were dismayed about what was going on. They raised concerns and were ignored. And now there are many Lacen 'evil spirit possession' cases in such communities. Lots of murder cases carried out by ex-combatants which would usually be averted if ceremonies/rituals were performed.
>
> (Sonia, 15 December 2013)

In her research journey into Mato Oput application in the civil war situation, she attended pre-Mato Oput, Mato Oput and post-Mato Oput ceremonies and rituals. She explains that the Mato Oput institution is well managed and works well because community members know what to do during ceremonies. In her explanation, the Ugandan government, for instance, resettled survivors, victims, returnees and ex-combatants all together in Internally Displaced People (IDP) camps. She continues to say that, in the Acholi beliefs and cultural practices, when there has been bloodshed, there are clear guidelines regarding rituals that must be performed and witnessed by all people, majorly in perpetrators' resettlement. In her explanation, there was no clear strategy set up by the Ugandan government to ensure all could live in harmony in a post-conflict era. Bedigen (2017) also reports concerns that South Sudanese Acholi religious leaders raised over government failures in handling LRA issues. Mato Oput, with its associated rituals, simplified the re-integration of LRA ex-combatants and returnees into IDP camps and Acholi villages in Uganda. This traditional institution is suitable for South Sudan civil war resolution and peacebuilding. Once ex-combatants went through the normal indigenous peacebuilding processes, the community and the returnees lived at peace.

Indigenous Peacebuilding Methods through Ceremonies and Rituals

The Nilotic Lwo South Sudanese indigenous peacebuilding methods consist of ceremonies and rituals without which peacebuilding cannot occur. This book contributes to knowledge by discussing peacebuilding methods through ceremonies and rituals. In support, Douglas' (1966) work points to the significance of rituals by pointing out that rituals create unity-in-experience. For instance, the Nilotic indigenous peacebuilding methods require all community members to attend ceremonies and rituals (Bedigen, 2020). However, a single ceremony or ritual may not address all aspects of peacebuilding; thus, disputing parties must engage in other associated rituals to accomplish the necessary peace processes. Such aspects begin with exploring the roots of conflicts, story- or truth-telling, confession, cleansing and re-integration ceremonies/rituals (Bedigen, 2017; Lacey, 2013). More generally, ceremonies and rituals aim to address four principles of indigenous peacebuilding (i.e. consensus, harmony, justice and restoration) (Focus Group Field Notes, December 2013). Ceremonies and rituals are diverse, unique to conflict types and are said to offer resolutions to local disputes (Gebre and Ohta, 2017; Jok, 2011).

While some, such as Mato Oput, are robust and can be utilised in all conflicts ranging from family to civil wars and overall management of the community's political, social and economic needs, the majority are specific or limited. For instance, Ekisil is for inter-ethnic cattle rustling, Nyono Tong Gweno is for cleansing and Cieng is majorly for a reunion. It is recognised that their specificity to the context can render them efficient or inefficient in addressing modern-day conflicts and civil wars. However, the principles and values can significantly contribute to the national peace processes. Overall, ceremonies and rituals utilise peace offerings and sacrifices. By their means, symbolic patterns are worked out and publicly displayed with social intentions of healing and co-existence, thus contributing to sustainable peace.

To gain more understanding of indigenous peace ceremonies/rituals and why this book considers it crucial at national levels of peacebuilding, we highlight Kamwaria and Katola's (2012:53) work which indicates that:

> Rituals of exculpation must be conducted to restore the broken relationship by appeasing the spirits and settling them in good status in the ancestral world. Rituals are a usual means of preventing anger and aggression by the spirits of the deceased. The rituals restore the health of the individual and the community by expunging the evils caused by the immoral acts of civil war. The rituals exhibit a strong bond between the mundane (physical world) and transcendent (spiritual world). The spirits of the dead are believed to interfere or intervene in the life of the living. If well propitiated, they protect and guide people, ensure harmony in the community, promote fertility of land and people, and give good agricultural yield. If not well appeased, they withdraw their protection and create a state of vulnerability to misfortunes, afflictions, and even cause death.

In the above quote, Kamwaria and Katola detail the significance of ceremonies and rituals in preventing, building and making peace. Ceremonies and

122 Indigenous Communities, Institutions, and Methods

rituals help create harmony between people and spirits, subsequently eliminating conflicts. In the light of Douglas' (1970) view of culture, the Nilotic utilisation of ceremonies and rituals is intended for peace and social good. On the other hand, scepticism surrounds applying traditional methods to stopping violence or conflict. For example, Gatkuoth (2010) indicates that traditional mechanisms are weak, therefore do not necessarily stop violence or wars. Adding, Bradbury et al. (2006:46) point to the fact that the Wunlit Dinka–Nuer peace conference of 1999 did not instantly stop violence, such that its principles had to be revisited four years later.

Assumptions on the incapabilities of indigenous peacebuilding methods contribute towards involvement of international bodies such as the African Union, United Nations Mission in the Sudan (UNMIS), not only in South Sudan but also in other parts of Africa. Quoting Machar (2015:5), 'It is not the lack of conflicts in a given society that guarantees peace. It is the manner in which a given society or state addresses its pressing problems that keep peace.' Adding to this argument, Latigo (2008) indicates that due to the significance of these Nilotic Lwo ceremonies, international communities, including United State Agency for International Development (USAID), sponsored the majority of traditional ceremonies. This act led to re-integration of more than 12,000 LRA ex-combatants and returnees into Acholi communities. Conflicts, in the Nilotic communities, are perceived to cause dissension between people, God, spirits and nature. This can be best addressed only through conflict resolution ceremonies and rituals. For instance, cited in the above quote, ceremonies and rituals offer indigenous peacebuilding methods that are critical in achieving sustainable peace. Therefore, ceremonies/rituals discussed below include the *Nyono Tong Gweno* and *Ekisil* rituals.

The *Nyono Tong Gweno* 'Stepping on Egg' Ritual

Sonia's view on how well traditional leaders managed the Mato Oput peacebuilding process is similar to views expressed in a report by the Mato Oput Project (2009). According to the report, the Acholi of northern Uganda used Mato Oput to resolve civil war crimes and re-integrate the LRA ex-combatants into the community. The LRA abducted children and forced them to murder and mutilate people. They were initiated into this by ordering them to kill their family members in most cases. As such, adaptations to traditional processes were made based on who committed the crime, what crime it was, how the offender became part of the militia and who their victims were. In disputes such as these, Nyono Tong Gweno, 'stepping on the egg,' was utilised (refer to Figure 5.3). This ritual deals with crimes involving sexual violence, abductee wives, children and those activities that abductees were forced to conduct against their family members, friends or strangers.

Additionally, indigenous ritual-cleansing methods are intended for the abductees, regardless of their roles and actions while with the LRA. It is

Indigenous Communities, Institutions, and Methods 123

Figure 5.3 Nyono Tong Gweno Ritual Setting

applicable for unintended crimes, unknown perpetrators and victims. In contrast, conventional methods are particular in dealing with war crimes because the perpetrator, victim and evidence have to be found before the justice procedure occurs. In this book's view, Nyono Tong Gweno, as evidenced here, is a general procedure that involves 'cleansing for all.' Considering Douglas (1999), rituals are positive contributions to atonement and sacredness. Rituals lead to the inclusion of perpetrators, in contrast to the conventional justice system in which they are imprisoned or excluded. It offers a unique contribution to the peacebuilding process, where victims and perpetrators are unknown or where evidence is lacking. Specifically, its contribution to forgiveness, re-integration and justice is very significant, given the nature of Sudan's civil war crimes, most of which cannot be compensated.

In support of the views above, Mosa's narrative of the Nyono Tong Gweno ritual is below. The LRA militia abducted Mosa at 19 years of age. He talks of his personal life story, where he underwent the Nyono Tong Gweno ritual 20 years ago. As mentioned earlier, Mosa's Nyono Tong Gweno experience as an ex-abductee was that of general cleansing. He indicates that, had he been forced to commit crimes, he would be obliged to reveal them to his father or a community elder, who decides on the appropriate ritual for cleansing him. Below is his story:

> One night, they (the LRA) collected us from our village, about 30 people. Living with them in the bush was traumatic. We started escaping one by one, sometimes in twos or threes. They killed those people they caught. I escaped on the 14th day when another ethnic group attacked us 'the LRA', and, amidst the confusion, they could not keep watch of us 'captives', so I escaped. When approaching our home, I could not be allowed into the courtyard, I was stopped as the ritual had to be

performed to cleanse me of bad luck. There are three types of Nyono Tong Gweno, you know: cleansing for bad luck or surviving a tragic situation are dealt with. Secondly, it is for re-joining the community. Thirdly, when someone has committed an abominable act, something like incest or someone was forced to commit murder. Additionally, this ritual is performed when the victim is unknown or if there is no evidence. There is feasting, interaction and re-establishing of old relationships during the ritual. One of my aunties pulled me aside and told me that I would not have returned had it not been for the mediums my parents consulted. Our elders have, of late, developed guidelines that determine the standards of these rituals ... but there are no mega changes.

(Mosa, 11 May 2013)

Given Mosa's narrative above, forgiveness and re-integration in post-conflict situations can be possible through one or all the above distinctive types of Nyono Tong Gweno. In previous chapters, it is noted that Nilotic Lwo peacebuilding processes are concerned with the truth. Where truth cannot be established, for example, in the conduct of these civil wars, each returnee can resettle into the community after undergoing Nyono Tong Gweno. It is believed that fresh egg inhibits no impurities. By stepping on it, one pronounces their innocence and willingness to transform.

After undergoing this ritual, one is believed to have been cleansed, therefore becomes a good person, fit to rejoin the community. The ritual contributes significantly in four ways:

i) It is a welcome home and reunion ritual that gives the returnee a sense of belonging.
ii) It protects all those suspected or associated with the crime from stigmatisation and fear of not being welcomed into the community.
iii) It relieves offences or strangers of the guilt and the spirit of vengeance, or Lacen.
iv) The offended who do not know their perpetrator are relieved of the bitterness as the ritual prepares them to forgive the offender.

Although Latigo (2008) indicates forgiveness is an aspect of Mato Oput, this book argues that it is in Nyono Tong Gweno, rather than in Mato Oput, that true forgiveness is evident. This is due to the argument that Nyono Tong Gweno does not demand compensation, nor does it subject the suspected or associated individuals to interrogation prior to reconciliation. Conventional peacebuilding processes could emulate this aspect, where similar circumstances apply.

Although Nyono Tong Gweno ritual is less known than Mato Oput to peace writers, it is a very effective peacebuilding method, particularly in the ongoing and post-civil war cases in South Sudan. According to Mosa, it is a cleansing ritual that may be performed with or without Mato Oput, but this depends on an individual's story. Anyone outside his community for one reason or the other must go through this ritual, as the Acholi believe one gets contaminated while outside the community. Moreover, an estranged person is believed to contaminate the home community, causing unexplained calamities, illnesses, deaths and murders on their return. Therefore, Nyono Tong Gweno's main aim is to preserve the Acholi homestead's sacredness and social stability. It is used to resolve both trivial disagreements and major disputes, as well as to administer justice. After a conflict or disagreement, Nyono Tong Gweno is applied, both as a reunion and reconciliation ceremony, where both the returnee and the community commit to restart a harmonious relationship. Considering concepts in cultural theory, hegemony and Afrocentricity, it is through rituals that sacredness or oaths in various Nilotic societies are instituted and used to control destructive behaviours or prevent conflicts.

Ensuring harmonious relationships is at the core of Nilotic Lwo peacebuilding culture. Traditionally, Nyono Tong Gweno is applied at a family or clan level, perhaps an example of Charlie's narratives previously indicated. As other interviewees point out, it has been utilised in mass ceremonies, specifically in the LRA situations. This mass applicability has not gone without criticism from the conservative Nilotic elders, who believe it should only be applied to the family or clan situation. Significantly, its values, which include community sacredness, welcoming long-lost relations, reconciliation, justice, forgiveness and the re-establishment of relationships, benefit peacebuilding. In this book's view, these values are part of Nilotic Lwo traditional peacemaking and peacebuilding measures. It is argued that this ritual can be incorporated into conventional peacebuilding processes, particularly in complex cases.

Ekisil and *Akigath* ('Breaking of Bones' and Prayers)

Sadrak indicates that Ekisil 'breaking of bones' is another significant ceremony utilised in the Nilotic Lwo inter-ethnic peacebuilding process. Efo's account elaborates by suggesting Ekisil ceremony is followed by Akigath (a responsive prayer). His story highlights that the breaking of bones is performed in preparation for Akigath, a prayer led by elders to seal a reconciliation ceremony. Efo gives an in-depth narrative of Akigath:

> After the breaking of bones, elders sit round in a circle. The senior takes the lead in Akigath 'prayer'. Others, including the youth and women, respond in agreement!
>
> We, and all other Nilotic neighbours here, use Akigath, but it is a Karamojong word, and I think we borrowed it from them. Akigath prayer goes like this ...
>
> *'Lead Elder:* May we live in peace again!
> *All:* May we live in peace again!

> *Lead Elder:* May you not be the first to cause hurt!
> *All:* May you not be the first to cause hurt!
> *Lead Elder:* May the crops grow!
> *All:* May the crops grow!
> *Lead Elder:* May the cows, goats, and sheep multiply!
> *All:* May the cows, goats, sheep multiply.
> *Lead Elder:* May the women bear children!
> *All:* May the women bear children!
> *Lead Elder:* May the children grow in good health! May they live in peace!
> *All:* May the children grow in good health! May they live in peace!
> *Lead Elder:* May those who engage in fights disappear with the setting sun curses!
> *All:* May those who engage in fights disappear with the setting sun!
> *Lead Elder:* May those who refuse to honour this peace die!
> *All:* May those who refuse to honour this peace die!
> *Lead Elder:* May the rains fall!
> *All:* May the rains fall!'

The elder concludes by saying, 'May those who disobey disappear with sunset', and he points the spear towards the sunset.

This pointing of the spear towards the sunset psychologically works on the youth, and it terrifies them. They will never engage in deadly fights again; it can take decades before they do.

He hands over the spear to another elder from another community, who prays his prayer but is related to the conflict, resolution and peace. This continues until all elders have said prayers.

(Efo, 15 December 2013)

Like other ceremonies discussed, this ceremony is characterised by socialising, feasting and inter-communal visits. Its uniqueness is that it brings together neighbouring communities that are not directly involved in the conflict. In this book's view, this ceremony is very applicable to South Sudan because all ethnic communities living in the region are brought together to work towards the region's much-needed peace. Importantly, it is not selective or concerned with regional alliances. All communities come to witness conflict resolution and join in the feasting and post-conflict peacebuilding. It contrasts with conventional peace processes, where a peace process is implemented based on friendliness or alliances. This can be divisive, as friendly neighbours may have their political agenda, which works against conciliation. For instance, interviewees point out that South Sudan's neighbouring countries, (i.e. Ethiopian and Ugandan), involvement in mediation and negotiation processes, have caused more harm than good to its national peace goal (Bedigen, 2017).

Indigenous Communities, Institutions, and Methods 127

This ceremony is practised among the Southern Nilotic Lwo groups, namely the Karamojong, Dodoth, Jie and Turkana (Bedigen, 2017; Harlacher, 2009). After fierce fighting, the elders of the warring parties decide to call an end to the fight; they seek to resolve it through non-violence. This is initiated through mediation, where elders visit each other's communities prior to the set date for the ceremony. On the scheduled day, the warring communities meet, but warriors are adorned with feathers and other traditional ornaments before the ceremony. A bull, previously selected by an elderly lady, is speared to death, cut to pieces, roasted without skinning and the meat is eaten/shared by disputing parties. The right thigh leg bones are kept in safety for the final ritual. Other ethnic communities eat the meat of animals they have contributed. After eating, the ceremony's climax is marked when the bones of the bull (whose meat was eaten ceremoniously during the feast) are brought and broken to pieces, signifying an end to war and the beginning of peace. This book argues that it is an indigenous Disarmament, Demobilization and Reintegration programme (DDR) (Takeuchi, 2011; Ingelaere, 2008:43). Efo explains that the bones signify strength, so breaking them symbolises an end to the use of physical strength or violence. Drinking, singing and dancing continue for three days, after which elders encourage everyone to visit each other's communities. Intermarriages are encouraged. These subsequently lead to further socialising and ceremonies; for instance, baby-naming ceremonies bring together these communities and maintain interaction and, therefore, peace. These aspects of socialising in indigenous processes are non-existent in conventional methods or the peace theories considered. In view of cultural and Afrocentric theories (Asante, 2003, Douglas, 1973, 1999), therefore, they should be included in the current South Sudan civil war resolution.

Ekisil, Akigath and other ceremonies discussed help us understand the significant role elders play in indigenous peacebuilding. Other South Sudanese traditional peace writers have written about elders; therefore, this book will not delve into the detail. However, their roles are summarised in the field notes below.

Elders' Role in Indigenous Peacebuilding

Odonge (elders) can be older family members, royalty, appointed or elected chiefs. Specific skills are required; one must be knowledgeable about customs and believed to be possessed by spiritual powers. In our peace culture, they negotiate, arbitrate, adjudicate and encourage disputants to forgive each other. They also organise compensation and make decisions on justice. Odonge must be wise, listen to other community members' views and consider them in making decisions. They seek spiritual guidance from the ancestral spirits and gods in complex situations through sacrifices. They can also adjust customary laws and practices, but this depends on the situation at hand. For example, we cannot accept any advice or practice from those we do not know. However, when the elders reassure us, it is ok because they work in the interest of everybody in the community. They always make sure that people and their neighbours live in good relationships. They command authority, but easy access to guns has at times made their work challenging, especially with the youth.

(Focus Group-M, 23 January 2013)

The fieldwork notes above were summarised from the focus group interviews conducted among the Nilotic Lwo men. Their narratives give full descriptions of what part elders play in peacebuilding. They have members' trust and steer the community in the right direction. The above field notes clarify that traditional leaders are very effective in organising and leading their communities through peacebuilding processes. Summarising from earlier interviewee narratives, Sonia indicates elders' organisational skills, Fred talks of their wisdom, Efo's description of Ekisil expounds on their authority and Pete stresses the fact that these traditional institutions work well under the leadership of traditional elders who play a significant role in arbitration, adjudication, negotiation and mediation.

Conclusion

This chapter has demonstrated that indigenous communities, institutions and methods, including ceremonies and rituals are vital in achieving sustainable peace in the region. These include the Nyono Tong Gweno Ritual ('Stepping on Egg'). The crucial role of elders in conducting a peacebuilding ritual, Ekisil and Akigath ('Breaking of bones' and prayers), is demonstrated. In discussing these findings, the book provides a deeper appreciation of indigenous peacebuilding in relation to its contrasts to conventional approaches and protocols. Such includes the role of institutions such as the International Criminal Court (ICC) and its unsustainable justice process and the involvement of peacekeeping forces in conflict zones. It argues that such international conventions ignore the significance of community, institutions, relationships, ceremonies/rituals and elders. This work emphasises that the Nilotic Lwo cultural peace practices should take centre stage and hegemony in peacebuilding. The implication is that the concepts analysed here can be theoretically conceptualised to find an 'indigene-centric' approach to peacebuilding.

Bibliography

Adebayo, A.G., Abdallah, M., Adesina, O.C., Adéyẹmí, O., Agena, J.E., Agbor, S.O., ... Danso, S.O. (Eds.), 2015. *Indigenous Conflict Management Strategies in West Africa: Beyond Right and Wrong*. Lanham, MD, Lexington Books.

Adebayo, A.G., Jesse, J.B. and Brandon, D.L. (Eds.), 2014. *Indigenous Conflict Management Strategies: Global Perspectives*. Lanham, MD, Lexington Books. Retrieved from https://rowman.com/ISBN/9780739188040.

Asante, M.K., 2003. *Afrocentricity: The Theory of Social Change*. Chicago, IL, African American Images.

Avruch, K., 2004. Culture as context, culture as communication: Considerations for humanitarian negotiators. *Harvard Negotiation Law Review*, 9, pp. 391–408.

Bedigen, W., 2017. Traditional conflict resolution: The Nilotic Lwo of South Sudan (PhD thesis). Leeds, Leeds Beckett University.

Bedigen, W., 2019. Youth (Monyomiji) and conflict resolution in the South Sudan Civil War. *Journal of African Cultural Heritage Studies*, 2(1).

Bedigen, W., 2020. Significance of societal customs in the south Sudan civil war resolution. Journal of Peacebuilding & Development, 15(1), pp. 3–17.

Belay, T., 2015. Conflicts, conflict resolution practices and impacts of the war in South Sudan. *International Journal of School and Cognitive Psychology*, S2, p. 13. doi: 10.4172/ijscp.S2-013.

Bradbury, M., Ryle, J., Medley, M., & Sansculotte-Greenidge, K., 2006. *Local Peace Processes in Sudan: A Baseline Study*. London, Rift Valley Institute.

Cashmore, E. and Rojek, C., 1999. *Dictionary of Cultural Theorists*. London, Hodder Arnold.

De Waal, A. and Flint, J., 2005. *Darfur: A Short History of a Long War*. London, Zed/International African Institute.

De Waal, A., 2014. When kleptocracy becomes insolvent: Brute causes of the civil war in South Sudan. *African Affairs*, 113(452), pp. 347–369.

Dogra, N., 2011. The mixed metaphor of 'third world woman': Gendered representations by international development NGOs. *Third World Quarterly*, 32(2), pp. 333–348. doi: 10.1080/01436597.2011.560472.

Douglas, M., 1966. *Purity and Danger: An Analysis of Concepts of Pollution and Taboo*. London, Routledge and Keegan Paul.

Douglas, M., 1970. *Natural Symbols. Explorations in Cosmology*, New York, Routledge.

Douglas, M., 1973. *Natural Symbols: Explorations in Cosmology*. London, Barrie & Rockliff.

Douglas, M., 1999. *Leviticus as Literature*. Oxford, Oxford University Press.

Douglas, M., 2004. *Natural Symbols: Explorations in Cosmology*. London, Routledge.

Edelstein, S., 2011. *Food, Cuisine and Cultural Competency for Culinary, Hospitality and Nutrition Professionals*. Mississauga, ON, Jones and Bartlett Publishers.

Francis, D., 2004. *Rethinking War and Peace*. London, Pluto Press.

Galtung, J., 1990. Cultural violence. *Journal of Peace Research*, 27(3), pp. 291–305.

Galtung, J., 1996. *Peace by Peaceful Means*. London, Sage.

Galtung, J., 2004. *Transcend and Transform: An Introduction to Conflict Work*. London, Pluto Press.

Gatkuoth, R.P., 2010. The Nuer traditional time: Social life and culture. Retrieved December 19, 2013, from: http://www.southsudannewsagency.com/opinion/articles/the-nuer-traditional-time-social-life-and-culture.

Gebre, Y.G. and Ohta, I., 2017. *African Virtues in the Pursuit of Conviviality: Exploring Local Solutions in Light of Global Prescriptions*. Langaa RPCIG, Bamanda, African Books Collective.

Gramsci, A., 1992. *Prison Notebooks (Vol. 2)*. New York, Columbia University Press.

Grawert, E., 2014. *Forging Two Nations Insights on Sudan and South Sudan*. Addis Ababa, OSSREA.

Harlacher, T., 2009. *Traditional Ways of Coping with Consequences of Traumatic Stress in Acholi Land: Northern Uganda Ethnography from a Western Psychological Perspective* (PhD thesis). Freiburg: University of Freiburg.

Ingelaere, B., 2008. The Gacaca courts in Rwanda. In L. Huyse and M. Salter (Eds.), *Traditional Justice and Reconciliation after Violent Conflict: Learning from African Experiences*. Stockholm, International IDEA, pp. 25–59.

Jok, J.M., 2011. *Diversity, Unity, and Nation Building in South Sudan*. Washington, DC, US Institute of Peace.

Kamwaria, A. and Katola, M., 2012. The role of African traditional religion, culture and world-view in the context of post-war healing among the Dinka community of Southern Sudan. *International Journal of Humanities and Social Science*, 2(21), pp. 49–55.

Lacey, L., 2013. Women for cows: An analysis of abductions of women in South Sudan. *Agenda*, 27(4), pp. 91–108.

Latigo, J.O., 2008. *Northern Uganda: Tradition-Based Practices in the Acholi Region*. Stockholm, International Institute for Democracy and Electoral Assistance.

Lederach, J.P., 1996. *Preparing for Peace: Conflict Transformation across Cultures*. New York, Syracuse University Press.

Lederach, J.P., 1997. *Building Peace: Sustainable Reconciliation in Divided Societies*. Washington, DC, United States Institute of Peace Press.

Lederach, J. P., 2003. *The Little Book of Conflict Transformation*. Intercourse, Good Books.

Lederach, J.P., 2012. The origins and evolution of infrastructures for peace: A personal reflection. *Journal of Peacebuilding and Development*, 7(3), pp. 8–13.

Leonardi, C., Moro, L.N., Santschi, M. and Isser, H.D., 2010. *Local Justice in South Sudan (Peaceworks Number 66)*. Washington, DC, United States Institute of Peace.

Longman, T., 2006. Justice at the grassroots? Gacaca trials in Rwanda. In: Roht-Arriaza, N. and Mariezcurrena, J. (Eds.) *Transitional Justice in the Twenty-first Century: Beyond Truth versus Justice*. New York, Cambridge University Press, pp. 206–228.

Machar, B., 2015. *Building a Culture of Peace through Dialogue in South Sudan*. Juba, South Sudan, The SUUD Institute.

Mbiti, J.S., 1970. *Concepts of God in Africa*. London, SPCK.

Nyerere, J.K., 1968. *Ujamaa–Essays on Socialism* (Vol. 359). Dar es Salaam: Oxford University Press.

Poku, N. and Mdee, D.A., 2013. *Politics in Africa: A New Introduction*. London, Zed Books Ltd.

Ramsbotham, O., 2005. The analysis of protracted social conflict: A tribute to Edward Azar. *Review of International Studies*, 31, pp. 109–126.

Simonse, S. and Kurimoto, E. (Eds.), 2011. *Engaging Monyomiji: (Bridging the governance gap in East Bank Equatoria)*. Torit, South Sudan. Proceedings of the Conference, Nairobi, Pax Christi Horn of Africa. 26–28 November 2009.

Takeuchi, S., 2011. *Gacaca and DDR: The Disputable Record of State-Building in Rwanda*. Tokyo, Japan International Cooperation Agency Research Institute (JICA).

wa Thiong'o, N., 1986. *Writing against Neocolonialism*. Nairobi, Vita Books.

List of Interviews Cited in the Text

1) Charlie, 2 May 2012
2) Efo, 15 December 2013
3) Focus Group Field Notes, December 2013
4) Fred, 12 January 2013
5) Kijo, 4 May 2013
6) Kilo, 11 March 2014
7) Mosa, 5 February 2015
8) Ngugi Wa Thiongo, 1986:10
9) Nyerere, 1968
10) Pete, 4 May 2013
11) Sonia, 15 December 2013

6 The Role of Youth (*Monyomiji*) in Indigenous Peacebuilding

Introduction

The *Monyomiji* indigenous cultural practice challenges conventional perceptions about youth and places the latter at the centre of community leadership and peacebuilding. This chapter seeks to demonstrate that they are an entity through which sustainable peace can be achieved, contributing new knowledge in this area. In view of Antonio Gramsci's ideas that include cultural practices and cultural hegemony, *Monyomiji* is a suitable political and social institution through which positive change can be realised in the society (Gramsci, 1992). In South Sudan, conflicts are enacted along inter-ethnic lines (e.g. Dinka, Nuer, Anyuak, Acholi, Shilluk, Lopit, Lotuho or Lotuko and Lulubo) over control of resources such as land, water, cattle, pastures, foraging and political disagreements (Grawert, 2014:144; Schomerus and Allen, 2010:20; Thomas, 2015:1). Therefore, their resolution requires a cultural intervention (Bedigen, 2020).

Whereas this chapter demonstrates that Monyomiji remains a formidable peacebuilding institution at local levels, various western-led or inspired peacebuilding attempts that exclude this institution have taken place at the national level since 1983. For example, to pursue a resolution, the Intergovernmental Authority on Development (IGAD), which includes governments of Eritrea, Djibouti, Ethiopia, Kenya, Somalia and Sudan, and which also involved the IGAD-partner forum (government representatives of the United States, some European countries and the United Nations), has led peace processes at national levels (Grawert, 2014:30). This IGAD peace process continues to pursue and implement conventional top-down methods of peacebuilding, such as negotiation and mediation (de Waal and Flint, 2005; Iyob, and Khadiagala, 2006:13; Ramsbotham et al., 2011; Young and Lebrun, 2006:8). Parallel to national negotiations are local levels, foreign-led NGO peace training workshops, seminars and conferences such as the Wunlit and Torit conferences of 1999 and 2009 (Bradbury et al., 2006:4; Simonse and Kurimoto, 2011:14; Wunlit conference, 1999). Despite peacebuilding efforts at national and local levels, peace processes remain lacking and in need of cultural contexts such as *Monyomiji*.

DOI: 10.4324/9781003133476-7

Monyomiji

An interviewee, Sellie, a Lulubo woman and medical practitioner who fled South Sudan during the conflict and took refuge in the UK, gives us a very relevant description of the *Monyomiji* institution.

> *Monyomiji* is our tradition; it is our way of dealing with our problems. In our culture, trust is put on the youth to handle these problems. They are of ages 15 to 45. *Monyomiji* is inclusive of women and we call them *Honyomiji*, who play a part in decision making. This system is everything to us ... It has now been copied by other tribes like the Shuli (Acooli/Acholi), Madi, Dinka, Langi and others. They offer security and if there is a problem, raid or an attack, they decide whether to go to war. They can also decide not to go to war by ... negotiation ... The *Monyomiji* keep law and order, they can even punish the rain chief for not bringing rain.
>
> (Sellie, 10 August 2012)

Sellie claims the practice stems from the Lulubo culture, one of the Nilotic Lwo ethnic groups in South Sudan. According to her, *Monyomiji*, as a word in the Lulubo language, means 'adolescence' or 'youth,' which is a valuable and celebrated stage in life within the Lulubo culture. For example, Sellie remarks that, traditionally, the death of a youth is commemorated with a special dance, as opposed to no dance at all for a diseased child. She says the youth's day of death is a day of tremendous feeling of loss and despair, because the community is robbed of the deceased's contribution to the community. She further expounds that *Monyomiji* also translates as 'security,' 'protection,' 'youthfulness,' 'energy,' 'toughness,' 'provision' and 'resilience.' Based on Sellie's description, *Monyomiji* encapsulates youth enthusiasm in community well-being and wellness, attributes central to the Nilotic concept of peace. In light of this, this book emphasises that *Monyomiji* forms a cultural basis upon which peace and peacebuilding philosophical heritage can be modelled, both among the practising communities and beyond. Monyomiji, therefore, is a word that describes both youth and a traditional institution led by youth.

As an institution, *Monyomiji* means the owners or fathers of the village (Bedigen, 2019). The Monyomiji has no formal leader; they settle conflicts, decide on land questions and protect the interest of the community (Grawert, 2014:144). The term also refers to youth and traditional youth governance or leadership systems. It is a political, social and economic management institution or tool. For instance, socially, they help the widows and orphans in choosing a guardian. Economically, they help gather fruits and wild honey, and hunt or organise community-fishing trips. Politically, they help implement the chief's policies, and at times the government's, when requested (Bedigen, 2019; Simonse and Kurimoto, 2011:9). Broadly, the majority of Nilotic Lwo communities, such as the Dinka, Nuer, Anyuak, Acholi, Shilluk, Lopit, Lotuko and Lulubo, of South Sudan, practise the Monyomiji system. It is an institution responsible for the transmission, teaching and implementation of peace values in dispute resolution, at family, intra- and inter-ethnic levels. Thus, the Monyomiji practice can vary from community to community as the very people who utilise it construct its principles. Generally, the system utilises a community's societal customs, laws, beliefs and practices to resolve issues of concern and restore relationships and bring tangible benefits (Deng, 2006:27; Bradbury et al., 2006:8). Despite their critical characteristics, the institution is underutilised in South Sudan's national peacebuilding processes (Simonse and Kurimoto, 2011).

Simonse and Kurimoto (2011) indicate that the Monyomiji institution predominantly consists of a handful of men aged between 18 and 45 years of age. They rule for a specified period (8–25 years), but change can occur after a few years. The outgoing Monyomiji community leaders hand over community responsibilities to the younger incoming Monyomiji group by means of political-like campaigns (Bedigen, 2019; Simonse and Kurimoto, 2011:9).

There are four main ways by which youth can join Monyomiji institution and they include:

i) Through joining a leadership aspirant age group who eventually take up community governance.
ii) At the retirement or deposition of an existing Monyomiji.
iii) Naturally gifted, spirit-possessed individuals appointed to join the team.
iv) By marriage, a capable woman can become a '*Honyomiji*'—female Monyomiji (Bedigen, 2019, 2020; Deng, 2006:27–32).

In the past decade, some grassroots NGO peace processes have recognised and increasingly engaged with the Monyomiji in community peace dialogues. Such NGOs recognise the Monyomiji to be knowledgeable of best solutions to conflicts, thus supporting their indigenous peace processes and authority (Francis, 2004:43; Simonse et al., 2010:1, 2). For instance, work by Simonse and Kurimoto (2011:8) indicates the crucial contribution Monyomiji institution could make in the political peace dialogues and have brought together Monyomiji and government personnel into western-style workshops, seminars and conferences such as the Torit, Loki and Wunlit Peace and Reconciliation Conference (WPRC) (Bradbury et al., 2006:12). While such peace efforts align with the bottom-up peacebuilding arguments that support inclusion, interdependence and cooperation, they exclude holistic peace cultures crucial in South Sudan's national peacebuilding (Lederach, 1995).

Among South Sudanese, a more general understanding of what youth is that it is a transitional stage from childhood to adulthood. The description given by the United Nations (2014) defines youth as 'a period of transition from the dependence of childhood to adulthood's independence and awareness of our interdependence as members of a community.' This description confines the meaning of the word 'youth' to immaturity, inexperience and passive. While some Nilotic Lwo people, African cultures and others hold this view, this book argues these descriptions have contributed to the relegation of youth into studentship. For example, interviewee narratives indicate that, among the Nilotic people, the youth learn from their elders. They depend on the wisdom of their mothers. Adding to this, UNESCO (2014) refers to youth as a group of people that has to be reached out to, and empowered, 'responding to their expectations and ideas, fostering useful and long-lasting skills.' Such connotation of youth has contributed to the west's reluctance to involve them in most critical issues facing the community.

However, in 1999, the United Nations designated an International Youth Day (IYD) which is celebrated on 12 August each year. Adopted in the UN resolution 54/120, it outlines youth policies and programmes that revolve around three issues: 'participation,' 'development' and 'peace.' IYD is a day in which global attention is drawn to legal and cultural issues affecting youth. This day is packed with activities, including workshops, concerts, cultural events and meetings organised between youth organisations, with local and national government representatives. To some extent, the significance the UN attributes to IYD bears similarities with that of the Lulubo culture. For instance, the findings here demonstrate that peace and security are *Monyomiji* major roles. Yet, empirical data shows that *Monyomiji* endeavours and specific roles in supporting their respective communities vary from one community to another.

In contrast to the UN description, a reflection on the Lulubo interpretation of youth in *Monyomiji* cultural practice implies it is more about characteristics of freshness, spiritedness, vigour and appearance of a young person. These attributes are passionately expressed in interviewees' narratives of the *Monyomiji*-practising individuals. This description agrees with that of Thomas, a psychologist, whose work on the 'Psychology of Adolescents' describes youth as a stage of self-concept construction, often influenced by many other variable factors, including culture, peers, lifestyle and gender. It is during youth that a person makes choices that affect their future. Here, we can see clearly that these views defy the views held by the world organisations and other African cultures. It is important to note that cynicism that surrounds youth today, both in the conflict zones and beyond, is because they are the main perpetrators of crimes (Mamdani, 2020). For instance, their involvement in civil war crimes is highlighted in the previous chapters.

In view of the above, we can argue that both Thomas' and Wing's concepts of youth fit well with the *Monyomiji* concept of youth as the front-line

136 The Role of Youth in Indigenous Peacebuilding

runners in peace and peacebuilding within their respective communities (Wing, 2012). As a cultural practice, male peers organise themselves into a traditional political group (*Monyomiji*) similar to modern political groups. They make an informed choice to take on community leadership, with the intention to shape and secure the community's future economically, socially and politically. For instance, anthropologists Simonse and Kurimoto's (2011) work on *Monyomiji* culture in South Sudan points out that this institution is underutilised by both local and international sectors.

To provide further understanding into *Monyomiji* traditional role, this book considers Gramsci's work on the role of culture and cultural practices in politics, moral leadership and authority or hegemony (Gramsci, 1992, 1955). In the light of Antonio Gramsci's cultural hegemony, this book suggests that, through the *Monyomiji* institution, the Nilotic Lwo beliefs, perceptions, norms, values and procedures can be influenced to facilitate South Sudan civil war resolution. These discussions demonstrate that the positive outcome of any social or political control by a 'ruling class' *Monyomiji* can be achieved by a local institution (such as *Monyomiji*), rather than a foreign one such as the UN and UNESCO.

In summarising the importance of *Monyomiji* cultural practice, members embrace this title in their traditional outlook (Figures 6.1 and 6.2). Monyomiji members' roles and responsibilities are symbolically represented in their traditional outfit of a hat adorned with white/blue feathers, a spear and a stick.

In most Nilotic cultures, white and blue represent peace. Therefore, white and blue feathers, stitched on the *Monyomiji* hat, symbolise their role in peacemaking, peacebuilding and peacekeeping. Blue, in some Nilotic communities, for example the Anyuak, represents peace. Among the Kalenjin

Figure 6.1 Monyomiji Hat

The Role of Youth in Indigenous Peacebuilding 137

Figure 6.2 Cultural and Modern Monyomiji

group of Nilotic-speaking people (Masai, Pokots and Samburu), it represents the blue sky, where the gods, who watch over the living and keep them at peace, dwell. The hat, made of cured cowhide, protects a human's head, symbolising protection. The spear represents security and provision because the community is defended by it. In hunting wild animals for community members' food, the spear is used as a tool to provide meat for sustenance and nourishment.

The stick represents support, which, in this case, implies community support for the *Monyomiji* institution and vice versa. In view of these carefully selected *Monyomiji* traditional dress code features, this book suggests that *Monyomiji* in itself embraces the whole Nilotic tenets of peace and peacebuilding.

Next, I shall discuss *Monyomiji* roles in peacebuilding.

Significance of the Monyomiji in Peacebuilding?

Monyomiji is a popular institution to whom all disputes (rape, murder, theft, witchcraft, land) and any disturbances are reported (Muratori, 1950:133). Monyomiji members often gather to seek a resolution according to societal customs. The Monyomiji peace process is flexible, 'take into account the particular social contexts of disputes, rather than any rigid application of written laws' (Leonardi et al., 2010:5). As such, up to 90% of criminal and civil cases in the family, intra- and inter-ethnic situations are resolved by the Monyomiji (Bedigen, 2017; Jok et al., 2004:6; Leonardi et al., 2010). Also, youth form 70% of the South Sudanese population (World Bank, 2014:1), the majority have engaged in combat and committed war crimes (Bedigen,

2017; Deng, 2006:27; Schomerus and Allen, 2010:54; Simonse and Kurimoto, 2011:7). As such, including them in the national peacebuilding becomes inevitable. Further, the Monyomiji characteristics correspond with the dominant conventional bottom-up peacebuilding theory propounded by Lederach. Lederach argues for an approach to peacebuilding that 'must be inclusive, embracing multiple facets, the interdependence of roles and activities, and a clear vision of the broader agenda in peace-making and peacebuilding' (Lederach, 1995:12). Drawing examples from Somalia, he points to the significance of sub-clans, storytelling, negotiation and compensation in peacebuilding discussions that led to the Grand Borama Peace Conference. This is important because such cultural peace characteristics, including ceremonies/rituals and socialising, exist in the Monyomiji peace practices (Bradbury et al., 2006:12). Notably, the Monyomiji inclusiveness and interdependence of actors such as the rain chief, war chief, Honyomiji (women), medicine man, and ceremonies or rituals are key in delivering sustainable peace in the region (Deng, 2006:31–32; Bradbury et al., 2006:16; Brunet-Jailly and Scherrer, 2018:73).

Fred, in his narrative, talks about his experience of elders and youth. He highlights that peacebuilding is a joint venture between the traditional leadership institutions of *Odonge* (elders) and *Monyomiji* (youth). It is what makes peace sustainable in community settings. Fred narrates:

> These young leaders tend to be very successful in bringing the community together and keeping peace, because the whole community shows them overwhelming support. They are also believed to be patriotic, with untainted political ambitions and community development aspirations.
> (Fred, 25 March 2013)

Although some work on Monyomiji role in community governance exists (Simonse and Kurimoto, 2011:129), very little is known about their peace roles implemented through political leadership, mediation, negotiation and ceremonies/rituals. Exploration of these roles is vital because in South Sudan, politics is shaped along tribal lines, and as such, the SPLM/A continues to have major difficulties in promoting national peacebuilding (Leonardi et al., 2010:3; Young, 2003:425; Young and Lebrun, 2006:13). But, Monyomiji can bridge this inter-ethnic gap because it is inclusive of all people and their cultures. Further, given the complexity of the conflict and failed resolution attempts, locals' view is that 'the government and the Monyomiji should co-operate in designing and implementing strategies for the non-violent transition' (Bradbury et al., 2006:19; Simonse and Kurimoto, 2011:3). For example, spearheaded by Monyomiji, Wunlit (Dinka and Nuer) peacemaking included armed forces, youth, chiefs, women and the Mabior 'white bull' ritual (Bradbury et al., 2006:16). Wunlit's success supports the argument that Monyomiji offers a cultural basis upon which peace and conciliation can be modelled in South Sudan. Thus, by discussing Monyomiji,

The Role of Youth in Indigenous Peacebuilding

this chapter contributes to knowledge in community peacebuilding and provokes further discussions on their potential at the national level.

Monyomiji Peacebuilding Roles

This section discusses the Monyomiji roles in conflict prevention and peacemaking in relation to interviewee responses and related literature. To iterate, they include cultural norms of leadership, mediation, negotiation implemented along with ceremonies/rituals. It uses interviews to illustrate how these cultural peace roles could benefit national peacebuilding. For easy follow-up of discussions, in-depth interviewees are nicknamed ('Fego,' 'Jona' and 'Sellie').

Leadership

According to a women's focus group, these communities

> have utilised the *Monyomiji* system for ages. It is the leadership our community members recognise. They do arbitration, negotiation, mediation, reconciliation ... to bring peace. We can't understand why it can't be utilised at national levels. When they call for workshops, all they talk about are some negative practices such as cattle raiding, gangs and militia groups. Not every *Monyomiji* system does these things, and some communities have punished their own *Monyomiji* who engage in these activities.
> (Focus Group-W, 17 March 2013)

Discussing Monyomiji cultural norms of leadership is essential because interviewees indicate they control the 'political, social and economic situation of the community' (Male Focus Group, LSCA), and the 'government and the Monyomiji should cooperate in designing and implementing strategies for the non-violent transition' (Simonse and Kurimoto, 2011:16). In doing so, this section looks at two aspects. (1) Apprenticeship: This includes good behaviour, age-grade progression and conflict transformation. (2) Re-integration, an aspect of Monyomiji leadership which includes pragmatic resettlement of ex-combatants, community conflict management, lawmaking and enforcement.

Apprenticeships

The fieldwork notes from a women's focus group highlight the role of youth apprentices in a Nilotic Lwo traditional setting and within the *Monyomiji* system:

> In Nilotic Lwo cultures, children stay with and learn from mothers until the age of about nine, the age at which boys get to join their fathers in

masculine activities, while girls remain with women and join women's activities. Boys can have family responsibility like protection as early as nine years of age. They join peers and conduct mock fights, aimed at instilling bravery, at the same time resolving their squabbles. The boys, or youth, can take up community responsibilities, such as provision (for example, hunting, fishing, and farming) and defence, from about 14 years of age. Generally, duties and responsibilities are allocated according to one's ability. Age does not matter, but one can be referred to as a boy or youth, even when they are over 45 years old. The determining factor is when they graduate from one stage of life to the other, with responsibilities. For instance, a man of over 45 years of age, if not married, is referred to as a boy, and will be looked after by his mother. Likewise, an unmarried woman of a similar age will be referred to as a girl. When a young man shows more mental and physical capability, he can be entrusted with public or community duties, for example leadership or resolving community problems.

(Focus Group-W, 7 March 2012)

Monyomiji apprentices should demonstrate good behaviour, age-grade progression and conflict transformation. While leadership peace roles can be inherited in some Monyomiji-practising communities such as the Shilluk, the first step in achieving this role is through 'apprenticeships' (Female Focus Groups, LSCA). Interviewee indicates 'elders initiate and work with youth aged 9–13 as apprentices in various aspects of life that emphasise interaction' (Fego, Juba). During the apprenticeship, the youth learn 'to work together in the family first, then community defence.' Working together and learning is an essential aspect of cleansing rituals such as the 'Cieng (togetherness) and Mabior' (Male Focus Group, LSCA). Apprentices are expected to participate in the identification and preparation of herbs, the animal to be sacrificed and venue for reconciliation ceremonies (Male Focus Group, LSCA; Parmar et al., 2010:276–277). When their time comes, they take up leadership and utilise previously learnt informal skills in stages (i.e. family, community and inter-community conciliation) (Female Focus Group, LSCA). Adding, interviewee responses indicate Monyomiji means 'youthfulness, energetic and toughness' (Female Focus Group, LSCA). In the context of South Sudan where financial resources and personnel are limited in facilitating peace processes, these attributes are vital in the training for and facilitation of peacebuilding. Monyomiji apprenticeship attributes contrast with the western perspective of youth as a group in need of formal training and empowerment, separate from indigenous settings (UNESCO, n.d.:1). Monyomiji were excluded from the recent IGAD-led negotiation (Amum, 2018:1). Although the UN seems to be aware of youth potential in ensuring sustainable peace, the UN youth enhancement programmes unwittingly support formal school and social activities, further narrowing opportunities for indigenous structures to thrive. Monyomiji apprenticeship is important in the context of South Sudan because the youth become part of a solution to societal problems early. For instance, Kemper (2005:11) suggests that 'communities can help to cater for youth's demand for life skills, education ... endowing them with a sense of belonging.' However, decades of war, lack of resources and high demands for reconstruction have meant the older members of Monyomiji are no longer deeply knowledgeable in their peace cultures and therefore deficient in peace values and skills to transmit to the younger. Regardless, it is observed that Monyomiji apprenticeship is a type of 'inclusion' and should be wholly implemented in national peacebuilding programmes (Lederach, 1995:12).

During the apprenticeship, each Monyomiji is expected to demonstrate good behaviour. Interviewees indicate Monyomiji are 'elders, lawmakers, lawmakers/enforcers or home guards/security with moral authority' (Female Focus Group, LSCA). Thus, their role in peace leadership is earned through hospitality and community service (e.g. digging wells, clearing roads). Contrary to other youth systems, for example, the violent nature of Niger Delta youth (Iwilade, 2014:588), the Monyomiji is expected to demonstrate exemplary behaviour at all times (Simonse and Kurimoto, 2011:9). Iwilade's analysis shows the Niger Delta youth are spirited, youthful groups that operate in a well-established network whose leadership is earned through notorious achievements. The Niger Delta youth are focused on the destruction of oil pipes, killings, rapes, robbery, neighbourhood terrorism as well as drug-related activities. As seen here, the idea of earning leadership is context based and varies. Further, in the context of South Sudan political and peace negotiations at national levels, good behaviour in leadership is lacking. For instance, Deng (2017:1) indicates that 'a personal problem between leading individuals, extended to regional relations between neighbouring communities, became incrementally connected to the responsibility of the national government,' thus impacting negatively on peacebuilding. The unique attribute Monyomiji can offer to the broader peace discipline is good behaviour in leadership that helps transform deadly conflicts into peaceful situations through hospitality and service (Fego, Juba; Grawert, 2014:144; Muratori, 1950:133; Simonse and Kurimoto, 2011:9). Like the Niger Delta youth, the Monyomiji have been accused of similar crimes, including cattle raids (Thomas, 2015:2). For example, Schomerus and Allen (2010:54) indicate among Dinka Gok, cattle are for food, marriage, property and perceived as 'life' so the youth do anything to acquire them. At times, the Monyomiji engage in cattle raiding activities affecting community and government confidence in the institution's ability to lead peacebuilding. However, because the Monyomiji draw from customs and history, it is observed that they revert to peaceful means after all (Deng, 2006:27). For example, history has it that Ngok Dinka and Lou Nuer ancestors broke a spear in two and each took half of it and 'invoked it with a conditional curse by which either side attacking each other would bring down supernatural vengeance' (Bedigen, 2019; Prichard, 1934:2). This is significant in the context of some South Sudanese communities where disputes over grazing land or water source flare civil wars.

In initiating peace aimed at transforming conflict situations, the Ngok Dinka and its neighbours continue this good neighbour tradition in the modern day, not only to honour ancestral practice but keep and build peace (Bradbury et al., 2006:16). This leads this book to argue that Monyomiji peace process broadly embraces the past and present to allow co-existence, as well as prevent inter-ethnic conflicts that stem from disputes over natural resources, contribution to sustainable peace (Bedigen, 2020). Examples of leadership initiatives by which Monyomiji revert to peace through community services are by setting up a neutral venue 'living peace village' or 'peace market' for negotiation (Bradbury et al., 2006:16) and providing security forces to allow uninterrupted peace discussions, for example, Wunlit peace village (Gebre and Ohta, 2017).

The context within which Monyomiji leadership peace role is understood is that 'family or community conflict management' determines 'age-grade progression and conflict transformation' youth achieve (Fego, Juba). The concept of conflict transformation is considered essential in the bottom-up peacebuilding (Lederach, 1995). The most effective way by which Monyomiji age-grade progression is assessed and rewarded is during peacebuilding ceremonies/rituals where individuals participate and progress to public conflict transformation. Achieved by confession, community service and responsibility to lead, the age-grade progression and transformation of conflict situations help 'address practices, issues and questions that are relevant to post-conflict contexts' (Stovel and Valinas, 2010:7). Further, Durham (2000:113) suggests that 'different societies do define and demarcate youth differently.' One of the main strengths presented in Durham's argument is that context is important in understanding the politics of youth and how youth navigate and transform specific spaces, violent or non-violent. Likewise, Iwilade (2014:573) highlights how youth are 'the most vocal social category' in the difficult Niger Delta environment. Thus, understanding contexts within the most rural of places in South Sudan, with populations of up to 65%, is fundamental (Bradbury et al., 2006:19). A focus on how Monyomiji participation in the age-grade system and leadership influence violent situations is essential in delivering sustainable peace in the region. This chapter argues that integrating the Monyomiji age-grade progression, conflict transformation ceremonial activities and rituals can help consolidate frameworks of the IGAD-led peace process (Deng, 2017:11; Rushohora, 2017:24).

Further to the above, the Monyomiji participation and leadership are contrary to the UN context that there must be policies that target youth 'participation' (Bedigen, 2019). The UN identifies youth as individuals aged between 14 and 25 years old (UNESCO, n.d.:1). Such narrow social groupings cannot be applied locally because of the importance of context recognition. By placing youth in an age bracket, the UN neglects any consideration of the social properties of local or Monyomiji culture that requires youth participation in matters of concern in their respective communities. This chapter highlights UN is ignorant of Monyomiji potential in embracing a central role in community service and transforming the South Sudan conflict situation. This ignorance is evident in the IGAD negotiations of the 2013 civil war, where male political leaders dominate negotiations, but no youth representation (Amum, 2018:1). This demonstrates that the conventional perspective of youth undermines their innovative and resourceful nature at local levels, thus the need to highlight its potential at national peacebuilding.

Although examples above show Monyomiji initiatives, participation, leadership abilities and responsibilities are visible and efficient at local levels, it requires a platform to show potential at national levels. Moreover, as an institution, social expectations within respective communities are not transferable to other communities or at state levels (Jok et al., 2004:22). Traditionally, the youth believe in themselves as responsible people, as does the community (Male, In-depth interview, LSCA). This social construction within which Monyomiji institution operates allows it to exploit its potential in maintaining community peace. However, the Monyomiji institution faces many challenges. Like the South Sudanese government, the Monyomiji are under significant economic, moral and political stress (Brunet-Jailly and Scherrer, 2018; Leonardi et al., 2010:12). For example, Monyomiji members are not salaried but rewarded whenever the community can afford. As such, some have used this title as a means of wealth accumulation by raiding neighbouring communities and levying higher charges for civil dispute resolution consultations, imputing negative perceptions of the institution. Politically, because they make decisions on consensus, are informal and perform roles interdependently, the institution appears to lack structure, particularly, to the outsiders hence its exclusion at the national peace negotiations. This chapter recognises that a redesign of its structure might be necessary if it is to be adopted at national levels of peacebuilding. On the other hand, a redesign might cause concerns in areas of hegemony as the state, not the Monyomiji institution, is likely to be in control.

Re-integration

Re-integration, an aspect of Monyomiji leadership, includes pragmatic resettlement of ex-combatants, community conflict management, law-making and enforcement. Although most Monyomiji groups joined militia groups voluntarily or due to peer pressures, it is typical for youth to be conscripted into the militia and forced to commit crimes (Bedigen, 2019). In narrating his conscription experience, Fego indicates the militia 'forced captives to burn houses, crops or kill. We were cleansed to re-join family; dug wells, roads to compensate' (Fego, Juba). Majority returnees needed to be re-integrated into communities or Monyomiji roles. However, the SPLA (predominantly Dinka) distrust towards ex-combatants of other non-Dinka groups led to targeted attacks on some Monyomiji groups. The SPLA impartiality meant re-integration benefits such as 'medical care, food security, education and road network' were promised but not provided to non-Dinka ex-combatants (Simonse and Kurimoto, 2011:7). This meant that the Monyomiji were not ready to participate in the government re-integration programmes because they preferred familiar peace values in resettling ex-combatants. In the context of the Monyomiji and South Sudan, social re-integration through community service (digging wells, clearing roads and supporting victims), and Mabior cleansing ritual, becomes inevitable in the community and national peacebuilding. Similar to Sierra Leone civil war, youth were 'brutally coerced into a military role,' but *Fambul Tok* (truth-telling) was utilised in the re-integration and peacebuilding through storytelling, sports and income-generating activities (Gebre and Ohta, 2017:161; Murphy, 2003:64).

'The Monyomiji are everything to us' (Sellie, LSCA). This assertion is significant because it situates the Monyomiji as a foundation for a more general, pragmatic and accepted approach to peacebuilding in the South Sudan civil war (Sellie, LSCA). Sellie's confidence in the institution helps point us to its efficiency at community-level dispute resolution. Also, the Monyomiji pragmatic peace and security role is evident in Muratori's description of Monyomiji as 'members of a warrior class,' and active participants in funeral dance, leading to conflict prevention (Muratori, 1950:133). In an attempt to resolve the Dinka–Nuer conflict during the civil war, this pragmatism was demonstrated in animal sacrifice, prayers, negotiation and compensation of victims (Bedigen 2017). After Wunlit, Dinka and Nuer communities resumed trade relations, strengthening communities' economic, political and social status. Further, in their practical application, Simonse's grassroots peacebuilding engaged Monyomiji from Lutuho, Bari-Acholi and other ethnic communities of Eastern and Central Equatoria state in local peacebuilding seminars (Simonse and Kurimoto, 2011:7). In the context of the civil war resolution, Monyomiji pragmatism at local levels can be used to assess the value of youth as significant actors in re-establishing relationships and national peacebuilding (Kemper, 2005:36). The concern here is their distinctiveness, as each community has its structure (Jok et al., 2004:22). Lack of uniformity in Monyomiji practice requires its modification as a framework for national conciliation.

When asked what she means by Monyomiji being 'everything to us,' Sellie maintains the Monyomiji 'addresses all the society's political, economic and social problems'—a view shared by others (Male Focus Group, LSCA; Sellie, LSCA). It is argued that these many responsibilities influence Monyomiji decision in maintaining peaceful conflict management within their respective communities and with other militia groups in the region (Kemper, 2005:37). For instance, Simonse and Kurimoto (2011:129) indicate Monyomiji as grassroots administrators, make by-laws consistent with neighbours and government policies to enhance cooperation between local

The Role of Youth in Indigenous Peacebuilding 145

Monyomiji groups and national governance (Deng, 2017:12). As such, Simonse and Kurimoto's argument for the need to preserve Monyomiji 'cultural heritage' is consistent with this chapter's 'relevance' claim (Simonse and Kurimoto, 2011:9). Monyomiji multifaceted role is important in the context of civil war resolution because Sellie's narratives and others' indicate that the Monyomiji system has vibrant cultural norms (cooperation, confession, songs, animal sacrifice, prayers and post-conflict interaction) which have been utilised in more recent inter-ethnic peacebuilding and management. For example, the Wunlit, Liliir and Abyei conferences (Deng, 2017:11; Bradbury et al., 2006:68). Further, interviewee responses demonstrate that the institution can effectively resolve civil war crimes through 'community warning, shaming, coercion or rejection' (Stovel and Valinas, 2010:16). Such was the case during Wunlit conference, where Chief Gaga named and shamed militia leaders, questioned their terrorist activities and political motives (Bedigen, 2017). Although interviewees speak of Monyomiji's significance as resolvers of 'all community problems,' this might only be limited to community conflict management, and most external or peace actors in the region perceive it as inadequate in the current situation. Further, the failure of Wunlit and Liliir conferences, in which traditional aspects of Monyomiji peacebuilding were utilised, but lasted for only nine and two years, respectively, arose criticisms of indigenous peace practise capability.

'Monyomiji maintain law and order during civil wars' (Female Focus Group, LSCA). During the two decades of the second civil war, locals depended on the Monyomiji who drew from societal customs to resolve all disputes, including civil war crimes (i.e. mutilation, rape, murder, theft, abductions and land grab) (Bedigen, 2020; Leonardi et al., 2010:11). Using customs as the primary source of social order, Monyomiji maintained stability in the region (Deng, 2006:27; Jok et al., 2004:6). This supports the argument that the Monyomiji system can be further modified to suit the modern context. For instance, Simonse, a traditional peace activist, organised the Torit Conference in 2009 where the Monyomiji and government officials participated (Simonse and Kurimoto, 2011). Focussing on lawmaking and enforcement, this conference intended to lay a foundation for better understanding between Monyomiji and local government officials in the East Bank, South Sudan. About 40 Monyomiji members from different communities engaged in dialogue with the same number of state and county officials responsible for the administration of the same communities—this was a step in the right direction (Simonse and Kurimoto, 2011). Many of these conferences, including workshops and seminars, have taken place in South Sudan, but the question is, have they made any positive contribution to the civil war situation? The common problem with these foreign-initiated conferences is that they disregard 'local social contexts' to the critical peace-related customary laws, the heritage of leadership, ceremonies/rituals and youth involvement (Bedigen, 2020), but consistently implement western-style techniques of negotiation and mediation (Brunet-Jailly and Scherrer,

2018:83; Giblin, 2014:502). It is argued that Monyomiji reliance on societal customs, law-making and enforcement, cooperation with other local groups and the government is significant in delivering sustainable peace at the national level. This can be possible when Monyomiji institution is contextually conceptualised. Borrowing from Rushohora's discussions on theorising landscapes, Monyomiji is 'a cultural construct ... given meaning by people ... It is conceptualised, experienced and remade.' It is 'the entire cultural history' of those who practise it (Rushohora, 2017:20). In the context of Monyomiji and South Sudan, focussing on local customs in conceptualising the institution is important because it allows one to analyse vital norms, laws and relationships relevant at national levels (Ochola and Macbaker, 2009).

Drawing from interviewee responses and related literature, this section has discussed local cultures through which the traditional roles of youth are manifested through Monyomiji peace role leadership. The context of this leadership peace role is understood in (1) Apprenticeship: This includes good behaviour, age-grade progression and conflict transformation. (2) Re-integration, an aspect of Monyomiji leadership, includes pragmatic resettlement of ex-combatants, community conflict management, law-making and enforcement. Using interviews, arguments indicate these cultural peace roles could be included in national peacebuilding to prevent decades of failed national, regional and international interventions. Next, the chapter discusses Monyomiji conflict prevention and peacemaking in relation to Jona's leadership experiences in mediation and negotiation.

Monyomiji Mediation and Negotiation Roles

One of the focus group members, Jona in their narrative, talks about his experience as a youth working with elders. The narrative highlights the great link between the traditional leadership institutions of *Odonge* (elders) and Monyomiji (youth). Jona's experience supports the idea of Monyomiji dynamic and multifaceted peace roles in peacebuilding through an apprenticeship in 'leadership, mediation and negotiation' (Jona, Juba). Jona, a youth in the Anyuak community leadership, tells of his experience within the community. He says that once a conflict existed between two women elders old enough to be his grandmothers. This conflict was over duties and responsibilities, as each one of the women claimed the other was overtaking her roles. Although these women were directly answerable to him, an older person had to be sent, to join him in the peacebuilding meeting. His enthusiasm, contribution and support from members were vital (Fego, Juba). He had to restructure and redefine roles, without offending either party to the conflict. He stresses that this kind of case handling by youth is not only practised within a given community but that their involvement can also be necessary for major conflicts. Jona's youth role in peacebuilding highlights how Monyomiji peace role can mature into higher level mediation and negotiation duties.

Mediation Role

> We have to learn from the elders. We work with our leaders for a start carrying messages from one place to the other .... We depend on our mother's wisdom ... and when the local youth talked during the meeting, we just listened ... we couldn't agree more.
>
> (Focus Group-Y, 5 June 2013)

Through the age-set and age-grade systems, practised in the *Monyomiji* institution, the youth play a unique role in traditional mediation. As indicated in the focus group notes above, the youth *Monyomiji* work alongside the outgoing *Monyomiji* elders. This contrasts with the UN view of youth. The UN's developmental policies should target the given *Monyomiji* institutional role as a peace and security organisation. *Monyomiji* initial involvement, as indicated in interviewees' narratives, is in carrying and delivering messages between disputants who are involved in peacebuilding discussions. In doing so, they learn aspects of indigenous peace and peacebuilding mediation. Interviewees indicate that, in some communities that practise the *Monyomiji* system, all the youth are expected to be part of an age-set from which they are initiated into age-grade. This can be attained individually or as a group in a series of levels. For instance, in males, boyhood, adolescence or warrior, early manhood and elder manhood are the principal levels. Procedures in youth age-grade are similar to elders (Bedigen, 2017). Note that individual age-grade progression, rather than collective, plays a significant role in enabling the identification of mediation skills and other special peacebuilding qualities and abilities in youth. From learners to performers, *Monyomiji* offers a practical example of how community values and responsibilities can be imparted to youth, not only in the South Sudan situation but in the wider world.

In some Nilotic Lwo communities, traditional peacebuilding is dominated by male elders. This is because, in these communities, age, masculinity and seniority are associated with experience, expertise and wisdom. Findings demonstrate that when a youth becomes a chief, through hereditary means, or as a *Monyomiji* member, his age does not matter, as he assumes the role of an elder immediately. Apart from playing the leadership role, he assumes other peacebuilding roles of peacemaking or mediator. In Nilotic culture, role inheritance is practised at family, extended family, clan and community levels. At each of these levels, it is believed to be a way through which societal values are passed onto the young. Heredity in chieftaincy can be gradual. The young in the chiefly lineage are prepared for leadership from an early age. This implies that peace values and peacebuilding skills are learnt through informal settings, an aspect conventional methods can learn from.

Further, traditional mediation involves identifying dispute causes, damages, a suitable resolution process and the mediator under the guidance of the spirits. Through the age-set and age-grade systems, the youth play a unique role in traditional mediation (Grawert, 2014:144; Muratori, 1950; Simonse and Kurimoto, 2011:2). Focus groups and Jona's story reveal 'Odonge (elders) and Monyomiji (youth) work together,' initially (Jona, Juba). For instance, they initially carry and deliver messages between disputants and in doing so, learn and perfect how to identify dispute causes, damages, suitable resolution process and the mediator (Jona, Juba). This contrasts with the UN assumptions and demand for legal classification of youth, and justifies the UN view of youth as a life stage, thus exclusively defining the youth population as between the ages of 15 and 24 (Kemper, 2005:8). Western notions of a 'normal' childhood are emulated in defining age chronologically, assuming a homogeneous view that people develop along a linear path, whereas in the context of Monyomiji and South Sudan, age-set and age-grade influence youth definition and roles. For example, boyhood, adolescence or warrior, early manhood and older manhood have different responsibilities (Male Focus Group, LSCA). A more experienced younger Monyomiji can mediate in complex cases such as murder by taking responsibility and apologising for wrongs done on behalf of perpetrators (Stovel and Valinas, 2010:16). Significantly, identifying mediation skills and other unique peacebuilding qualities and abilities in younger Monyomiji like Jona who demonstrate a high future potential is crucial. From learners to performers, Monyomiji offers a practical example of how community mediation values and responsibilities can be imparted to youth. Monyomiji involvement in traditional mediation is significant in the context of South Sudan because it frames youth as a 'part of the struggle for influence, authority, and control' (Christiantine et al., 2006:11). Thus, the UN peace and developmental policies should target Monyomiji institution as a peace and security organisation crucial in nurturing future mediators.

Further, interviewee responses indicate 'the Nilotic Lwo younger Monyomiji mediators can be as competent as an elder mediator' because, in their African Traditional Religion (ATR) belief, god gives societal rules and regulations (Male Focus Group, LSCA; Deng, 2006:27). Cultural beliefs hold that, for a successful mediation, the gods, spirits and ancestors work through leaders so must be included and appeased in concluding the process (Deng, 2017:11; Stovel and Valinas, 2010:17). Additionally, they are believed to be possessed by the spirit, communicate directly with god who gives wisdom to all those in public duty (Deng, 2006:28; Hutchinson, 2001:312). This highlights the significance South Sudanese accord spiritual authority and the belief that spirits have interest in humans and societal concerns. During mediation, many spiritually connected cultural rituals continue to be practised in South Sudan villages because locals revere spiritual authority (Deng, 2006:27; Parmar et al., 2010:276). However, at the national level, local churches through the New Sudan Council of Churches (NSCC) have been part of many mediation processes, as they are perceived to represent all beliefs (Bradbury et al., 2006:6; Simonse and Kurimoto, 2011:8). ATR, which is a significant aspect of Monyomiji mediation practice, belief and

The Role of Youth in Indigenous Peacebuilding 149

values, is excluded at the national level as it is perceived irrelevant to the tangible civil war economic and political struggles. Regardless, this chapter demonstrates the Monyomiji mediation is important because it helps in identifying dispute causes, damages and ensuring a suitable resolution process, thus allowing locals' ownership.

Negotiation Role

Traditional negotiation progresses from mediation and focuses on dispute settlement and the future by determining compensation type, amount and customary law amendment (Ingelaere, 2008:43; Jona, Juba). Monyomiji peace negotiations start with the 'ceremonial sacrifice of a great white bull' or Mabior ritual, followed by discussions, compensation agreement and food sharing (Bedigen, 2017; Bradbury et al., 2006:12; Wunlit, 1999:3). Traditional negotiation offers a means by which Monyomiji resolve various incidents without inciting hostilities; discipline individuals causing disturbances and ensure abducted women, children and missing cattle are returned, to prevent revenge (Bradbury et al., 2006:72). As mentioned earlier, the negotiation process is flexible and takes into account the contextual aspects of disputants' motives, goals as well as the impact of ruling on family, Monyomiji specific role and priorities (Leonardi et al., 2010:17). By using customary laws, Monyomiji has implemented context-based negotiations through people-to-people conferences to resolve farmers–pastoralists disputes in Abyei, Aweil and Twic Counties, halting civil wars (Bradbury et al., 2006; Thomas, 2015:1). Thus, Monyomiji as an institution with a heritage of peacebuilding should have priority not only at the inter-ethnic but national level of peacebuilding. Generally, in post-conflict situations, youth have been excluded from the hierarchical decision, creating negative peace that is easily threatened by militia groups lacking full engagement in negotiation. The local South Sudan peace initiatives have often represented Monyomiji via government-appointed chiefs/leaders or politicians, yet youth remain misrepresented. Although the CPA provides for Monyomiji involvement, this provision remains largely on paper (Bedigen, 2019). For instance, IGAD peace negotiations continue to exclude the Monyomiji institution, which may support intra- and inter-ethnic conflict reconciliation through both technical and soft means (Grawert, 2014:144). It unwittingly continues to place South Sudanese traditional peace values at the peripheries, preventing sustainable peace from happening.

Monyomiji negotiation team consists of high levels of specialised leadership within the Monyomiji system, including the 'rain chief, war chief, and medicine man' (Jona, Juba). They negotiate access to natural resources (namely: water, pasture and fruit trees), trade, village boundaries, as well as peacebuilding treaties with neighbouring communities (Bradbury et al., 2006:20). Each of these leaders may be called upon to execute their role during a negotiation process. For example, during the second civil war, Riek

Machar (the Nuer militia leader-war chief) negotiated trade routes to allow supplies into communities and militia zones (Hutchinson, 2001:314). Also, when concluding a negotiation process, the medicine man can be called upon to offer sacrifices and conduct cleansing rituals that help deter feelings of revenge and exclusion (Graybill, 2004:1126). Adding, in line with Lederach's argument, flexibility and interdependence of roles during negotiation are important in the context of farmers–pastoralists who rely on each other's goodwill to share scarce resources (Lederach, 1995:12). For example, seasonally many Missiriya pastoralist groups pass through Abyei (Dinka settlements) in search of grazing pasture (Bradbury et al., 2006:17; Craze, 2011). To avoid cattle feeding on crops, the Dinka and the Missiriya prevent conflicts by negotiating and agreeing to safe passage routes pastoralists must follow (Bradbury et al., 2006:17; Deng, 2017:17; 58Wilson, 2014). Furthermore, in cases where animals damage the crops, compensation type and amount are negotiated (Ingelaere, 2008:43). However, these seasonal agreements are precarious and prone to failures due to unpredictable changes in the environment, community needs and their lack of permanency may not offer sustainable peace at national levels (Bradbury et al., 2006:12).

The Monyomiji specialised organisation is vital in ensuring the smooth handling of the inter-community interaction. Specialisation prevents conflicts from arising due to the confusion of duties and responsibilities. For instance, when negotiators' involvement in intra-ethnic conflicts is needed, each specialist must make themselves available. These specialist duties are only recognised within a community, not at an inter-ethnic level where youth like Jona, who may not necessarily have any specialities, become part of the negotiation process, thus rendering the system limited in certain situations.

This chapter agrees with the argument that Monyomiji as a cultural heritage needs to be preserved because they modify and enforce pro-peace laws (Simonse and Kurimoto, 2011:9). During the negotiation, they help determine compensation type and amount without which peacebuilding cannot start. In the past, compensation for a minor case such as theft required one ram, but ten sheep in grievous crimes such as murder, witchcraft and poisoning (Muratori, 1950:138). Moreover, change in customs and beliefs may affect Monyomiji modern-day roles and practices (Asante, 2003:5). Any such changes should reflect in Monyomiji ruling (Jok et al., 2004:22). As such, the system allows for constant reflection on new ideas and learning, therefore making it a legitimate moral institution. This is important in the context of South Sudan dynamic conflicts and leads to the argument that Monyomiji institution is still significant as some civil war crimes are too grievous for any compensation type or amount. To keep the peace, the Monyomiji give compensation claim due consideration in each court case (Jok et al., 2004:22).

For instance, interviewee indicates that, in the past, 'a girl was given as compensation for murder' (Sellie, LSCA). Considering decades of war that have led to significant loss of property, the Monyomiji have adjusted these compensation requirements over the years. Payment of goats and cows replaced 'girl compensation.' Likewise, in the past, the Monyomiji took anybody's goat for customary rituals, but, in recent years, they provide, thus, conflict prevention. Similar institutions such as the Gacaca traditional courts in Rwanda made such adjustments in compensation to re-establish unity (Ingelaere, 2008:31). For example, perpetrators could be asked to build a house for the victim/victim's family (Graybill, 2004; Raper, 2005).

These discussions have shown that mediation develops into negotiation and that youth involvement from a young age into specific peace roles within Monyomiji institution can benefit South Sudan's complex civil war situation. Next, we discuss a funeral dance ritual through which mediation and negotiation are instigated and pursued to enable peacebuilding.

Monyomiji Funeral Dance

Sellie's and focus group's responses mentioned earlier show 'Monyomiji peace practices are normative and without coded laws' (Sellie, LSCA). Jok et al. (2004:6) affirm this by saying 'very few customary law systems exist in written form.' In implementing normative uncoded laws, this chapter demonstrates that Monyomiji ensure their respective communities function well and prevent aggression or conflicts without any need for external intervention. One such uncoded lawless peacebuilding measure is through a funeral dance. Muratori (1950:133) indicates that the Lotuko Monyomiji hastily organises a funeral dance to resolve an issue brought to their attention. The purpose of a funeral dance, where mourning songs are sung and danced to by children, youth and adults, is to 'invite' the unknown perpetrator(s) to confess before a mediation process. With almost no investigation, the perpetrator(s) on hearing the sounds of mourning songs often reveal themselves to the Monyomiji for fear of being cursed or excessively punished if discovered.

For example, among the Lotuko, a funeral dance is a public announcement of the planned attack on the neighbours, if they did not voluntarily reveal perpetrators (Bedigen, 2017). Once the funeral dance songs are heard by neighbours, and to avoid an indiscriminate attack, Monyomiji of neighbouring communities interrogate their members in a bid to find the unknown perpetrator. The Lotuko neighbours (Toposa, Acholi, Lango, Boya, Lopit, Madi and Pari) without being consulted help keep or make peace by initiating a negotiation process that will culminate into targeted and proportionate justice (Muratori, 1950). This suggests that informality within traditional systems can be productive, unlike ceasefires that have not delivered peace in places such as Nuba Mountains (Bradbury et al., 2006:9). It demonstrates there needn't be a peace envoy or special investigation unit as often witnessed in conventional approaches.

Also, peace songs, randomly started by an individual and joined by others, are known to break tense moments, for example, during Abyei and Wunlit peacebuilding processes (Deng, 2017:11; Bedigen, 2017). Practices such as funeral dance and peace songs are ideal in South Sudan, a country bogged by war and unable to meet costs of conflict prevention and peacemaking. Funeral dance, as a peace cultural heritage feature, prevents post-conflict reconstruction challenges as community consultations and meditation begin spontaneously.

Further, a funeral dance allows creative work in peace to commence. As a heritage, it propels the Monyomiji to deliver a clear path to societal change from violence to non-violence and from conflicts to peace. The argument here is, the Monyomiji commitment to expected duties and responsibilities effortlessly translates into peace and peacebuilding approaches, namely mediation, negotiation and the implementation of restorative justice. Considering the time frame, amount and scarcity of resources required to achieve a civil war resolution in conventional approaches, non-Eurocentric approaches such as the funeral dance can be of benefit to South Sudan for they are less costly and are contextual (Asante, 2003:5; Giblin, 2014). Adding, Deng (2017:11) indicates 'all rituals imply that the reconciliation was complete and binding.' Local customs' popularity allows Monyomiji hegemony in that the local people and their roles, customs, beliefs, practices and values are central; therefore, rituals such as a funeral dance are essential in realising sustainable peace (Deng, 2017:18). There is an indication that although local rituals such as funeral dance lead to confession and accountability, it is coercive as all members are recognised as belonging to the same 'moral universe' (Stovel and Valinas, 2010:18). Thus, this unconventional conflict prevention method may instigate indiscriminate punishment and unnecessary conflict if neighbours do not respond.

Youth Marriage and Peacebuilding

Interviewee narratives demonstrate that, traditionally, youth are encouraged to marry into enemy communities for reconciliation purposes. The Nilotic Lwo believe that inter-marriage can help resolve intermittent conflicts. Fulo, an interviewee, tells how this kind of marriage is practised in her community:

> A young girl will offer to leave her own family to go and live at the victim's family. If she is of a marriageable age, marriage arrangements are made and negotiations of both marriage and conflict take place. However, if she's too young to be married, her parents will support her choice, and a ceremony in which she is handed over to her new family is held.
> (Fulo, 17 August 2012)

The young girl is initiated into this new family; all ties are cut with the original family as she is given new names. She is raised into adulthood and when her time for marriage comes, a dowry is paid to her new family. While traditional negotiation is dominated by the elders, this story shows the significance of youth involvement in its process. It is important to note that, from an early age, youth understand the need to resolve disputes, their role and what it takes to be involved. These findings confirm that the young are neither victims nor spectators, when it comes to peacemaking. In conventional standards, traditional practices such as these can be perceived as a human rights violation.

Further, what made the role of young unmarried girls distinctive, in traditional societies, is that they are perceived not to belong to their birth families, but destined to live and fulfil their lives in someone else's—their husband's. This implies a girl has to possess qualities, or virtues, such as compassion, discretion, patience, gentleness, modesty and self-control. These societies place very high expectations on girls. The above qualities are considered inherent in womanhood, only needing reinforcement through upbringing, to enable them to fulfil their roles as wives and mothers as well as peace roles. For instance, interviewee narratives demonstrate that the role of transmitting cultural values fell on the family first, then the community. From childhood, therefore, girls' duties and responsibilities in marriage become their passion. They are brought up in preparation for this ultimate goal. Based on this belief and expectations, girls or women are considered peacemakers. For instance, field notes demonstrate that

> the Nilotic Lwo word for woman, '*dako*' or '*daho*', means 'traveller', 'to move'. In their birth families, they are considered temporary family members. Family plans focus on the boys, and girls are constantly reminded of how they should grow into good marriageable women, or refrain from any undesirable behaviours, such as quarrelling, meanness and disrespect, before they marry. These behaviours can cause marriage tensions, separation or even divorce.
> (Focus Group-M, 21 March 2013)

It is highly likely that the society's belief and expectations in young girls are the reasons why, in some communities, young girls spearhead mediation or expect to be used as stratagems in peacebuilding (Achebe, 1958). Most significantly, peace duties and responsibilities are expected to continue throughout the young girl's lifetime. Both her birth and marriage communities expect her to contribute positively towards the well-being and peaceful relationships with family members and others, as demonstrated in Efo's and Mosa's narratives above. Her new home becomes her personal long-term ambition. It is in her interest to make it a peaceful living environment or community. Importantly, through marriage, alliances are created between two families or communities. This is a traditional conflict prevention measure that offers a foundation upon which peacebuilding processes can be based.

154 *The Role of Youth in Indigenous Peacebuilding*

Further, Bedigen (2007, 2021) indicates that, during conflict, the young Somali unmarried women (*Heerin*) from one of the warring clans paid visits to the enemy clan without the knowledge or consent of their families. They told the enemy clan that they were unmarried women, to be married. Generally, this is a well-known tradition to help start a conflict mediation process. Thus, the young women on approaching the enemy camp are welcomed. Following, mediation for the payment of a dowry and conflict resolution is commenced. This was followed by a marriage proposal, ceremony and subsequent reconciliation (Bedigen, 2021). As indicated in Sellie's narratives, these practices are not alien to South Sudan communities. They stabilise conflict situations and can lead to sustainable peace. Although the Nilotic Lwo traditional practices of peacebuilding marriages are relied on traditionally, they may not sit well with human rights laws. This opens another chapter for academic debate.

Next, I discuss the role of youth in a peacebuilding ceremony.

Youth and *Kwero Merok* 'Cleansing of Ex-combatants'

Similar to the *Nyono Tong Gweno* ritual, discussed in the previous chapter, interviewee narratives cited the *Kwero Merok* ritual where youth involvement is key (see Figure 6.3). It is a ritual that can be utilised to cleanse, re-integrate and avoid post-traumatic stress of a former soldier. Although it is not a direct peacebuilding ritual, its purpose is to prevent evil spirits, or

Figure 6.3 Preparation for Kwero Merok Ritual

Lacen, or *Nueer*, from possessing individuals. In the Nilotic communities, it is believed that evil spirit possession can cause one to murder. This ritual must involve a teenage virgin girl, a relation to the perpetrator. Her role is to accompany the offender, symbolically demonstrating his willingness to purify himself of the evil spirits.

The purpose of this ritual is conflict prevention in a post-conflict situation. In support of this, Kamwaria and Katola (2012) indicate that the Dinka concepts of health and illness encapsulate cleansing rituals that are aimed at conflict prevention. Throughout the Nilotic Lwo cultures is a strong belief that the murder spirit inhabits the killer. If not driven out by cleansing, it can cause the killer to repeat the offence. Sonia's work uncovers this missing link in conventional peacebuilding efforts in northern Uganda. Further, it is believed the *Kwero Merok* ritual cleanses the killer's family, clan or community from calamities, diseases, tragedies and illnesses—these have at times exacerbated conflicts. This ritual signifies individualism and collectiveness in traditional peacebuilding.

Similar to other rituals, already discussed, its values are deeply rooted in conflict prevention and peacebuilding from within. A significant point this ritual brings out is that both personal (individual) and public (community) peace are correlated. Peace is not viewed as an entity. In conflict situations, it is the duty and responsibility of those affected, or concerned, to cause it to exist through ceremonies and rituals. Each and every step in the traditional peacebuilding process contributes towards a common goal. Before the ritual, returnees are obliged to tell their stories. These include all killings. In situations where an ex-combatant does not reveal any killings, his behaviour is watched to see if he shows signs of 'abnormal behaviour,' such as withdrawal, mood swings or unnecessary aggressiveness, and the elders can decide to perform this ritual on him. While conventional methods have focussed on economic empowerment of ex-combatants in South Sudan, the *Kwero Merok* ritual demonstrates Nilotic Lwo's indigenous approaches are more concerned with an individual's psychological state of mind and well-being. The Nilotic perception is that an individual's conscience resonates with peace and peacebuilding, in both community and environment (Bedigen, 2017).

Conclusion

Findings discussed in this chapter demonstrate that youth, or *Monyomiji*, play a significant role in indigenous peacebuilding. They start as learners but through the *Monyomiji* structure graduate into skilful negotiators and mediators. Further, they are creative and participate fully in the leadership and organisation of their communities. In doing so, they prepare to face social challenges. Youth can be fully involved in community cleansing ceremonies and rituals that help in the re-integration of ex-combatants. Therefore, the *Monyomiji* system, originally practised among the Lulubo ethnic groups of

Eastern Equatoria, encapsulates the significance of the Nilotic traditional peace and peacebuilding institution. Other South Sudanese ethnic groups, including the Nuer, Shuli (Acooli/Acholi), Madi, Dinka and Langi, have adopted the *Monyomiji* system. Based on this and if we are to heed Sellie's claim that '*Monyomiji* is everything' to the Lulubo, it is not a mere institution, but a system that enables communities to thrive in peace. Adding, it is argued that *Monyomiji* is not just an alternative dispute resolution system, but an age-old reliable source of moral, cultural and philosophical heritage, instrumental in conflict prevention, peacemaking and peacebuilding. The *Monyomiji* system promotes and enhances creative solutions to peace and peacebuilding challenges, not only among the Nilotic ethnic communities, but to other African ethnicities and the wider world.

Further, this chapter demonstrates that traditional roles of youth in peacebuilding through the Monyomiji institution are preferred at the inter-ethnic level and should be included at national peace dialogues. Discussions show that the dynamic and multifaceted Monyomiji peace roles in peacebuilding through leadership, mediation, negotiation, implemented along with ceremonies/rituals, are essential in bonding communities and delivering lasting peace at the national level. However, South Sudan national peace processes continue to exclude Monyomiji, pursue and implement conventional top-down methods of peacebuilding, such as negotiation and mediation. With limited sample and distinctiveness of the Monyomiji practice in various South Sudanese communities, the chapter does not explore Monyomiji governance or political set-up but focuses on their popularity in local peace activities and rituals, and potential at national levels. Success in Monyomiji peace practices during the South Sudan civil war includes the Wunlit, Liliir, Torit and Abyei local peace processes. Other community-based peace success stories in the region include Sierra Leone (*Fambul Tok*), Northern Uganda (Mato Oput) and Rwanda (*Gacaca*). Moreover, the chapter highlights Monyomiji challenges (e.g. economic, moral and political), and therefore its legitimacy as a local-based peacebuilding institution at the national level.

To emphasise, South Sudan civil war sustainable resolution requires a bottom-up approach that is context based. It is observed that Monyomiji reliance on societal customs: inclusiveness, interdependence roles, local peace cultures and community support are bottom-up characteristics that could benefit the IGAD peace processes (Deng, 2006:27; Lederach, 1995:12). This is because this war is flared by inter-ethnic conflicts which the locals have historically resolved using local institutions and practices. In doing so, the chapter discussed findings on what the Monyomiji traditional peacebuilding roles are and if these traditional peace roles can be useful in civil war resolution. Engaging Monyomiji institution holistically is significant in telling what and how peacebuilding should be implemented at the national level (Female Focus Groups, LSCA). As stipulated in the CPA, and demonstrated in Simonse's local peace processes, there is a possibility for Monyomiji–government or Monyomiji–IGAD partnership (Bradbury et al., 2006:13; Simonse and Kurimoto, 2011; Young and Lebrun, 2006:28). Further, engaging Monyomiji in national negotiations and peacebuilding creates acceptance, affirms locals' values, and removes the burden of peacebuilding from agencies such as IGAD (Schomerus and Allen, 2010:81). Simonse and Kurimoto (2011:16) indicate that, 'ensuring Monyomiji participation in the councils would be proportionate to their role in the community.' In utilising Monyomiji, this chapter puts emphasis on their conflict prevention and peacemaking, and critical of these are the use of ceremonies/ rituals in transforming violent situations into non-violence. This chapter's contribution to knowledge is that local institutions are crucial in the identification and implementation of relevant peace practices at local and national level. Also, local institutions are essential in integrating cultural heritage into modern peacebuilding approaches.

Bibliography

Achebe, C., 1958. *Things Fall Apart*. London, Heinemann.
Amum, P., 2018, April 23. South Sudan's planned election violates peace process. *Sudan Tribune*. Retrieved from http://www.sudantribune.com/spip.php?article65259.
Asante, M.K., 2003. *Afrocentricity: The Theory of Social Change*. Chicago, IL, African American Images.
Bedigen, W., 2017. *Traditional Peacebuilding. The Nilotic Lwo of South Sudan* (PhD Thesis). Leeds, Leeds Beckett University.
Bedigen, W., 2019. Youth (Monyomiji) and conflict resolution in the South Sudan civil war. *Journal of African Cultural Heritage Studies*, 2(1). Retrieved from https://www.jachs.org/articles/abstract/47/.
Bedigen, W., 2020. Significance of societal customs in the South Sudan civil war resolution. *Journal of Peacebuilding and Development*, 15(1), pp. 3–17.
Bradbury, M., Ryle, J., Medley, M. and Sansculotte-Greenidge, K., 2006. *Local Peace Processes in Sudan: A Baseline Study*. London, Rift Valley Institute.
Brunet-Jailly, J. and Scherrer, O., 2018. Protecting architectural heritage in Djenné: A civil society point of view. *Journal of African Cultural Heritage Studies*, 1(1), pp. 72–94. doi: 10.22599/jachs.15.
Christiansen, C., Utas, M. and Vigh, H., 2006. Introduction. In C. Christiansen, M. Utas and H. Vigh (Eds.), *Navigating Youth, Generating Adulthood: Social Becoming in an African Context*. Uppsala, Nordiska Afrikainstitutet, pp. 9–30.
Craze, J., 2011. *Creating Facts on the Ground: Conflict Dynamics in Abyei*. Geneva, Small Arms Survey.
de Waal, A., 2014. When Kleptocracy becomes insolvent: Brute causes of the civil war in South Sudan. *African Affairs*, 113(452), pp. 347–369.
de Waal, A. and Flint, J., 2005. *Darfur: A Short History of a Long War*. London, Zed/International African Institute.
Deng, F., 2017. *Abyei Dialogue: Bottom Up and Top Down*.
Deng, F.M., 2006. *Talking It Out: Stories in Negotiating Human Relations*. London, Routledge.

Durham, D., 2000. Youth and the social imagination in Africa: Introduction to parts 1 and 2. *Anthropological Quarterly*, 73(3). Retrieved from https://www.jstor.org/stable/pdf/3317936.pdf (Accessed 12 December 2018).

Francis, D., 2004. *Rethinking War and Peace*. London, Pluto Press.

Gebre, Y.G. and Ohta, I., 2017. *African Virtues in the Pursuit of Conviviality: Exploring Local Solutions in Light of Global Prescriptions*. Langaa RPCIG, African Books Collective.

Giblin, J.D., 2014. Post-conflict heritage: Symbolic healing and cultural renewal. *International Journal of Heritage Studies*, 20(5), pp. 500–518. doi: 10.1080/13527258.2013.772912.

Gramsci, A., 1992. *Prison Notebooks (Vol. 2)*. New York, Columbia University Press.

Grawert, E., 2014. *Forging Two Nations Insights on Sudan and South Sudan*. Addis Ababa, OSSREA.

Graybill, L.S., 2004. Pardon, punishment, and amnesia: Three African post-conflict methods. *Third World Quarterly*, 25(6), pp. 1117–1130.

Grueb, A., 1992. *The Lotuho of the Southern Sudan, an Ethnological Monograph*. Stuttgart, Steiner.

Hutchinson, S.E., 2001. A curse from god? Religious and political dimensions of the post-1991 rise of ethnic violence in South Sudan. *The Journal of Modern African Studies*, 39(2), pp. 307–331.

Huyse, L. and Salter, M., 2008. *Tradition-Based Justice and Reconciliation After Violent Conflict: Learning from African Experiences*. Stockholm, International IDEA

Ingelaere, B., 2008. The Gacaca Courts in Rwanda. In *Traditional Justice and Reconciliation After Violent Conflict: Learning from African Experiences/Huyse, Luc [edit.]; ea*, pp. 25–59. Stockholm, Sweden, International IDEA.

Iwilade, A., 2014. Networks of violence and becoming: Youth and the politics of patronage in Nigeria's oil-rich delta. *The Journal of Modern African Studies*, 52(4), pp. 571–595. doi: 10.1017/S0022278X14000603.

Iyob, R. and Khadiagala, G.M., 2006. *Sudan: The Elusive Quest for Peace*. Boulder, CO, Lynne Rienner Publishers.

Jok, A.A., Leitch, A.R. and Vandewint, C., 2004. *A Study of Customary Law in Contemporary Southern Sudan*. Rumbek, South Sudan, World Vision International.

Jok, J.M. and Hutchinson, S.E., 1999. Sudan's prolonged second civil war and the militarization of Nuer and Dinka ethnic identities. *African Studies Review*, 42(2), pp. 125–145.

Kamwaria, A. and Katola, M., 2012. The role of African traditional religion, culture and world-view in the context of post-war healing among the Dinka community of Southern Sudan. *International Journal of Humanities and Social Science*, 2(21), pp. 49–55.

Kemper, Y., 2005. *Youth in War-to-Peace Transitions: Approaches by International Organisations*. Berghof, Berghof. Research Center for Constructive Conflict Management.

Lederach, J.P., 1997. *Building Peace: Sustainable Reconciliation in Divided Societies*. Washington, DC, US Institute of Peace Press.

Lederach, J.P., 1995. *Preparing for Peace: Conflict Transformation across Cultures*. Syracuse University Press.

Leonardi, C., Moro, L.N., Santschi, M. and Isser, H.D., 2010. *Local Justice in South Sudan*. Peaceworks Number 66. Washington, DC, United States Institute of Peace.
Mamdani, M., 2020. *When Victims Become Killers*. Princeton, NJ, Princeton University Press.
Muratori, C., 1950. A case of magical poisoning in a Lotuko village. *Sudan Notes and Records*, 31(1), pp. 133–136.
Murphy, W., 2003. Military patrimonialism and child soldier clientalism in the liberian and Sierra Leonean civil wars. *African Studies Review*, 46(2), pp. 61–87. Retrieved from https://www.jstor.org/stable/1514826?seq=1#page_scan_tab_contents (Accessed 26 December 2018).
Ochola II, M., 2009. *Spirituality of Reconciliation: A Case Study of Mato Oput within the Context of the Cultural and Traditional Justice System of the Nilotic Acholi/Central Luo People of Northern Uganda*. Lecture. October. Kitgum, Uganda.
Parmar, S., Roseman, M.J., Siegrist, S. and Sowa, T. (Eds.), 2010. *Children and Transitional Justice: Truth-Telling, Accountability and Reconciliation*. Cambridge, MA, Harvard University Press, pp. 276–277.
Prichard, E.E., 1934. Sudan notes and records. *Nuer Tribe and Clan*. Part 1. Volume 17. London, Hawkes and Co., Ltd.
Ramsbotham, O., Miall, H. and Woodhouse, T., 2011. *Contemporary Peacebuilding*. Polity, Bradford Scholars.
Raper, J., 2005. The gacaca experiment: Rwanda's restorative dispute resolution response to the 1994 genocide. *Pepperdine Dispute Resolution Law Journal*, 5, p. 1.
Ross, S.D. and Tehranian, M. (Eds.), 2011. *Peace Journalism in Times of War 1*. London, Transaction Publishers, pp. 4–11.
Rushohora, N.A., 2017. Theorising the Majimaji – Landscape, memory and agency. *Journal of African Cultural Heritage Studies*, 1(1), pp. 19–31. doi: 10.22599/jachs.11.
Schomerus, M. and Allen, T., 2010. *Southern Sudan at Odds with Itself: Dynamics of Conflict and Predicaments of Peace*. London, UK, Development Studies Institute, London School of Economics and Political Science.
Schwartz, S., 2010. *Youth and Post-conflict Reconstruction*. Washington, DC, United States Institute of Peace Press.
Simonse, S. and Kurimoto, E. (Eds.), 2011. Engaging 'Monyomiji', bridging the gap in East Bank Equatoria: Proceedings of the Conference 26–28 November 2009. Nairobi. Pax Christi Horn of Africa, pp. 2–129.
Simonse, S., Verkoren, W.M. and Junne, G., 2010. *NGO Involvement in the Juba Peace Talks: The Role and Dilemmas of IKV*, : pp. 1–2. Basingstoke, PAx Christi.
Stemler, S., 2001. An overview of content analysis. *Practical Assessment, Research and Evaluation*, 7(17), pp. 137–146.
Stovel, L. and Valiñas, M., 2010. *Restorative Justice after Mass Violence: Opportunities and Risks for Children and Youth*. Florence, UNICEF Innocenti Research Centre.
Thomas, E., 2015. *South Sudan: A Slow Liberation*. London, Zed Books Ltd.
UNESCO, n.d. About the youth programme. Retrieved from http://www.unesco.org/new/en/social-and-human-sciences/themes/youth/about-youth/ (Accessed 23 May 2014).

UNESCO, n.d. What do we mean by 'youth'. Unesco.org. Retrieved from http://www.unesco.org/new/en/social-and-human-sciences/themes/youth/youth-definition/.

Wheeler, S., 2010. *South Sudan: Changing of the Guard*. Torit, South Sudan. Retrieved from ipsnews.net; http://www.ipsnews.net/2010/01/south-sudan-changing-of-the-guard/.

Wilson, J.H., 2014. *Local Peace Processes in Sudan and South Sudan*. Washington, United States Institute of Peace.

Wing, Jr, J. 2012. "Youth" Windsor review. *A Journal of the Arts*, 45(1), p. 9.

World Bank, 2014. Factsheet: South Sudan. Definition of Youth. Retrieved from http://www.youthpolicy.org/pdfs/factsheets/south-sudan.pdf (Accessed 12 June 2018).

Wunlit Peace and Reconciliation Conference, 1999b. Appendix: Wunlit recommendations on abductions. From the Dinka Nuer West Bank Peace and Reconciliation Conference in Wunlit. Available from: http://southsudanfriends.org/wunlit/index.html (Accessed 7 April 2014).

Young, J., 2003. Sudan: Liberation movements, regional armies, ethnic militias & peace. *Review of African Political Economy*, 30(97), pp. 423–434.

Young, J. and Lebrun, E., 2006. *The South Sudan Defence Forces in the Wake of the Juba Declaration*. Geneva, Small Arms Survey.

List of Interviews Cited in the Text

1) Focus Group-W, 17 March 2013
2) Fulo, 17 August 2012
3) Fred, 25 March 2013
4) Sellie, 10 August 2012

7 The Role of Women (*Honyomiji*) in Indigenous Peacebuilding

Introduction

Conventional peace theories and methods analysed in previous chapters highlight the involvement of women in local peace processes (Bedigen, 2021), but they do not explore the significance of their indigenous, traditional and domestic roles. With this in mind, this chapter seeks to make a contextual contribution by discussing indigenous women's institutions and their subtleties in peacebuilding. These include motherhood, organisation, facilitation, peace education, leadership, divination, social support roles and decision-making, and their contribution to national peacebuilding. The chapter stresses that the Nilotic Lwo communities' functionalities are dependent on women's subtle roles. Significantly, these roles are inclusive of customary laws, beliefs and practices in peace and peacebuilding. Therefore, their inclusion in national peacebuilding could deliver sustainable peace. Overall, this chapter aims to elucidate the role of the Honyomiji institution and its possible contribution to national peacebuilding. Before then, it discusses the UN's Women Peace and Security (WPS) agenda.

Women Peace and Security Agenda

The majority of debates on the Women Peace and Security (WPS) agenda show that women in conflict zones are highly vulnerable, continuously at risk or passive victims to be protected (Ibok and Ogar, 2018; Oosterom, 2017; Pankhurst, 2008). Leonardi et al. (2010:11) highlight the intermittent ethnic conflicts and civil wars the South Sudanese women have experienced since 1955. Their plight prompted the United Nations Security Council (UNSC) to reaffirm its commitment to the WPS agenda. Fulfilled through Resolution 1889, whose aim was to strengthen the implementation and monitoring of Resolution 1325, the resolution reiterates its mandate for the increased participation of women, particularly during all stages of post-conflict peace and decision-making. Its primary focus is protecting women and girls during armed conflict and in post-conflict situations (Bedigen, 2017). In effecting this resolution, the United Nations (UN) aims to appoint more women to senior positions, particularly in field missions, as a tangible step towards providing leadership and implementing Resolution 1325. Adding, the UN Resolutions 1889 and 1325 place emphasis on:

i) Encouraging states to design strategies to address the needs of women and girls during post-conflict situations, including access to education, socio-economic provisions and gender equality.
ii) To promote the participation of women in peace processes, particularly in conflict resolution, post-conflict planning and peacebuilding (United Nations, 2009; Arabi, 2011).

Such moves demonstrate the UN's increasing interest in women's inclusion. Moreover, they are implemented as subsidiaries of the 'high-level' conventional methods that ignore existing indigenous institutions but select a few grassroots women who are facilitated and empowered to participate in national peacebuilding processes (Duriesmith, 2015; Hancock, 2017). Such discriminatory approaches to women's participation reinforce the continued oppression and marginalisation of sub-Saharan African women and their indigenous institutions from major decision-making on peace and the future of their communities or nations (Barry and Grady, 2019). The UN's discriminatory approach to women's engagement in peacebuilding is not isolated. Some South Sudanese ethnic groups, such as the Lotuko, exclude their women from security decisions, yet women can positively influence both the *Amangat* (or male decision-makers) and the Monyomiji (Aldehaib, 2010; Ibok and Ogar, 2018; Pankhurst, 2008; Oosterom, 2017).

Whereas the UN women and peacebuilding concepts have developed alongside the WPS agenda, such concepts have matured into gender mainstreaming and peacebuilding industry agendas that lack 'normative commitment' to grassroots women's contexts (Hudson-Weems, 2019). Also, the meaning of gender, security and peacebuilding related to indigenous institutions and women's role in peace processes is blurry (Dogra, 2011). The UN peace initiatives in conflict zones continue to view women as merely passive victims to be protected, trained/educated or empowered to fit conventional standards of peacebuilding (Ibok and Ogar, 2018; Oosterom, 2017; Pankhurst, 2008). Their everyday cultural peacebuilding lifestyle is not recognised (Mac Ginty, 2014; Bedigen, 2017; Ibok and Ogar, 2018). It can be argued that such conceptualisations are entrenched in the liberal feminist Eurocentric assumptions that undermine women's indigenous institutions' structural and organisational obligations to national peacebuilding processes (Hancock, 2017), further putting the whole project of peacebuilding at risk.

Moreover, studies indicate that ethnic or 'interpersonal conflicts were structurally similar to those between states' (Denskus and Kosmatopoulos, 2015:220; LeVine, 1961), and that local resources and capacities demonstrated by local institutions such as clan elders, for example, in the

Somaliland peacebuilding remain exemplary (Njeri, 2019). This chapter proposes that such subtle roles can be modified to meet national peacebuilding, development, security and human rights needs (Bedigen, 2017; Coe et al., 2013; Simonse and Kurimoto, 2011).

By discussing indigenous peacebuilding and the culturally constitutive nature of the Honyomiji institution, this chapter views indigenous women's 'visible and invisible' roles and practices as key in peacebuilding, even at conflict intensities. For instance, Simon Simonse provides examples of Monyomiji power handover ceremonies in various practising communities. These include Mak village, Lomohidang South Payam Ikwota County in 1998, Wiatuo village, dance ceremony in January 2009, Hothoro Monyomiji of Ngangala village in 2005, Lofithufere of Ngulere village in 2004, Taruha III of Liria village in 2003 and Kipiya of Lowe village in 2002, among others (Bedigen, 2017; Simonse and Kurimoto, 2011). While the UN WPS agenda dominates national peacebuilding, some Monyomiji/Honyomiji-practising communities believe that the main challenges facing their indigenous institutions' functionality are UN 'imported cultural norms that disrupt the traditional system of rule' (Simonse and Kurimoto, 2011:60–61). This chapter suggests that local resources and capacities in peacebuilding (family, motherhood and ceremonies/rituals) utilised at ethnic levels have greater legitimacy and sustainability at the national level. Before discussing these local resources and capacities, the meaning of Honyomiji is discussed.

Honyomiji: *Women's Traditional Institution*

> In our Lulubo culture, there are female Monyomiji. They are called Honyomiji. They are very powerful; they can make final decisions on war and peace. They once took a stand, in Juba, during a community meeting. They told men they were the ones who had lost their husbands, sons and time to look after crops. The Honyomiji said they should be the ones to decide when it comes to negotiating and mediating peace.
>
> (Sellie, 20 March 2013)

Sellie's narrative generally indicates that Honyomiji is a formal or technical Nilotic Lwo woman's role. These roles include arbitration, adjudication, negotiation and mediation (conducted by males). Other grassroots peace writers, Bradbury et al. (2006), Iyob and Khadiagala (2006), Itto (2006) and Mazurana et al. (2005), have discussed these technical roles extensively—thus, they will not be discussed in detail here. Before this book delves into such subtle peace roles, it elaborates on the meaning of Honyomiji.

Honyomiji is a term or a brand name applied to 'women leaders' or women's institutional governance or indigenous leadership groups practised by a dozen ethnic groups in the Eastern and Central Equatoria States of South Sudan (Bedigen, 2017:232; Simonse and Kurimoto, 2011:9). Sellie's narrative and some authors indicate that indigenous institutions such as

Honyomiji are community-centred problem-solving entities (Alexander-Floyd and Simien, 2006; Barry and Grady, 2019; Blackmon, 2008; Hudson-Weems, 2019; Joyce, 2001). Honyomiji was originally practised by a few Nilotic ethnic groups such as the Lotuho, Lukoya and Lango but was later on adopted by other Nilotics such as the Dinka, Nuer and Acholi (Simonse and Kurimoto, 2011). While relevant examples of the Honyomiji institution are drawn from practising communities, interview data is primarily from the Dinka and Nuer ethnic groups for many reasons. First, they have historically lived side by side and engaged in ethnic conflicts and civil wars. Second, their political and socio-economic activities, which are defined by pastoralism and cultivation, exacerbate conflict over resources. Third, according to the 2013 South Sudan population census, they are the largest ethnic groups: the Dinka represent 35.8% and the Nuer 15.6%. Also, the incapability of the newly formed state to provide security for all led to locals' over-dependence on indigenous peacebuilding methods, furthering its popularity (Kelly, 1985; Zanen and van den Hoek, 1987).

The Honyomiji male counterparts are known as Monyomiji, which means 'the owners or fathers of the village' (Bedigen, 2019:2). While traditionally, members are female (i.e. spouses of Monyomiji, gifted women, diviners, herbalists or rainmakers), the institution can operate as a dual-sex leadership system where males may be part of or participate in masculine roles. Created by the community, these institutions envisage women as pivotal members whose contribution makes communities thrive (Bedigen, 2017; Ibok and Ogar, 2018). Working with all women and community members (Blackmon, 2008; Oosterom, 2017), the Honyomiji institutional task is to maintain the community's history, cultural awareness and sense of political, social and economic independence. The institution is primarily responsible for the leadership, education, religious and social support of the whole community. Women leaders within this system facilitate, train, organise, make decisions and participate in associated community-building rituals.

The ruling Honyomiji work together with the preceding set of Honyomiji/Monyomiji. The practitioners regard the institution as the cornerstone of stability and promote the unity of clans. It sets and enforces society's rules. They resolve disputes over natural resources, property and human conflicts. It has the power to 'discipline wrong-doers' by expelling them into exile (Interview with Nekye, 2012). The institution promotes a notion of a public cause whereby community values that transcend the private interests of individuals, families or clans are used to enforce decisions on justice and reconciliation, not international law or culture. In the Honyomiji system, both women leaders and their subjects work together for the community's good and peacebuilding is part of the responsibility of every woman's daily lifestyle. Given these, the Honyomiji view the government, peace and development agencies and community members living outside the community or diasporas as intruding on their 'sovereignty' (Simonse and Kurimoto, 2011:12). As such, the institution can be a force of local resistance against the government or conventional intervention. Whereas their resistance against outside help, reinforced by a community-centred approach to problem-solving, can be beneficial in that it allows the institution to be innovative, it can exacerbate conflict escalation leading to further deaths, limited humanitarian work, medical services and extreme poverty.

As an institution and during the South Sudan second civil war, women who felt excluded and marginalised by the male Monyomiji system 'formed their own Monyomiji system as a countervailing power to the men' (Simonse and Kurimoto, 2011:12). Thus, Honyomiji 'continued to debate on the gender inclusiveness of customary law and traditional institutions,' and the Honyomiji/Monyomiji institution 'can be an important asset in post-war peacebuilding, reconstruction and development' (Simonse and Kurimoto, 2011:127, 17). In reality, however, communication, coordination, coherence and complementarity gaps exist within the Honyomiji/Monyomiji institution and between the government and agencies (Newman, 2013). This leads to misunderstanding and doubts over Honyomiji's potential in national peacebuilding and compels peace actors to create new hybrid or Western-style peacebuilding initiatives that are less inclined to cultural practices, consequently furthering frictions (Millar et al., 2013). It is argued that if properly coordinated within itself and with the government, peace and development agencies, the institution can be a significant asset to the national peacebuilding process.

Interviewees indicate that 'culture is what unites South Sudanese.' Yet, peace and development agencies are often ignorant of this unique resource for mobilisation for peacebuilding (Interview with Nuer and Dinka Honyomiji, 2014). For instance, Denskus and Kosmatopoulos (2015:221) indicate that 'international culture' has dominated peacebuilding. These include military and financial support for major political parties, the Sudanese People's Liberation Movement/Army (SPLM/A) and the Sudan People's Liberation Movement-in-Opposition (SPLM-IO) (Bedigen, 2019). Such international push for immediate peace in the region majorly depends on the multiagency intervention that excludes indigenous institutions—thus, which has at times caused conflict escalation and furthered cultural and ethnic divide in the recent wars. Also, it has significantly impacted the Dinka and Nuer Honyomiji authority, including kingdoms and chiefdoms. Moreover, misunderstanding of the respective roles indigenous women play and their competencies under the Honyomiji institution have resulted in mistrust and lack of coordination, cooperation or incorporation into national peacebuilding efforts.

Also, because each community develops its own Honyomiji system, there is no uniform leadership style, legislation or policy framework to regulate these various ethnic institutions and provide a sense of inter-community direction. While this heterogeneity can also influence competition among villages that seek to dominate others, interviewees indicate that many Honyomiji generic groups are not open to expanding their diversity outlook, as doing so could 'dilute' community norms. Such an inward-looking attribute can lead to its rejection by the annexed/minor communities. It is suggested that diverse context-based training and mentorship that is inclusive of all Honyomiji groups and conventional agencies could produce a more sustainable peacebuilding process in the region. Before we delve into the Nilotic women's peacebuilding roles, the following discussions demonstrate that they have historically participated indirectly or directly in inter-ethnic wars.

The Role of Nilotic Women in Wars

Before discussing the Honyomiji or women's role in peacebuilding, it is important to note that they contributed to inter-ethnic conflicts and civil wars. Thus, the argument that women should not be treated as guests at the negotiation tables. They deserve to sit at negotiation tables because they contributed to the success of wars (Itto, 2006; Mazurana et al., 2005). In addition, they play an active role in post-conflict reconciliation. These authors indicate that, during the South Sudan civil wars, hundreds of South Sudanese women joined the liberation struggle as spies, combatants, porters, messengers, nurses and wives. Further, they claim that in Khartoum, women contributed gold in support of the jihad. They encouraged their sons to join the civil war. Adding to these claims, Bedigen (2021) indicates that during the civil war, women formed their own battalion, locally known as Katiba Banat. Additionally, South Sudanese women contributed food and encouraged their sons to join the SPLA to fight marginalisation and oppression by the government in Khartoum. These claims are supported by Fred's account that demonstrated how the political situation affected whole communities in South Sudan; therefore, women used various means to ensure men stayed on the battlefield to win the war. For instance, he explains that civil war had taken many years, therefore, causing demoralisation in the men who were at the battlefront. One of the ways through which women intervened was by threat and coercive language. He says that women said:

> You men, if you do not want to fight, then we shall do so. We shall shed blood again. We have shed blood in childbirth, but we are ready to re-live the experience. We have lost everything and will not tolerate your 'womanly' behaviour. We would rather live with lions than 'fellow women.'
>
> (Fred, 20 December 2012)

He continues to say that, in the Nuba Mountains, where his wife comes from:

> Women sang songs to encourage men to go to fight. In the Nuba Mountains, they told men off, saying, 'if you are tired, give us the guns,

and you look after the children ...'. The men had to go back to war. They started overtaking garrison after garrison, and they won eventually.

(Fred, 20 December 2012)

Adding to Fred's narratives above, Sadrak's story demonstrates that, irrespective of women's encouragement, coercion and warnings, men from certain communities gave up hope. He explains that, at the height of the intensity of the civil war, Toposa men (one of the Nilotic ethnic communities in South Sudan) ran away from the front line. Consequently, women, in their desperation, took up arms voluntarily and were recruited into the military.

Other women, he explains, left the comfort and security of their homes not simply to accompany their husbands to battlefields but to fight for freedom, democracy, equality, justice, rights and dignity. Here is his account:

> Most Toposa men sold their guns and ran away. In response, women took up guns, some alongside their husbands. The SPLA recruited women, and some women joined forces voluntarily. Toposa women became very knowledgeable about guns. Others supported the civil war, playing roles such as front-line mums, nurses, messengers and businesspersons, who brought essentials to the front line. When it came to negotiation, they demanded their representation at the negotiation table.
>
> (Sadrak, 15 December 2012)

Both Fred's and Sadrak's accounts of the roles South Sudanese women played during the civil war are not new. In the Nilotic Lwo tradition, women can encourage, support, facilitate and cause men to go to battle if this is the only viable option to restore peace and security. Nilotic Lwo interviewees' accounts demonstrate that this mostly happens in inter-ethnic conflicts. In addition, Branch (2011), in her work on the Pokot–Marakwet inter-ethnic conflicts, indicates how the *Loketio* or *Logedio* (pregnancy support belt) is a 'double-edged sword.' It can be utilised to encourage men to go to war, as well as build peace.

Loketio or *Logedio* (Pregnancy Support Belt)

> When a mother removes Loketio and, like the womb opens in childbirth, it is believed she exposes her sons to the elements, which include curses or even death. When a mother passes on beads or cowrie shells from her Loketio, they are sewn into the son's belt, hat or bangle. He will wear this at all times for his own protection and safety.
>
> (Kilo, 28 April 2013)

He explains that a Loketio is a woman's belt, which is tied around the belly from the time of pregnancy and throughout life. In his description,

Nilotic communities that utilise Loketio include the Masai, Turkana, Samburu, Pokot and Marakwet. The Loketio belt is made from a bull's skin that is killed ceremoniously. It is decorated with cowrie shells and beads. Kilo states that men are obliged to follow women's decisions when they are wearing them. He explains that when women are in favour of war, they will wear it (see Kilo's account below). This symbolically implies that men are protected. They will not be killed in battle but will be successful and return home to their families.

> Men have to inform women of any planned raids in the event of cattle raids or inter-ethnic conflicts; when women are in support of the invasion, they wear Loketio. It gives men reassurance that they are protected and will be victorious in battle.
>
> (Kilo, 2 April 2013)

Kilo's narratives demonstrate that the Loketio provides a perfect example where Nilotic Lwo symbolic beliefs and practices can be harnessed to create or keep harmony at family, community and inter-community levels. Woven by women, Loketio contains white cowrie shells, which represent both sustenance (milk) and peace. This specially crafted belt is made by other women in the community and presented to the bride as a wedding gift. The bride, once married, is to wear this belt at all times. However, she can remove it 'to curse' a person who has displeased her. Also, she can remove it to protest her husband's or son's decision to go to war. This item has been utilised in this way at family, community and inter-community levels by the Pokot, Marakwet and Masai to prevent, keep and build peace (Bedigen, 2017).

Further, Nilotic Lwo women do not only make contributions to peace and conflict resolution, but they also prepare for war. Traditionally, their role is to initiate boys into warrior groups. For instance, the Nuer male adolescent is scarred (during initiation) by distinguished women. This scar signifies warrior-like capability or bravery and inspires boys to participate in war. Additionally, women prepare the warriors by organising pre-war rituals/ceremonies. They sing war songs that encourage their sons and husbands to go to war. According to a Dinka interviewee, they have, at times, threatened not to fulfil their marital duties if their husbands do not destroy the enemy. When the warriors are back from the battlefield, songs are sung in praise of those who demonstrated bravery. At times, ornaments artistically designed by women are used to adorn these individuals. Mothers can offer such men their daughters to marry as a symbol of honour. Such men are encouraged to acquire more wives. Scars incurred in battle are regarded as signs of manhood, bravery and security. Women adore war scars; likewise, they are a source of pride to men.

As illustrated in Figure 7.1, it can be argued that women's support for war contributed to intermittent inter-ethnic conflicts and civil wars. Therefore, it is not correct to portray them as innocent and vulnerable victims. For

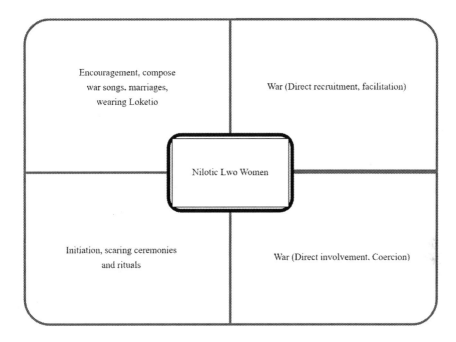

Figure 7.1 Nilotic Lwo Women and War

instance, women in the Middle East and Muslim-practising regions of Sudan have offered themselves to martyrdom. Adding, in South Sudan, they have joined the front lines to fight for their country. In support of this, Blumberg et al. (2006:41) write that 'Across cultures, women are traditionally seen as pacifists, seeking to build and maintain a peaceful society through reconciliation.' Pieces of evidence highlighted here demonstrate that women in conflict zones are capable and not necessarily at risk.

Moreover, this book recognises that, while women participated in wars, customs offered them some sort of protection. For instance, according to the Nilotic Lwo customary laws, the killing of women, children, disabled people or the elderly in battle is an abomination (Bedigen, 2017). On the other hand, while earlier discussions demonstrate that women engaged in conflicts from 1983 (the second civil war), intermittent inter-ethnic conflicts and civil wars exposed women and their children to extreme violence, including hunger and isolation from neighbouring communities (Leonardi et al., 2010). In this war, women and children became victims of violence, bombing, landmines, hunger and diseases (Blumberg et al., 2006). Moreover, many conventional approaches designed to help this situation and stop violence against women may not have been very effective either. This brings us to the discussions on local resources and capacities in peacebuilding.

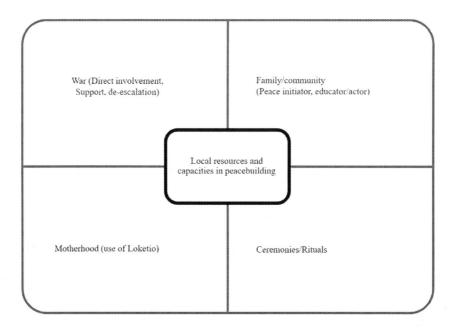

Figure 7.2 Nilotic Lwo Women, Local Resources and Capacities in Peacebuilding

Local Resources and Capacities in Peacebuilding

As represented in Figure 7.2, local resources and capacities in peacebuilding include women, family, motherhood, Loketio or Logedio and ceremonies/rituals.

Women and Family

Field notes indicate that a family is a child's first place to learn about life and life skills applied in the family. It is women's duty and responsibility to ensure this happens. Sellie, for instance, says that 'Youth depend on the wisdom of mother' (sic). Adding to this, Sadrak says that, during the second civil war, women offered support through cooking, looking after children and teaching them cultural values throughout the day. Heron (1976) indicates that mother's songs and father's stories told around the fireplace influenced Okot p'Bitek, one of Africa's greatest novelists. Important to note, the African [Banjul] Charter on Human and Peoples' Rights, adopted on 27 June 1981, urges the state to support families and their human and moral rights.

Further interviewee stories demonstrate that family is where children first come to understand what society holds dear and what it shuns. It is where the basis of their identity is formed. The family's role is to consolidate peace

The Role of Women in Indigenous Peacebuilding 171

and unity among its members and community. Its responsibility is to ensure every member's existence and security. Everyone is born into and grows to achieve their full potential in the family. The family plays a vital part in the development of a child's personality. It is where children are trained and encouraged to work and thrive in all areas of life (Bedigen, 2017).

When it comes to marriage, intense research is done on the bride and her family. This is because unstable families or lifestyle is initially attributed to that person's mother, then to the family as a whole. Consequently, such failures reflect badly on the wider community. Further, wedding songs are composed in praise of a 'bride's beauty,' or laberna, in the Acholi language. This is not outward beauty but an inner character trait. For instance, in Sellie's account, the word ber 'beauty,' sung during wedding ceremonies, refers to the bride's good character. She explains that a true Nilotic Lwo girl is well behaved and good natured. The bride is not only a treasure to the groom but to his family and community. The bride's beauty, or character, is praised with reference to her parents, aunties, grandparents and clan. This points to the significant role a bride is expected to manifest peaceful behaviours at all times. Whenever conflicts arise, she is expected to unite the family or community. Further, this conforms to the Nilotic Lwo belief that raising a child is the whole community's duty and responsibility. A girl with good character is an asset to the community's peaceful existence.

These views are expressed in Efo's story below:

> A woman is the peace-maker in all circumstances. Young girls are brought up with values that make them feel they are part of that next society, not to look back. For example, my mother – their home was just across the road, but my mum never visited her mother. I suppose it is a concept of belonging to her marital home, fitting in or having a voice in her new community. When a woman is absent or badly behaved, a lot of problems, children are wild; the family is not at peace. My brother's kids never achieved; they are alcoholics and jobless because of their mother. She was badly behaved and never disciplined them. When my brother used to try, she would shout at him, always standing up for the kids. My brother gave up, and the children are now lost; they steal from both their own family members and the neighbourhood. Only one turned out well. He lived with my other sister from the early age of seven; he is now a medical doctor. I wish she could come back from the grave to witness what her kids have turned into. Girls are constantly reminded of how they should grow into good marriageable women or refrain from any undesirable behaviours, such as quarrelling, meanness and disrespect, before they marry. And divorce can lead to tensions, raids, and enmity.
> (Efo, 17 April 2014)

While Efo's account may point to male dominance in patriarchal societies, Bedigen (2022) affirms that women are regarded as pillars of a community

172 *The Role of Women in Indigenous Peacebuilding*

and, therefore, play a crucial part in ensuring harmony within the family and neighbourhood (Bedigen, 2017). Efo demonstrates that the absence of a woman in any given family implies that trivial disputes are not tamed, so the family lacks peace. It is believed that a lack of peace within a family reflects on the community as a whole. He further explains that Nilotic Lwo girls are taught to serve and respect but not to confront, regardless of the situation. Additionally, girls/brides are expected to make a success of their marriages. On the contrary, being good natured is not a characteristic emphasised to boys/grooms. Focus group field notes, conducted among women, indicate that a man is considered lucky if he married a good wife. Overall, Nilotic Lwo's cultural belief is that it is women who keep families and communities together, implying that peace originates from the woman and family settings.

In contrast, while young girls' behaviours are watched, male children are told certain myths that emphasise their authority, masculinity and good leadership and are not directly held responsible for peacebuilding. Boys hold their meetings in open, neutral places to discuss such myths further. The imbalanced high expectation appears to place more responsibility on girls. For instance, girls can drop out of school for early marriages just to ensure their family benefits from dowry payments or acquire for their brother a wife. Such customary demands can be contradictory to conventional norms, as they appear to assert masculinity and patriarchy in local settings, thus maintaining gender marginalisation (Bedigen et al., 2020; Bedigen, 2022).

Fulo narrates that in the evening, they hurried to her grandmother's house to listen to such character-building stories. She narrates that most stories exposed greed and individual interests as major sources of conflict. Stories formed a reference point for morals. Some stories spelt out negative aspects of violence or conflicts, which mothers encourage children to avoid. For example, bad behaviour, such as theft, murder, incest or witchcraft, is intolerable. Those whose behaviour disrupted the peace and harmony of the community are seriously punished. Such punishments could range from beating or the payment of a fine to expulsion from the community. In exceptional circumstances, such as defilement, rape and murder, the death penalty could be issued by women (Bedigen, 2017). Generally, the manner in which communities deal with sexual violence or crimes at the family or inter-ethnic conflict level is contradictory to human rights laws. For instance, Pete, a human rights lawyer, refers to them as re-victimisation. He says that:

> There have been cases of abuse of the system, where there is re-victimisation of the victims, for instance, in rape, where you have a male-dominated system, and the victim is forced to marry the perpetrator of the crime.
>
> (Pete, 19 May 2013)

Overall, women's engagement at family and community levels equips them with skills that enable them to view conflict as an opportunity to build relationships with the wider community (Bedigen, 2017). Augsburger (1992) indicates that when it comes to the use of power, femininity and peacebuilding, women are wired differently. This is demonstrated through their utilisation of Loketio or Logedio in peacebuilding.

Motherhood and *Loketio or Logedio*

Today, the role of mothers is somehow confined to family and home boundaries, yet, in view of Nilotic Lwo cultures, this role extends beyond family circles. Emphasis is put on a mother's role as a peacemaker, conflict preventer and peacebuilder. Thus, a mother's role goes beyond childbearing and rearing. This section examines three different stages of motherhood, namely pregnancy and childbirth, children's upbringing and menopause. This work demonstrates that these stages can be exploited to positively influence connections in social and political inequalities as well as peacebuilding. This work highlights the significance of Loketio, or Logedio, a pregnancy support belt, which can be utilised in conflict prevention, peacemaking and peacebuilding. Its use follows the communities' strict cultural norms, practices and beliefs intended to maintain peaceful communities and co-existence. Remarkably, motherhood and Loketio is a means by which women can manipulate socio-cultural practices. This view is supported by Kofi Annan, UN secretary-general, at the panel discussion on 'Afghan Women Today: Realities and Opportunities.' He stated that:

> While women must be protected from the impact of armed conflict, they must also be recognised as a key to the solution. We must work harder to include them fully in all our strategies for peace-making, peacebuilding and reconstruction.
>
> (United Nations, 2004)

The Concept of Motherhood

The concept of motherhood in Nilotic Lwo's understanding is not different from the literal meaning of motherhood (mother, maternity). As indicated by psychologists (Gergen and Davis, 1997, 2013), motherhood is a form of nurture that is not confined to the nuclear family. These authors explain that motherhood embodies maternity, family and community relationship, which extends to the inter-community relationship. Among the Masai, Pokot and Marakwet of Kenya, motherhood is conceptualised through Loketio. In the absence of peace theories specifically addressing the importance of motherhood in indigenous peacebuilding, this book utilises views from Mary Douglas' work (Douglas, 1970, 1973, 2004). Such include her analysis of the significance of symbols, blood, rituals and ceremonies in building relationships. For example, Nilotic Lwo interviewee stories reveal that, among the Masai, Pokot and Marakwet, mothers choose to 'wrap up' their unborn foetus with a Loketio belt from the time of conception. When babies are born, mothers take the responsibility to weave into their children's bracelets, belts, necklaces and other items—symbols that are believed to offer protection, health and peace. These items are not only mere symbolic representations but can be utilised by mothers in times of need to change the course of events from bad to good (Bedigen, 2020). Mothers emphasise attributes of peace, which, in the Nilotic Lwo context, include wellness, caring, sensitivity, fairness, kindness, honesty, respect, patience, generosity, responsibility, purity, forgiveness and integrity. In the long run, these attributes influence the political, economic and social situations affecting the community.

Ultimately, the above Nilotic Lwo view challenges the conventional thinking that mothers' roles preclude traditional women's roles in contributing to communities' peace processes. In this book's view, this discord presents women and children as vulnerable. This has led to campaigns and support for women in war zones through 'facilitation,' 'participation' and 'empowerment' by international agencies (Bedigen, 2021). Yet this book demonstrates that in the absence of such external support, mothers play a central role in ensuring inter-community peaceful living and co-existence. It is recognised that the high levels of crime may have negatively impacted subtle interventions in modern-day conflicts, making them less evident at national scenes. Nevertheless, discussions in this chapter demonstrate that the starting point for peacebuilding is conflict prevention through motherhood. It is suggested that this traditional role can effortlessly influence national peacebuilding, as shall be evidenced in the role of Honyomiji in peacebuilding.

Honyomiji Peacebuilding Obligations

In this section, the chapter discusses Honyomiji four key roles in peacebuilding, i.e. leadership, education, religion and social support. Manifest in family, community and inter-community relationships, these key roles meet locals' everyday needs beyond physical needs such as food, water, clothing and housing. In performing these roles, Honyomiji led and worked with other women, youth, children and men to achieve a common goal. As such, these obligations are a demonstration of indigenous women's active role in peacebuilding and that their inclusion in all stages of national peace processes is essential. Whereas some authors indicate that these traditional obligations cause women to be excluded from national peacebuilding by peace agencies, Porter's (2003) work seeks to highlight that if the international peace agencies focused on pre-conflict, conflict and post-conflict informal and formal stages of peacebuilding activities, these practices would be automatically included. This is because they are interwoven in Honyomiji functionality (Julian et al., 2019).

Proposing Honyomiji's significance in peacebuilding does not imply that the institution is flawless. Oosterom's (2017) analysis of Latuko

Monyomiji-practising communities indicates that the system discourages power-sharing and excludes some women or male counterparts (Monyomiji). Other studies highlight their role in mob justice, e.g. killings of suspected witches, support for an education system that inspires violence and the majority of its customs, practices and values have eroded over time (Bedigen, 2017). Moreover, the system is not homogeneous across South Sudanese ethnic groups and is the opposite of the conventional linear, formal, logical or structured methods. Additionally, the majority of international agencies often associate Honyomiji roles with informality, disorder, chaos, ineffectiveness or subsidiaries. It is thus important to emphasise that, in the context of gender and peacebuilding, the non-linearity of indigenous institutions is not associated with sub-standardness, as demonstrated in the leadership, education, religious and social support role discussions below.

Leadership

The primary responsibility of the Honyomiji system is the leadership and organisation of all women in the community. While the leadership establishes community laws and practices, organises women in age-sets, facilitates and makes critical decisions, this is based on consensus, and those who oppose could be excluded or severely punished. Some sub-Saharan scholars show the potential for traditional female community leadership in maintaining peace and development. For instance, Ibok and Ogar (2018) indicate that women are agents of peace. Lund and Agyei-Mensah (2008) show that, historically, African communities thrived under the traditional leadership, where kings' and chiefs' wives and princesses played notable roles in ensuring women and children's well-being, as well as the community's peaceful living. Others, though, have shown that indigenous women's leadership can be undermined during conflicts and in post-conflict situations. For example, De La Puente (2011) indicates that in the camps for internally displaced people in Darfur, western Sudanese indigenous women leaders were largely ignored by the humanitarian agencies and sidelined in national peace decision-making (Erzurum and Eren, 2014; Porter, 2003). Adding, in line with UN Resolution 1325, the South Sudan government-appointed women into civil service leadership positions, but they merely held posts without power (Arabi, 2011).

While the Honyomiji institution is a predominantly women's affairs department, it holds power to handle other issues that threaten the community's peace, for example, 'drought, famine, plague, witchcraft and conflict' (Interview with Nuer Honyomiji, 2012). For instance, Otuho community is made up of up to 10,000 people living in divided and independent villages. Honyomiji leadership in each village develops its own generic name and set of policies that are based on the community's immediate threats mentioned earlier. Examples include the Hothoro Monyomiji of Ngangala village, Taruha III of Liria village and Kipiya of Lowe peace mediators during the second civil war (Bedigen, 2017; Simonse and Kurimoto, 2011). However, the entire village is led by a village headman who may also be a woman (or Aboloni/Nabobni). Such a leader is expected to ensure that villages uphold their own history, philosophy, traditions and customs through war songs and other ritualistic practices. The Honyomiji institutional leaders may not necessarily lead/head the Monyomiji male or community's umbrella institution but work alongside Monyomiji. In some Honyomiji-practising communities, when the king dies, his spouse, the queen, is expected to take over the leadership of the community. For example, when the Lopit king, Mayya, died in 1959, his wife, the late queen Sabina lhure ljura, succeeded the throne.

Further, Simonse and Kurimoto (2011:50) indicate that the Lopit Honyomiji institution, well known as Iratu, plays various vital roles in community cohesion. Similar observations where the queen mothers or royal women assume responsibility for the community are indicated by Ma'at-Ka-Re Monges (1993), Schiller (1990) and Stoeltje (1997). Such roles include communicating important messages to the community, supervising the chief or queen in times of drought and pestilence as well as setting prices for the agricultural and women's artisan products. In Dinka communities, while some mature males prefer to remain in the cattle camps for longer, women take root in the community by developing stronger leadership networks. It is observed that Honyomiji institutional leadership roles interactively take care of women's affairs by advocating for their social, political and economic needs (Afisi, 2010). For example, among the Monyomiji of Torit, women have the opportunity to advocate for any emergencies and are involved in administering justice at the community level.

Whereas Honyomiji leadership has been deeply impacted by the proliferation of weapons, gender-based violence and anarchy, historically, they ensure the rule of law, democracy and governance are maintained (Bedigen, 2017). For instance, Oosterom (2017) indicates that women took up leadership roles in the 2013 civil war. Once women make a decision, all women are obliged to obey. If not, other women can impose fines on fellow women who violate set rules. Any woman who refuses to participate in community affairs such as cultivation, harvesting and preparations for social events is punished. Overall, Honyomiji's leadership role in making laws and critical decisions and organising and facilitating community activities demonstrates their creativity in resolving problems sustainably. For example, through subtle peace negotiations, mediation, arbitration and diplomacy, women can effectively and sustainably contribute to achieving authentic peace. The South Sudanese government and non-governmental organisations would ultimately benefit from building and enhancing the capacity of the Honyomiji institution as a legal and justice body. Considering its progressive nature in the East Bank Equatoria region, the government should officially recognise and formalise the system within its national leadership frameworks. By doing so, this institution can become an exemplary indigenous framework that helps make local women's leadership abilities visible internationally. Also, the institution could serve as a traditional underpinning of good governance, democracy and the rule of law. Moreover, its contexts offer great potential for the hybrid framework suitable for post-conflict national justice and peacebuilding.

Education

Historically, ethnic groups fought each other; however, indigenous education is used as a means to prevent, manage conflicts and build peace. This education is aimed at various social values such as the physical, artistic, creative, moral, mental and spiritual development of members (Okoro, 2010; Mosweunyane, 2013). In the Honyomiji educational system, all women, youth and children's education are based on community ethos. It thrives when communities are peaceful, unlike in the past decades when women could not have time to educate the young due to frequent flights and deaths of knowledgeable adults—thus erosion of community norms. Significantly, the education system is a means by which the Honyomiji provide 'auxiliary human resources to Monyomiji and the community' as a whole (Interview with Dinka Honyomiji, 2012). For example, honesty, respect for others, property, nature, environment, hard work, productivity, generosity and self-reliance are some of the attributes taught (Afisi, 2010; Katola, 2014; Okoro, 2010). To build mentally stronger members, counselling, resilience and management of community resources, including food, were encouraged. Also, apprenticeship, where children learn by observing and working with adults (mostly mothers) or participating as messenger boys, is a necessary aspect of this education. Motherhood or women (mostly of childbearing age) are expected to pass community values or discipline to any child found in the wrong. Overall, 'all women have a say in the upbringing and socialisation of their children,' particularly in the transmission of the community's history, language, cultural norms and values through songs, stories and proverbs (Interview with Dinka Honyomiji, 2012). Some authors support the view that this experiential knowledge must be included in peacebuilding (Julian et al., 2019).

Education can be a double-edged sword. For instance, Smith (2014) shows that education can contribute to post-conflict reconstruction, for example, in Sierra Leone or exacerbate conflicts, e.g., in Mozambique and Rwanda. In the case of South Sudan, grassroots researchers such as Iyob and Khadiagala (2006) point out that during the second civil war, women contributed to various peacebuilding educational activities such as reconciliation rituals/ceremonies and discouraged their sons from inciting violence through peace songs. Although Honyomiji education is largely developmental, it also serves as a means of instilling acts of bravery through skin cuttings, mock fights and war songs. These encourage youth conflicts, cattle rustling and engagement in the civil wars, particularly between the

Dinka and Nuer ethnic groups (Jok and Hutchinson, 1999). Also, spiritual education at times concerns itself with witchcraft, resulting in expulsion and even killings of the accused in the Lotuho communities (Bedigen, 2019).

International agencies, such as the United Nations Children's Fund (UNICEF), promote education and peacebuilding (Novelli et al., 2015). However, this type of education is placed under state or international management (Newman, 2013), and it excludes indigenous institutions, education or the involvement of indigenous women who have not attained formal or western education. Recently, local women from Misseriya and Ngok Dinka communities taught and utilised songs, stories and poems in inter-ethnic peacebuilding. However, when national peace negotiations commenced, indigenous women were excluded (Bedigen, 2019; Hancock, 2017; Nassanga, 1997). It is recognised that the UN system is designed to include women in decision-making and 'all' gender-related development issues outlined in the Sustainable Development Goals (SDGs) (Novelli et al., 2015). However, its western approach does not include 'all women' in the decision-making of what norms should be incorporated into training programmes for peacebuilding (Bedigen et al., 2020). The international initiative for education and peacebuilding at times disregards traditional or indigenous knowledge (Narayanaswamy, 2016) and enforces exclusion of indigenous voices or consensus decision-making and promotion of minority values. Although the UN and its agencies view education as key in peacebuilding, practically, their initiatives provide education whose context is less compatible with local histories, culture, customs, ideologies and philosophies (De Coning, 2016), effectively delineating Honyomiji from their traditional education roles.

Further, the internationally led education for peacebuilding has become another way by which western cultures are enforced on the sub-Saharan states. It is an education that fits the peacebuilding ideas of international agencies, not local norms (Donais and Knorr, 2013; Hancock, 2017). For instance, western types of education for peacebuilding seek to impart technical peace skills such as negotiation, mediation, arbitration and the signing of agreements (Bedigen, 2017). Workshops, seminars and conferences may impart conventional norms and skills but not values related to the actual needs or morals of the people. This is viewed as an extension of western values, which contribute to more direct control of peace initiatives by international NGOs who majorly seek to attract donor funding.

The Honyomiji education system is designed to develop an individual's mind, soul and body to be fully responsible, useful and fit into the community; however, this might be limited to one's locality—therefore not benefiting the wider society (Katola, 2014). Within domestic environments, fulfilling their household chores and farm activities, mothers morally guide their children on how to 'manage all aspects of life' (interview with Nekye, 2013). It is suggested this indigenous type of education can effectively contribute to achieving South Sudanese child soldiers' re-integration (Wessells, 2005).

Whereas there is distinctiveness in ethnic cultures and lifestyles, values that teach and encourage cohesion are similar, for example, respect and tolerance of others. Also, through work parties, Honyomiji education takes place anywhere, anytime and by any older person to children or learners. Overall, the benefits of Honyomiji indigenous peace education are that:

i) It provides an open and unlimited space for oral transmission of knowledge, skills, positive attitude or resilience that encourages creativity.
ii) It limits the organisational and logistical costs often experienced in formal systems and draws from familiar ideologies, philosophies and practices.
iii) Its contextual nature is supported by locals and thus offers a platform for sustainable peacebuilding at national levels.

Religion and Rituals/Ceremonies

Coe et al. (2013) indicate that conflicts damage social relations and that women utilise religion and culture through ancestral spirits, kinship and rituals of reconciliation to repair relationships. Schirch (2015) shows that rituals and traditional religion are essential in peacebuilding because their symbolism and reliance on nonverbal nature help defuse tensions between disputants. These include symbolic sacred spears, or 'spears of sacrifice,' war, general calamity and reconciliation rituals (Evans-Pritchard, 1953:3). Religion is concerned with the social life and with the relation of the individual/community to God, who is believed to keep communities at peace (Evans-Pritchard, 1953:3). Honyomiji's religious role involves promoting morality and belief in God and spirits through African Traditional Religion (ATR), and it utilises ceremonies/rituals in rebuilding relationships between humans, God, spirits and the environment. Spiritual beliefs, derived from peoples' own experiences of divine revelations, are inseparable from customary practices (Bedigen, 2017). Honyomiji spirituality and cultural obligations include spiritual mediation between humans, ancestral spirits, the environment and ceremonies/ritual leadership.

Calamities such as drought, less production, illness, epidemics, stressful life, deaths, failures in life, quarrels, murders and intra-ethnic conflicts are signs that the community lacks peace, sources of which are attributed to evil spirits. So, women act by organising for the appeasement of spirits through cleansing ceremonies/rituals intended to rid the evil spirits from the community. Also, such calamities can be contributors to inter-ethnic and protracted conflicts, and in such instances, rituals can be limited due to diversities in customs or the magnitude of the conflict. For instance, Simonse and Kurimoto (2011) indicate that among the Lopit community, rain chief and rainmaking are spiritual issues. Drought causes famine and, consequently, food theft, cattle rustling and ethnic instabilities by Monyomiji. To prevent such conflicts, Honyomiji has the power to summon and punish the rain chief, demand him to expose the witch who has withheld rain or make him/her offer rituals to appease the spirits and bring rain. It is observed that to ensure sustainable peace, such a ceremony/ritual is based on oral, spiritual and customary laws as well as the principles of truth, accountability and restoration of relationships (Bedigen, 2017; Coe et al., 2013).

Further, Honyomiji religious practices support the sacredness of nature (mountain/rocks, rivers, lakes, big trees and animals). Diligent observance of these prevents overuse or fights over resources. When conflicts occur, religious and ceremonial activities are utilised to 'influence forgiveness, healing and examination of conscience' (Bedigen, 2017). Honyomiji peace and cultural practices are 'incomplete' without supernatural involvement, a significant aspect that integrates local's experiences, meaning and purpose of life (Interview with Mama Dunia, 2013). The omission of religious/spiritual elements from peacebuilding results in something less authoritative and thus not respected by locals. This demonstrates that beliefs and spiritual connections are essential for a community to thrive. Whereas all good is believed to originate from a supernatural being Rwoth, all evil is believed to originate from evil spirits Nueer (the Dinka word for evil spirit) or Lacen (an Acholi word for evil spirit). Honyomiji's philosophy is that evil deeds, crimes or conflicts are spiritually influenced—thus, requiring a spiritual remedy. Thus, Mabior undefiled or young bull sacrifice is essential in resolving evil deeds, disputes and crimes, as well as rebuilding relationships (Bedigen, 2021). Also, religious and cleansing rituals such as Mato Oput encourage conscience examination and forgiveness to enable sustainable peace (Interview with Dinka and Nuer Honyomiji, 2012, 2014).

Schirch (2015) indicated that in peacebuilding, 'rituals and rational approaches' are essential. Ouellet (2013) suggests the significance of religion in peacebuilding and how the Liberian women utilised religion at both local and national levels to achieve peace. Religious moral teachings on respect for others/property, forgiveness and reverence for the supernatural are significant in securing sustainable peace. During the civil wars, South Sudanese women approached peacebuilding not only through ATR but through Christian and Muslim religions. For example, in Darfur, Muslim women engaged in the *Judiyya* (Muslim local justice system) and peacebuilding debates. Additionally, in East Equatoria, Christian women were involved in the Wunlit Peace and Reconciliation Conference (commonly known as Wunlit), Liliir and Abyei conferences traditional and Christian peacebuilding processes (Bedigen, 2017; Coe et al., 2013; Wunlit, 1999). Yet, at national levels, African traditional religion, ceremonies/rituals and their implementers, women, remain excluded (Bedigen, 2017; Hancock, 2017; Ouellet, 2013). The Honyomiji-practising communities remain relatively peaceful due to the immediate implementation of post-war cleansing and purification rituals, consequently leading to the successful re-integration of ex-combatants, restoration of public order and security. It is argued that the Honyomiji spirituality and cultural obligations, which are inclusive of humans, ancestral spirits, environment and ceremonies/rituals, historically enable communities to re-establish relationships or co-exist and can deliver sustainable peace and development.

Social Support

Conflicts, be it family, intra-, inter-ethnic or civil wars, ruin social relations (Bedigen, 2021; Coe et al., 2013). To rebuild relationships, Okoro (2010) shows that the socio-political philosophy of indigenous African society that revolves around the concept of social solidarity and belonging offers the solution, and Bedigen (2017) indicates that it is women's role to mend these broken relationships. Oosterom (2017) adds to this by suggesting that during the 2013 civil war, women in Monyomiji-practising communities took up economic and social support roles to maintain families and co-existence. Social support is not only expected at family levels but community political leadership levels. Through the community's leadership, education and cultural system, a sense of social responsibility is expected: first, to the community and, next, to the individual members. In peace, conflict and post-conflict situations, the Honyomiji social support system cares for the community, ensuring everyone can access the most basic, e.g. food and healing herbs. As Simonse and Kurimoto (2011:64) indicate, the exemplary woman is expected to provide motherly care, social support and leadership at all times. Honyomiji social support obligations are to 'keep the family, unify, and demonstrate loving-kindness in serving members' as well as connect and be part of a whole (Interview with Nuer Honyomiji, 2014). Among the Olu'bo society, for example, girl initiation is highly regarded due to its social and economic benefits. It encourages the making and trading of artefacts for associated ceremonies as well as socialising by bringing together girls of the same age and their parents (Bedigen, 2017).

Whereas social support promotes solidarity, Oosterom's (2017) analysis of Latuko Monymiji-practising communities indicates that the solidarity of a few can contribute to gender-based violence, dominance, non-sharing of power and exclusion, particularly where an individual or a few express a dissenting opinion. The implication of this is that the institution appears disorganised to the outsiders, therefore disregarded as a crucial aspect in national peacebuilding. Significantly, Honyomiji philosophy is not purposed for maintaining political–gender balance but social support for the common good. For example, in the Lotele Honyomiji institution, while the landlord or landlady, rainmaker and the diviners share power and make unifying decisions on issues that threaten community peace, the latter two are not wholly embraced by a few members who do not practise ATR (Simonse and Kurimoto, 2011:64). Yet, it is argued that in the long run, this type of solidarity helps strengthen community cohesion and offers a solid framework for both local and national peacebuilding.

Sustainability in providing social support for effective peacebuilding is only possible where 'people share a common socio-cultural, national or civic bond' (De Coning, 2016). The Jie Monyomiji have contributed to peacebuilding meetings and rituals, including support for community development activities such as the construction of health centres, schools and roads. They have provided grain, food, water, sand and stones (Simonse and Kurimoto, 2011). Also, during the Wunlit traditional peacemaking conference, the Dinka and Nuer women and their children contributed firewood, water, cooked food and participated in the Mabior ceremonial cleansing ritual (Bedigen, 2017). This reinforces a subtle form of social and community connectedness, suggesting that women's moral obligations, by default, transcend beyond their vulnerability and are dependent on other societal members. Honyomiji duties of social support and cultural practices of moral responsibility are intertwined and influenced by the entire societal fabric, harmonising social structures, community and members' well-being.

Whereas commonality and national bond exist in the struggles for peace, it becomes more challenging when set against the reality of a state carved out in the shadows of colonialism, deeply rooted ethnic conflicts and weak leadership. It is recognised that this is a historical legacy that perhaps Honyomiji cannot undo singly, at least not in the short term. Yet, this study acknowledges that the Honyomiji social support system that interlinks its leadership, education and religious practices promotes functional relationships between humans, spirits and the environment (areas in which peace must exist to realise sustainable peace). Adding, informal frameworks/roles/obligations discussed here can provide channels for external support, whether in technical and human resources, as well as offer a foundation for hybrid sustainable peacebuilding.

Conclusion

This chapter states what Honyomiji means and discusses the role of Nilotic women in wars, motherhood and their utilisation of Loketio or Logedio (pregnancy support belt) in peacebuilding, including the United Nations Women Peace and Security (WPS) agenda. It demonstrated that women's indigenous or traditional roles and obligations such as motherhood, leadership, education, social support and involvement in religious/cultural ceremonies are crucial in the intra-ethnic and inter-ethnic conflicts—thus it suggests that their inclusion in the national peace initiatives is core in delivering sustainable peace in the region.

This chapter acknowledges that some flaws exist in the Honyomiji institution. For instance, the exclusion of women by fellow women, or male indigenous institutions, killings of suspected witches and an education system that inspires violence. Also, traditional/indigenous customs, practices and values have eroded over time, are not homogeneous across South Sudanese ethnic groups and are the opposite of the conventional linear, formal, logical or structured methods. However, it is essential to emphasise that, in the context of gender and peacebuilding, the non-linearity of indigenous institutions is not associated with disorder or sub-standardness. As demonstrated here, indigenous approaches and women's traditional roles are an essential ingredient in the processes of conflict prevention, management and peacebuilding and that it generates sustainability in complex conflict situations. Moreover, the Honyomiji institution presents a perfect example of local women fully engaged in communities' well-being. They are not passive victims to be protected but are capable women who utilise communities' ideologies, philosophies and practices in carving peace. The institution is a significant asset in bottom-up and national peacebuilding (Bedigen, 2021; Coe et al., 2013).

Bibliography

Adebayo, A.G., Benjamin, J.J. and Lundy, B.D. (Eds.), 2014. *Indigenous Conflict Management Strategies: Global Perspectives*. Lanham, MD, Lexington Books. https://rowman.com/ISBN/9780739188040.

Afisi, O.T., 2010. Power and womanhood in Africa: An introductory evaluation. *The Journal of Pan African Studies*, 3(6), pp. 229–238.

Aldehaib, A., 2010. Sudan's comprehensive peace agreement viewed through the eyes of the women of South Sudan. JSTOR.org.

Alexander-Floyd, N.G. and Simien, E.M., 2006. Revisiting "what's in a name?": Exploring the contours of Africana womanist thought. *Frontiers: A Journal of Women Studies*, 27, pp. 67–89.

Arabi, A., 2011. In power without power: Women in politics and leadership positions in South Sudan. In *Hope, Pain and Patience: The Lives of Women in South Sudan*. Wynberg, Fanele Publishers, pp. 193–213.

Augsburger, D.W., 1992. *Conflict Mediation across Cultures: Pathways and Patterns*. Louisville, KY, Westminster/John Knox Press.

Barry, F.B. and Grady, S.C., 2019. Africana womanism as an extension of feminism in political ecology (of health) research. *Geoforum*, *103*, pp. 182–186.

Bedigen, W., 2017. *Traditional Conflict Resolution. The Nilotic Lwo of South Sudan* (PhD thesis). Leeds, Leeds Beckett University.

Bedigen, W., 2019. Youth (Monyomiji) and conflict resolution in the South Sudan civil war. *Journal of African Cultural Heritage Studies*, 2(1), pp. 18–35.

Bedigen, W., Mdee, A., Temlong R., Thorley, L., and Tshomba, P., 2020. The failure of externally-driven advocacy initiatives to contextualise sub-Saharan "marginalised women". *Development in Practice*. DOI: 10.1080/09614524.2020.1836129.

Bedigen, W., 2021. Honyomiji: the local women's peacebuilding institution in South Sudan. *Peacebuilding*. DOI: 10.1080/21647259.2021.1895613.

Bedigen, W., 2022. Indigenous South Sudanese understanding of women empowerment. *World Development Perspectives*, 25, p. 100389. https://www.sciencedirect.com/science/article/abs/pii/S2452292921001053.

Blackmon, J.L., 2008. *I Am Because We Are: Africana womanism as a Vehicle of Empowerment and Influence* (Doctoral dissertation). Virginia Tech.

Blumberg, H.H., Hare, A.P. and Costin, A., 2006. *Peace Psychology. A Comprehensive Introduction*. Cambridge, Cambridge University Press.

Bradbury, M., Ryle, J., Medley, M. and Sansculotte-Greenidge, K., 2006. *Local Peace Processes in Sudan: A Baseline Study*. London, Rift Valley Institute.

Branch D., 2011. *Kenya: Between Hope and Despair, 1963-2011*. New Haven, Yale University Press.

Coe, K., Palmer, C.T. and ElShabazz, K., 2013. The resolution of conflict: Traditional African ancestors, kinship, and rituals of reconciliation. *African Conflict and Peace Building Review*, 3(2), pp. 110–128.

De Coning, C., 2016. From peacebuilding to sustaining peace: Implications of complexity for resilience and sustainability. *Resilience*, 4(3), pp. 166–181.

De La Puente, D., 2011. Women's leadership in camps for internally displaced people in Darfur, western Sudan. *Community Development Journal*, 46(3), pp. 365–377.

de Waal, A., 2017. Peace and the security sector in Sudan, 2002–11. *African Security Review*, 26(2), pp. 180–198. doi: 10.1080/10246029.2017.129758.

Denskus, T. and Kosmatopoulos, N., 2015. Anthropology & peacebuilding: An introduction. *Peacebuilding*, 3(3), pp. 219–223.

Dogra, N., 2011. The mixed metaphor of 'third world woman': Gendered representations by international development NGOs. *Third World Quarterly*, 32(2), pp. 333–348. doi: 10.1080/01436597.2011.560472.

Donais, T. and Knorr, A.C., 2013. Peacebuilding from below vs. the liberal peace: The case of Haiti. *Canadian Journal of Development Studies/Revue Canadienne d'Études du Développement/Revue canadienne d'études du développement*, 34(1), pp. 54–69.

Douglas, M., 1970. *Natural Symbols. Explorations in Cosmology*. New York, Routledge.

Douglas, M., 1973. *Natural Symbols: Explorations in Cosmology*. London, Barrie & Rockliff.

Douglas, M., 2004. *Natural Symbols: Explorations in Cosmology*. London, Routledge.

Duriesmith, D., 2015. Building peace with warlords in South Sudan: A gendered structure. In J. I. Lahai (Ed.), *African Frontiers*. London, Ashgate, pp. 157–166.

Erzurum, K. and Eren, B., 2014. Women in peacebuilding: A criticism of gendered solutions in postconflict situations. *Journal of Applied Security Research*, 9(2), pp. 236–256.

Evans-Pritchard, E.E., 1953. Nuer spear symbolism. *Anthropological Quarterly*, 26(1), pp. 1–19.

Galtung, J. and Fischer, D., 2013. Positive and negative peace. In J. Galtung (Ed.), *Springer Briefs on Pioneers in Science and Practice, vol 5*. Berlin, Heidelberg, Springer, pp. 173–178.

Galtung, J., 1976. *Three Approaches to Peace: Peacekeeping, Peacemaking, and Peacebuilding.Peace, War and Defense: Essays in Peace Research, Vol. II*, Johan Galtung (Ed.), pp. 297–298. Copenhagen, Christian Ejlers.

Gebre, Y.G. and Ohta, I., 2017. *African virtues in the pursuit of conviviality: Exploring local solutions in light of global prescriptions*. Langaa RPCIG, Cameroon, African Books Collective.

Gergen, M.M. and Davis, S. (Eds.), 1997. *Toward a New Psychology of Gender*. London, Routledge.

Gergen, M.M. and Davis, S.N., 2013. *Toward a New Psychology of Gender: A Reader*. London, Routledge.

Hancock, L.E., 2017. Agency & peacebuilding: The promise of local zones of peace. *Peacebuilding*, 5(3), pp. 255–269.

Heron, G.A., 1976. *The Poetry of Okot p'Btek*. New York, African Publishing Company.

Hudson-Weems, C., 2019. *Africana womanism: Reclaiming Ourselves*. London, Routledge.

Ibok, A.K. and Ogar, O.T., 2018. Traditional roles of African women in peace making and peace building: An evaluation. *GNOSI: An Interdisciplinary Journal of Human Theory and Praxis*, 1(1), pp. 41–58.

Itto, A., 2006. Guests at the Table? The Role of Women in Peace Processes. In Mark Simmons and Peter Dixon (Eds.), *Peace by Peace: Addressing Sudan's Conflict*, 18, pp. 56–59.

Iyob, R. and Khadiagala, G.M., 2006. *Sudan: The Elusive Quest for Peace*. Boulder, CO, Lynne Rienner.

Jok, A.A., Leitch, A.R. and Vandewint, C., 2004. *A Study of Customary Law in Contemporary Southern Sudan*. Rumbek, South Sudan, World Vision International.

Jok, J.M., 2011. *Diversity, Unity, and Nation Building in South Sudan*. Washington, DC, US Institute of Peace.

Jok, J.M. and Hutchinson, S.E., 1999. Sudan's prolonged second civil war and the militarization of Nuer and Dinka ethnic identities. *African Studies Review*, 42(2), pp. 125–145.

Joyce, A. J., 2001. African-centred womanism: Connecting Africa to the diaspora. In I. Okpewho, C. B. Davies, and A. A. Mazuri (Eds.), TheAfrican Diaspora: African Origins and New World Identities, (pp. 538–554). Bloomington, IN, Indiana University Press.

Julian, R., Bliesemann de Guevara, B. and Redhead, R., 2019. From expert to experiential knowledge: Exploring the inclusion of local experiences in understanding violence in conflict. *Peacebuilding*, 7(2), pp. 210–225.

Katola, M.T., 2014. Incorporating of traditional African cultural values in the formal education system for development, peace building and good governance. *European Journal of Research in Social Sciences*, 2(3), pp. 2056–5429. Nairobi. University of Nairobi.

Kelly, R.C., 1985. *The Nuer Conquest: The Structure and Development of an Expansionist System*. Ann Arbor, University of Michigan Press.

Leonardi, C., Moro, L.N., Santschi, M. and Isser, H.D., 2010. *Local Justice in South Sudan (Peaceworks Number 66)*. Washington, DC, United States Institute of Peace.

LeVine, R.A., 1961. Anthropology and the study of conflict: An introduction. *The Journal of Conflict Resolution*, 5, pp. 3–15.

Lund, R. and Agyei-Mensah, S., 2008. Queens as mothers: The role of the traditional safety net of care and support for HIV/AIDS orphans and vulnerable children in Ghana. *GeoJournal*, 71(2), pp. 93–106.

Ma'at-Ka-Re Monges, M., 1993. Reflections on the role of female deities and queens in ancient Kemet. *Journal of Black Studies*, 23(4), pp. 561–570.

Mac Ginty, R., 2008. Indigenous peace-making versus the liberal peace. *Cooperation and Conflict*, 43(2), pp. 139–163.

Mac Ginty, R., 2010. Gilding the lily? International support for indigenous and traditional peacebuilding. In O.P. Richmond (Ed.), *Palgrave Advances in Peacebuilding*. London, Palgrave Macmillan, pp. 347–366.

Mac Ginty, R., 2014. Everyday peace: Bottom-up and local agency in conflict-affected societies. *Security Dialogue*, 45(6), pp. 548–564.

Mac Ginty, R. and Firchow, P., 2016. Top-down and bottom-up narratives of peace and conflict. *Politics*, 36(3), pp. 308–323.

Mazurana, D., Raven-Roberts, A. and Parpart, J. (Eds.), 2005. *Gender, Conflict, and Peacekeeping*. Oxford, Rowman & Littlefield Publishers.

Millar, G., Van Der Lijn, J. and Verkoren, W., 2013. Peacebuilding plans and local reconfigurations: Frictions between imported processes and indigenous practices. *International Peacekeeping*, 20(2), pp. 137–143.

Mosweunyane, D., 2013. The African educational evolution: From traditional training to formal education. *Higher Education Studies*, 3(4), pp. 50–59.

Narayanaswamy, L., 2016. Whose feminism counts? Gender(ed) knowledge and professionalisation in development. *Third World Quarterly*, 37(12), pp. 2156–2175.

Nassanga, L.G., 1997. Women, development and the media: The case for Uganda. *Media, Culture & Society*, 19(3), pp. 471–476.

Newman, E., 2013. The international architecture of peacebuilding. In R. Mac Ginty (Ed.), *Routledge Handbook of Peacebuilding*. London, Routledge, pp. 319–332.

Newman, E., 2013. The violence of statebuilding in historical perspective: Implications for peacebuilding. *Peacebuilding*, 1(1), pp. 141–157.

Njeri, S., 2019. Somaliland; the viability of a liberal peacebuilding critique beyond state building, state formation and hybridity. *Peacebuilding*, 7(1), pp. 37–50.

Novelli, M., Lopes Cardozo, M. and Smith, A., 2015. *A Theoretical Framework for Analysing the Contribution of Education to Sustainable Peacebuilding: 4Rs in Conflict-Affected Contexts*. Amsterdam, University of Amsterdam.

Okoro Kingsley, N., 2010. African traditional education: A viable alternative for peace building process in modern Africa. *Journal of Alternative Perspectives in the Social Sciences*, 2(1), pp. 136–159.

Oosterom, M., 2017. Gendered (in) security in South Sudan: Masculinities and hybrid governance in Imatong state. *Peacebuilding*, 5(2), pp. 186–202.

Ouellet, J.X., 2013. Women and religion in Liberia's peace and reconciliation. *Critical Intersections in Education*, 1(1), pp. 12–20.

Pankhurst, D., 2008. Post-war backlash violence against women: what can "masculinity" explain?. In D. Pankhurst (Ed.), *Gendered Peace: Women's Struggles for Post-War Justice and Reconciliation*. New York, Routledge.

Porter, E., 2003. Women, political decision-making, and peace-building. *Global Change, Peace and Security*, 15(3), pp. 245–262.

Schiller, L.D., 1990. The royal women of Buganda. *The International Journal of African Historical Studies*, 23(3), pp. 455–473.

Schirch, L., 2015. Ritual, religion, and peacebuilding. In A. Omer, R.S. Appleby and D. Little (Eds.), *The Oxford Handbook of Religion, Conflict, and Peacebuilding*. Oxford, Oxford University Press.

Simonse, S. and Kurimoto, E. (Eds.), 2011. Engaging 'Monyomiji', bridging the gap in East Bank Equatoria: Proceedings of the Conference 26–28 November 2009. Nairobi, Pax Christi Horn of Africa, pp. 2–129.

Smith Ellison, C., 2014. The role of education in peacebuilding: An analysis of five change theories in Sierra Leone. *Compare: A Journal of Comparative and International Education*, 44(2), pp. 186–207.
Stoeltje, B.J., 1997. Asante queen mothers. *Annals of the New York Academy of Sciences*, 810(1), pp. 41–71.
Tadesse, B., Yeneneh, T. and Fekadu, B., 2010. Women in Conflict and indigenous conflict resolution among the Issa and Gurgura clans of Somali in Eastern Ethiopia. *African Journal on Conflict Resolution*, 10, pp. 85–110.
Vaittinen, T., Donahoe, A., Kunz, R., Bára Ómarsdóttir, S. and Roohi, S., 2019. Care as everyday peacebuilding. *Peacebuilding*, 7(2), pp. 194–209.
Wessells, M., 2005. Child soldiers, peace education, and postconflict reconstruction for peace. *Theory into Practice*, 44(4), pp. 363–369.
Wunlit Peace and Reconciliation Conference, 1999. *Appendix: Wunlit Recommendations on Abductions*. From the Dinka Nuer West Bank Peace and Reconciliation Conference in Wunlit, March 1999. Retrieved from http://southsudanfriends.org/wunlit/index.html (Accessed 2 March 2013).
Zanen, S.M. and van den Hoek, A.W., 1987. Dinka dualism and the Nilotic hierarchy of values. In R. de Ridder and J.A.J. Karremans (Eds.), *The Leiden Tradition in Structural Anthropology*. Leiden, Brill, pp. 170–196.
Zartman, I.W. (Ed.), 2000. *Traditional cures for modern conflicts: African conflict "Medicine"*. London, Lynne Rienner Publishers.

List of Interviews Cited in the Text

Interview with Dinka Honyomiji, 2012, 2014
Interview with Efo, 17 April 2014
Interview with Fred, 20 December 2012
Interview with Kilo, 28 April 2013
Interview with Mama Dunia, 2013
Interview with Nekye, 2013
Interview with Garad Nunow, 2013
Interview with Nuer Honyomiji, 2012, 2014
Interview with Pete, 19 May 2013
Interview with Sadrak, 15 December 2012
Interview with Sellie, 20 March 2013

8 Social Capital, Resilience and Proximity in Peacebuilding

Introduction

This chapter argues that resilience, proximity and social capital are crucial in peacebuilding. It utilises migrants' perspectives and reflections of their past, current and future concerns. Adding it highlights the steps some South Sudanese refugees in the Diasporas have taken in contributing to peacebuilding at local levels in their home country. It seeks to demonstrate that resilience and proximity concepts are inbuilt in peoples' cultures, beliefs and everyday peace practices and that these two are strengthened by social capital.

The inclusion of such concepts in the analysis of indigenous peacebuilding is significant in many ways. First, ethnic communities under study have historically experienced intermittent conflicts but prevailed—thus testifying to their resilience (Bedigen, 2017). Second, when government or peace agencies are absent (Bedigen, 2019), local resiliences demonstrated through cultures of proximities have enabled inter-ethnic peacebuilding to happen. Third, these concepts are quite well analysed in other disciplines but remain less discussed in peacebuilding—thus their analysis here contributes to new knowledge in indigenous peacebuilding. This chapter concludes that interviewees' perspectives (those at home or in the diaspora) are essential in maintaining peacebuilding networks.

First, this section analyses the concept of social capital in peacebuilding.

Social Capital

The term social capital dates back to the pioneering works of Bourdieu (1986), Coleman (1988, 1990), Fukuyama (1995) and Newton (1997), who describe social capital as any aspect of the social system that generates values, networks and outputs that promote peoples' activities within that social system. In the social science discipline, the term is related to other concepts such as civic culture (Almond and Verba, 1963) and civil society (Seligman, 1992). Putnam (1993:167) describes social capital as 'features of social organisations, such as trust, norms, and networks that can improve

DOI: 10.4324/9781003133476-9

the efficiency of society by facilitating coordinated actions.' Further, Seibert et al. (2001:1) and Fukuyama (1995) conceptualise social capital in terms of 'network structure and social resources,' where the informal-interpersonal behaviours, trust and unity play a key role in enabling individuals to go through tragedy/disasters.

In the security, peacebuilding and development nexus, for example, Lederach in his book *The Moral Imagination* provides examples of communities such as Dagoma, Konkomba and the Wajir who utilised their network structures and social resources (through interconnectedness, reflection and corporation) to transform conflict situations into peace and therefore development (Lederach, 2005). Bedigen (2019) indicates that among the communities in the Horn, social capital is not confined to the community's leadership, kinship and provisions but rather depends on the spirit of generosity and empathy. Social capital is an individual's resource embedded in relationships with like-minded others. For instance, Clark and Lisowski (2019:1) refer to social capital in migration situations as the 'giving and receiving aid in local contexts,' and those expectations of giving and receiving from a neighbour provide 'social capital.' This book's view is what David et al. (2010) term 'local social capital,' where individuals have stronger ties with their families, friends, locality and customary norms. The more helpful an individual/community or network is to the other (including former enemies), the stronger the relationship (Bedigen, 2019; Clark and Lisowski, 2018).

On the other hand, if investment (i.e. the giving and receiving) is not maintained, social capital depreciates (Coleman, 1990), consequently rendering proximities and resiliences unproductive. This implies that, in confronting and managing tragedies/disasters/conflicts, social capital may demand those normal relationships that facilitate crucial actions to be adoptive or resilient. Significant to maintenance is the relative level of wealth/resources and kind acts. Thus, in the refugee/migration situations, individuals objectively deal with their needs by adopting necessary survival skills/knowledge and capabilities. Achieving success is further enhanced by their knowledge, resources (human and material), resilience and proximities to situations.

It is argued that social capital influenced the need for South Sudanese refugees in Leeds, UK, to create a national association and venue where men, women and youth meet weekly for social events such as prayers, cooking, tailoring and IT classes. Moreover, social events enable members to create their national identities, historical traditions and social and cultural–political aspirations (Cox, 2008:6). According to Winter (2006), social events or practices bound people together. Here, narratives reveal peace cultures, social and ceremonial/ritual practices and norms that introduce 'new meaning in political and cultural life' in peacebuilding (Winter, 2006:154). In the post-conflict South Sudan, local peacebuilding initiatives and social events through sports, such as wrestling, football, marathons, cultural fashion shows, have brought together diasporas and enabled them to create their national identities and historical traditions, social and cultural–political aspirations (Cox, 2008:6). Interviewees indicate that such peace practices are essential and should be included in the conventional peacebuilding processes. Whereas this book draws from interviewees' shared past of cultural and civil war experiences, some interviewees, particularly immigrants, express less confidence in their own current direct/indirect or remote peace roles. Immigrants' concerns over conflict dynamics that they argue require modification of peace approaches is not an isolated case and does not imply that social capital is no longer adequate. Thus, individuals doubt their peacebuilding abilities. Yet, this work argues that cultural peace education can build confidence in peacebuilding (Bedigen, 2021).

Interactions in social events strengthen proximities and resiliences. The majority of attendees of the South Sudanese community centres believe that such venues are more than a home away from home. As such, members of ethnic groups from the region have forged unity, unlike in their home country, where historical animosities and ethnic rivalries fuel divisions or feed into civil wars. These situations present a sharp contradiction between the South Sudanese at home and the diaspora. It does imply that, theoretically, peacebuilding can be forged between rival groups or locations; however, translation of such might remain a challenge due to the dynamics of conflicts and their impact on the locals at home.

Moreover, social capital does not imply similarity in views. Individuals or groups expressed varying perspectives on indigenous peacebuilding and its suitability in modern contexts. The challenge remains in finding common ground in both the diasporas' and locals' views about what can work as dichotomies that cut across proximities, resiliences and social capital may render national peacebuilding elusive.

For instance, the older men in the diasporas believe that traditional methods are still applicable and can be applied to South Sudan's national peacebuilding processes. However, they express fears of competition from other non-indigenous institutions (such as government and agencies) and how the elders resident in South Sudan struggle to fit into government political structures, mainly for personal or financial gains. As Bedigen (2017) argues, some elders are appointed by the government or political leaders and may not be committed to indigenous norms—thus revealing another level of dichotomy in South Sudan diasporas and locals' views on the nation's peacebuilding.

Likewise, diaspora women indicate the significance of indigenous methods of peacebuilding but express limitations in their role as women and mothers in maintaining native cultural values in a foreign land. Also, questions arise around which culture offers a suitable methodology for diaspora and local women's peacebuilding activities (Reagon, 1986). Women indicate that, despite their efforts in wearing cultural peace jewellery such as waist beads, involvement in the events at Leeds Sudanese Community Centre and regular visits to South Sudan, they feel incompetent. This is because demands and cultures in the host country often cause distractions from peacebuilding opportunities that arise in family and community. The need to learn new ways of life may cause distrust in indigenous approaches. Moreover, approaches or peacebuilding methodologies in host communities remain technically and practically different from South Sudanese indigenous approaches, restricting social capital influence on proximity and resilience. Notably, women are nervous about getting it wrong in rituals and ceremonial activities because they are rarely practised in the diaspora, yet it is through such activities that South Sudanese are bound to their common origin.

Further, women explain that structures in the UK (such as the education system, social services, media and the host's local cultures) streamline women or mothers' traditional duties and responsibilities, placing indigenous norms in a secondary position. Yet this work does not claim that diaspora African women are purely cultural or possess homogeneous views but recognises that women's peacebuilding efforts are leaning towards a transnational shift. For instance, Erickson and Faria's analysis of the role of the South Sudan Women's Empowerment Network (SSWEN) in the post-conflict reconstruction following the 2005 Comprehensive Peace Agreement (CPA) (2011, p, 627) indicates that SSWEN's peacebuilding activities demonstrated a transnational shift in the South Sudanese women engagement along diasporic and local lines (Bedigen, 2021). In his argument for transnationalism and recreation of home, Osirim (2008) indicates how transnational ties in the form of pan-Africanism, customary norms and social capital lead African women immigrants to make significant contributions to cultural revitalisation, mainly as observed at the Leeds Sudanese Community Centre. It was clear that, in their daily lives, they are strongly committed to improving the lives of their children, families and communities both at home and in their new environments (Osirim, 2008).

Similarly, by their later years, women remainers in South Sudan will have experienced many difficult and unavoidable losses, thus inventing coping strategies. However, despite adversity, many older women adjust successfully and continue to embrace life with enthusiasm. Their exemplary lifestyles encourage younger women facing similar new challenges to do so with strength and determination (Bedigen, 2020). Overall, the elusive force of resilience in most South Sudanese women seems to make a difference as individuals confront life challenges (Wagnild and Young, 1990). For instance, some women in less or like circumstances are crushed by the weight of their lives. Thus, they become vulnerable and helpless, thus withdrawing into themselves. It is suggested that such women's plight is often generalised in the western rhetorics while the majorities' resilience and contribution towards peacebuilding are marginalised.

Winter (2006) indicates that both older men and women express a feeling of strong ties with the mother country; the implication of not being able to maintain cultural integrity and having limited hands-on practice of native cultural norms and values in the diasporas is that it leads to cultural loss—thus lessening the contributions of social capital to peacebuilding. To mitigate any shortfalls requires re-cultivation of cultural peace practices and re-education of all members.

On the other hand, the youth are adamant that the South Sudan civil war can only be resolved through political means. South Sudanese youth have contributed towards national peacebuilding through social media, organising and supporting local sports events. Bedigen (2019:5) analyses Youth (Monyomiji) cultural norms of leadership as essential in influencing the nation's political, social and economic situation. In doing so, youth have participated in apprenticeships and re-integration of ex-combatants (Simonse and Kurimoto, 2011:16). Yet, some elders argue that youth 'should stay in school to gain knowledge and experience' but not interfere so much with the political, social and economic situations. Placing youth in studentship helps maintain the conventional ideas that have continuously relegated youth from national peacebuilding.

Resilience

Resilience concept originates from psychology and health developments and is likened to salutogenesis, a concept developed in sociology. Both concepts address how people can manage their lives or adapt in the face of adversity (Lindstrom, 2001). However, the application of the resilience concept is not exclusive to these two disciplines but to others, such as conflict and peacebuilding. Resilience is related to hardiness, adaptation, adjustment, mastery, plasticity, invulnerability, person–environment fit or social buffering (Losel et al., 1989:187; Anthony, 1987). Yet, as Glantz and Slobada (2002) warn, 'There is no consensus on the referent of the term, standards for its application, or agreement on its role in explanation, models, and theories.' Further, Windle (1999:174) argues that the resilience literature offers

> no organizing framework for integrating studies, evaluating common and unique findings across different subject populations, variable domains, or spacing intervals, or studying the impact of alternative operational definitions and classification procedures on the identification of resilient individuals.

The concept attracted scholarly interests over the years, as its application appears interdisciplinary (Cicchetti and Garmezy, 1993; Masten, 2001). On the other hand, others indicate that the resilience concept has provoked scepticism. For instance, Kaplan (1999:72) argues it is 'a concept whose time has come and gone.' While the resilience concept in development faces many challenges, this work focuses on the ability to rebound in post-conflict peacebuilding and reconstruction (Masten, 2001). For instance, Evans and Lunn (1997:46), in their book, *War and Memory in the Twentieth Century*, indicate that interviewees' 'memories are constructed and reconstructed.'

Social Capital, Resilience and Proximity 193

While this could negatively influence the quality of data, in reality, it is claimed such stories of resiliences directly/indirectly contributed to positive outcomes in peacebuilding. This book recognises that positive impacts of construction and reconstruction are personal and national, immediate and long term. They include rights to asylum/refugee status and sustenance, lobbying for the host nation and international support to end the civil war and the right to a referendum.

Rights to asylum/refugee status gave South Sudanese refugees rights to European protection and human rights as far as the law was concerned. These laws offered many opportunities to South Sudanese refugees to better themselves through education, vocational trainings and political awareness. With the end of Sudan's second civil war, the international community (the USA, UK, UN and other agencies) contributed to the 2005 CPA that granted South Sudan autonomy. The CPA provided hope for national independence to many South Sudanese. For the first time, South Sudanese were recognised as distinct citizens (from Sudan) and, in effect, gained the right to vote for the 2011 national independence. Apart from this, South Sudanese had the right to establish their political parties and seek international relations with other states. Without the refugees' resilience to claim their rights to asylum/refugee status and sustenance and lobby for political support to end the civil war and a referendum, these achievements might not have been realised.

Further, in applying the resilience concept to peacebuilding, this book draws from a study on violence in the Latino community, which indicates that cultural factors act as a buffer against violence (Clauss-Ehlers and Levi, 2002). The study observed cultural-community resilience factors such as family, respect and personal character. It argues that this helps protect against destructive forces in the environment and reinforces cultural-community resilience or collective resilience.

These factors (family, respect and personal character) are significant in helping individuals reconstruct and maintain social relationships that strengthen social capital during tragedy (Hernandez, 2002). Adding, Radke-Yarrow and Sherman (1990:100) observe that at a community level, 'successful coping behaviours are those that contribute to the survival and wellbeing of others.' Adding these authors argue that 'positive coping behaviours contribute to the wellbeing of the self' at a personal level. The resilience concept envisages survivors/individuals as happy about themselves and positive in contributing to their community. Anthony (1987) indicates that absence of resilience denotes vulnerability to disaster, however parties to conflict ought to be resilient for peacebuilding to succeed.

Resilience and social capital depend on network structures and resources. The study on strategies for the stabilisation, recovery and resilience of the Boko Haram-affected areas of the Lake Chad basin region indicates that addressing the short-, medium- and long-term needs of the conflict zones to ensure stabilisation, resilience and recovery must involve local communities in the implementation of development programmes (Ogbozor, 2016).

Studies from Somalia and Darfur indicate that local coping strategies are the most critical component in people's survival in many crises and that families in such conflict-prone regions use mixed strategies to balance short-term needs and long-term survival concerns (Bedigen, 2017). Longley and Maxwell (2003) indicate that despite the impact of the war that caused massive displacements from the Kambia District, those who stayed worked the farms and showed resilience in negotiating peace and reconciliations. Also, the remainers/stayers often develop a complex set of strategies useful in reducing and coping with risks—thus continue to carry out their usual tasks amidst intense conflicts (Justino, 2009, 2012). Stayers' resiliences are determined by access to resources and opportunities related to ethnic culture, gender, status, ownership of assets, networks, knowledge and historical life experience (Bene et al., 2014).

Both natural and man-made disasters in the Horn have exposed many individuals to extreme circumstances that have necessitated communities' resilience. South Sudanese have historically experienced economic, social and political extremities. Such examples include wars, poverty, killings and assaults that caused the majority to take refuge in neighbouring countries, migrate to Internally Displaced People's camps (IDPCs) or further afield (Bedigen, 2017).

This book recognises various dimensions of the resilience of individuals at home and the diasporas and how both experiences can consequently contribute to tangible outcomes in peacebuilding. Both home/diaspora environments require adaptations, hardiness, adjustment, mastery, plasticity, invulnerability, person–environment fit, social buffering or strong-willed individuals (Losel et al., 1989:187; Anthony, 1987). This book observes that resilient people can tell their stories to compel third parties to intervene or act towards peacebuilding.

Proximity

The concept of proximity, commonly applied to economic geography and regional economics disciplines, draws from spatial studies that include regional clusters and urban studies (Zamyatina and Pilyasov, 2017). Authors argue that there are many dimensions to the proximity concept, i.e. cognitive, physical, organisational and institutional/political (Boschma, 2005; Shaw and Gilly, 2000). Relevant to peacebuilding is the psychological/emotional, political and cultural proximities (Böhmelt and Bove, 2020; Jensen and Jacobsen, 2020). Authors argue that these proximities are rooted in cultures that include 'the sharing of a common identity, feeling of belonging, and to the degree of affinity between' ethnicities (Bedigen, 2017; Felbermayr and Toubal, 2010:280). Böhmelt and Bove studies indicate that 'similarities in societal norms, customs, or beliefs seem likely to induce trust' in the social, economic and political interactions between migrants and hosts. Thus, 'cultural closeness between migrants and host societies' provides a platform for peacebuilding between different South Sudanese ethnic refugee groups translated to the home nation (2020:251).

While it is argued that emotional proximity transcends cultural differences, networks individuals and creates universalism, Lee et al. (2018:245) indicate that mobilising people to resolve 'issues that occur in physically distant' places in conflict or post-conflict zones can be a challenge. For example, poverty, famine, drought, disease or gender-related issues may be considered 'too far away to be relevant to many people's lives.' In contrast, other issues like climate change may be urgent in some western world citizens' everyday life due to their 'global nature,' thus making such issues psychologically distant (Spence et al., 2012).

Adding, psychological distance is a subjective experience that something in proximity or not from the self, here and now, is claimed to influence people's views, priorities and behaviours related to social issues such as conflict, refugees and humanitarian crises (Trope and Liberman, 2010). For instance, it is argued that people with less psychological distance towards an issue have stronger cognitions about and more supportive actions towards the issue. This is because perception, comprehension and interpretation of issues based on their feelings of closeness are likely to encourage participation in actions they believe will help resolve the issue (Liberman et al., 2007). For instance, due to a common Christian faith, the USA and UK governments, including related NGOs, have engaged the South Sudanese government and citizens towards peaceful resolutions and humanitarian assistance (Bedigen, 2017). Additionally, prominent social media campaigns during the Arab Spring influenced revolutions that toppled dictators in countries such as Egypt, Zimbabwe and Sudan, allegedly reducing psychological distance about such issues of concern and encouraging people with limited or no previous involvement to participate. Likewise, in the diasporas, refugee associations, community centres, workshops or vocational training centres such as the Leeds Sudanese Community Centre are shown to cultivate psychological proximity because they provide refugees with opportunities to create personal, social, economic and political networks among various South Sudanese ethnic groups who share mutual interests (Bedigen, 2017).

Further, conflicts such as the Rwandan genocide, the Lord's Resistance Army (in northern Uganda) and the Sudan civil wars have often been viewed by the west as 'distant others' (Sorenson, 1991). However, through cosmopolitan political proximity, refugees from these regions and international peace agencies networked the western citizens, diasporas and stayers with 'distant others' through perceptions of cultural/ethical/political similarities. Also, such networking has cultivated proximity and the need for international agencies to act. Cosmopolitan political or proximity politics refers to political–cultural problems that we experience due to globalisation (Tomlinson, 2000). Globalisation draws the world closer through its structurally complex institutional inter-connections, particularly communications and media technologies. However, in some contexts, cultural differences consist of their politics. It attempts to map some of this emergent terrain, focusing on some recent debates about cosmopolitanism. Here it explores, for instance, problems of conflicting cultural–political principles thrown up by the structural impact of enforced proximity. For instance, international/'ethical' interventions vs sovereignty, global governance vs localism or state vs traditional institutions. Uncertainties of incompatibility of such principles may often be exaggerated, leaving room for the theoretical conceptualisation of cosmopolitan political peacebuilding (Tomlinson, 2000). While Böhmelt and Bove (2020:252) highlight that 'migrants' cultural proximity to the host society mitigates the diffusion of terrorism,' this book argues for its significant political contribution to the home country through ethnic–political networks. For instance, the Rwandan genocide piled criticisms over delayed western interventions, yet over 100 local NGOs sprang up during post-conflict reconstruction.

While utilising cultural/ethical/political situations benefits cosmopolitan peacebuilding primarily, it facilitates the designation of a few western-educated experts, 'a direct progeny of the violence of modernity and the conventional systems' (Souffrant, 2016:6). This is mainly because cosmopolitan peacebuilding concentrates on consolidating peace with political leaders or agents in global environments and neglects indigenous institutions (Souffrant, 2016:4).

Further, proximity focuses on analysing potential interaction of various features such as societal, institutional and ethnic relations in war or peacebuilding. In particular, Vasquez (1995:1) indicates that 'most interstate wars are fought or begin between neighbours.' Others add to this argument by claiming that 'proxy cultural ties, such as common language, religion, or ethnicity' are double-edged swords that cause conflicts and build and sustain peace (Felbermayr and Toubal, 2010:279; Bedigen, 2017). Significant to note, South Sudan's experiences of civil wars have been caused by or fed into ethnic or neighbourhood conflicts in Chad, Uganda, Ethiopia and DRC, respectively (Bedigen, 2017, 2021). Considering the arguments presented here, the proximity concept, which concerns itself with relationships, can help provide an understanding of its contribution to post-conflict peacebuilding.

In applying the proximity concept here, spatial memory/migrant views, cultural and axiological sustainable peace by means of co-existence and social networks are considered (Zamyatina and Pilyasov, 2017). Such spatial memories interweave relationships and bind 'macro, meso and micro actors to the common purpose of building peace' (Braniff and Byrne, 2014:45). However, this can only be possible when a certain level of proximity that ignores ethnic diversities but allows co-existence and social networks is maintained. Moreover, where micro actors or the indigenous views and social networks are excluded from national peacebuilding, as is often the case, the consequence is unsustainable peace. It is argued that the fruitfulness of proximity is realised in relationships and activities that serve to reduce elements of peace processes contradictory to indigenous views and practises.

A study by Felbermayr and Toubal (2010) highlights that songs influence cultural proximity. Likewise, the Nilotic Lwo songs of war or peace highlight cultural and societal achievements that discourage or improve meaningful social relations. Songs of similar cultural attributes encourage cultural proximity, a significant aspect of peacebuilding. Cultural proximity, not geographical distance or external intervention, captures familiar contextual pieces of knowledge (such as rituals/ceremonies), which this book considers to be significant in delivering sustainable peace. The South Sudanese refugees in the diasporas project the view that cultural proximity is a social capital through which national unity can be built, starting from the diasporas to their home country. In line with this argument, Krishna attributes cultural proximity to associations that 'enable citizens to engage the state and agencies' (2002:1).

Above all, most authors argue for the contribution of proximity concept in building relationships or networks in social sciences (Braniff and Byrne, 2014; Krishna, 2002; Zamyatina and Pilyasov, 2017). For instance, Braniff and Byrne's (2014) analysis of the significance of 'circles of friends' that continues after the post-conflict agreements are signed supports an argument for proximity. However, Boschma (2005) indicates some conceptual and empirical challenges. For instance, its many dimensions might not be easily distinguished, therefore requiring multidisciplinary approaches in the analysis. Also, whereas the emotional proximity compels diasporas to want to do something to stop conflicts and build peace in the home country, the relevance of their approach remains questionable.

Moreover, Boschma adds that proximities 'emerge, develop and disappear' and can contain adverse effects that may potentially harm contributions from proximity (2005:41). Whereas this work argues that proximity is crucial in delivering sustainable peace, post-conflict reconciliation processes appear to focus on national reconstruction rather than individual rehabilitation. Thus, its capacity to deal with 'trauma and reduce the causes of division and segregation' is inadequate (Braniff and Byrne, 2014:46). This might explain the South Sudan 2013–2015 civil war, whose ultimate triggers started just after the nation's independence in 2011.

Conclusion—Migrant Perspective

This book conceptualises indigenous peacebuilding situations in communities emerging from inter-ethnic conflicts and civil wars. It identifies and conceptualises the 'indigene-centric' or the core set of indigenous institutions, customs and practices that underpin the historical and foundational peace values in the Nilotic Lwo ethnic groups and the South Sudan justice system.

This chapter has demonstrated that the peacebuilding skills and desires of South Sudanese in the diaspora are supported by resilience, proximity and social capital, which are 'indigene-centric' attributes. Significantly, the interviewee's location, being far away from South Sudan, allowed them to reflect freely on the level of exploitation that the community, next-of-kin or military leaders exert on citizens. They explain that, although these military leaders try to improve the image of how inter-ethnic conflicts and the civil war should be perceived, the war memories are freshly engraved in individuals' minds and social environment. The ongoing conflicts worsened this situation. In the conventional attempts at peacebuilding and post-conflict reconstruction, the current atmosphere of coming to terms with the painful past experiences through co-existence and reconciliation by means of unfamiliar foreign practices only nurtures ambiguities. For instance, the South Sudanese have, on the one hand, to reconcile themselves to the atrocities caused by inter-ethnic and civil war and, on the other hand, to bridge the gap between individuals, various ethnic groups, plus the past, present and future. This may not be possible without common cultures within which resiliences, proximity and social capital thrive. The South Sudan conflict complexity affirms this book's argument that the locally sourced cultures offer sustainability. This is because communities and their cultures are often subjected to various challenges that consequently reshape them.

Bibliography

Almond, G.A. and Verba, S., 1963. *The Civic Culture: Political Attitudes and Democracy in Five Nations*. Princeton, NJ, Princeton University Press.

Anthony, E. J., 1987. Risk, vulnerability, and resilience: An overview. In E. J. Anthony and B. J. Cohler (Eds.), *The Invulnerable Child*, pp. 3–48. The Guilford Press.

Ayazi, T., Lien, L., Eide, A.H., Ruom, M.M. and Hauff, E., 2012. What are the risk factors for the comorbidity of posttraumatic stress disorder and depression in a war-affected population? A cross-sectional community study in South Sudan. *BMC Psychiatry*, 12(1), pp. 1–12.

Bedigen, W., 2017. Traditional conflict resolution. The Nilotic Lwo of South Sudan (PhD thesis). Leeds, Leeds Beckett University.

Bedigen, W., 2019. Significance of societal customs in the South Sudan civil war resolution. *Journal of Peacebuilding and Development*. doi: 10.1177/1542316619866422.

Bedigen, W., 2020. Significance of societal customs in the South Sudan Civil War resolution. *Journal of Peacebuilding and Development*, 15(1), pp. 3–17.

Bedigen, W., 2021. Honyomiji: The local women's peacebuilding institution in South Sudan. *Peacebuilding*, 9(4), pp. 457–476.

Béné, C., Newsham, A., Davies, M., Ulrichs, M. and Godfrey-Wood, R., 2014. Resilience, poverty and development. *Journal of International Development*, 26(5), pp. 598–623.

Block, J.H. and Block, J., 1980. The role of ego-control and ego-resiliency in the organization of behavior. In W. A. Collins (Ed.), *Development of Cognition, Affect, and Social Relations*. Hillsdale, CZ, Lawrence Erlbaum Associates, p. 48.

Böhmelt, T. and Bove, V., 2020. Does cultural proximity contain terrorism diffusion? *Journal of Peace Research*, 57(2), pp. 251–264.

Boschma, R., 2005. *Role of Proximity in Interaction and Performance: Conceptual and Empirical Challenges*, Vol. 39, Regional Studies, pp.41–45. London, Routledge.

Bourdieu, P., 1986. The forms of capital. In J. Richardson (Ed.), *Handbook of Theory and Research for the Sociology of Education*. New York, Greenwood Press, pp. 241–251.

Braniff, M. and Byrne, J., 2014. Circle of friends: Unravelling the networks of peacebuilding in Northern Ireland. *Peacebuilding*, 2(1), pp. 45–63.

Cicchetti, D. and Garmezy, N., 1993. Prospects and promises in the study of resilience. *Development and Psychopathology*, Cambridge University Press, 5(4), pp. 497–502.

Clark, W.A. and Lisowski, W., 2018. Wellbeing across individuals and places: How much does social capital matter? *Journal of Population Research*, 35(3), pp. 217–236.

Clark, W.A. and Lisowski, W., 2019. Extending the human capital model of migration: The role of risk, place, and social capital in the migration decision. *Population, Space and Place*, 25(4), p. e2225.

Clauss-Ehlers, C.S. and Levi, L.L., 2002. Violence and community, terms in conflict: An ecological approach to resilience. *Journal of Social Distress and the Homeless*, 11(4), pp. 265–278.

Coleman, J., 1988. Social capital in the creation of human capital. *American Journal of Sociology*, 94, pp. 95–120.

Coleman, J.S., 1990. *Foundations of Social Theory*. Cambridge, MA, Harvard University Press.

Cox, M. (Ed.), 2008. *Social Capital and Peace-Building: Creating and Resolving Conflict with Trust and Social Networks*. London, Routledge.

Curran, D. and Woodhouse, T., 2007. Cosmopolitan peacekeeping and peacebuilding in Sierra Leone: What can Africa contribute? *International Affairs*, 83(6), pp. 1055–1070.

David, Q., Janiak, A. and Wasmer, E., 2010. Local social capital and geographical mobility. *Journal of Urban Economics*, 68(2), pp. 191–204.

Erickson, J. and Faria, C., 2011. "We want empowerment for our women": Transnational Feminism, Neoliberal Citizenship, and the Gendering of Women's Political Subjectivity in Postconflict South Sudan. *Signs: Journal of Women in Culture and Society*, 36(3), pp. 627–652.

Evans, M. and Lunn, K. (Eds.), 1997. *War and Memory in the Twentieth Century*. Oxford, Berg Publishers.

Felbermayr, G.J. and Toubal, F., 2010. Cultural proximity and trade. *European Economic Review*, 54(2), pp. 279–293.

Fukuyama, F., 1995. *Trust: The Social Virtues and the Creation of Prosperity*. New York, The Free Press.

Glantz, M.D. and Sloboda, Z., 2002. Analysis and reconceptualization of resilience. In M.D. Glantz and J.L. Johnson (Eds.), *Resilience and Development. Longitudinal Research in the Social and Behavioral Sciences: An Interdisciplinary Series*. Boston, MA, Springer. https://doi.org/10.1007/0-306-47167-1_6.

Hernandez, P., 2002. Resilience in families and communities: Latin American contributions from the psychology of liberation. *The Family Journal*, 10(3), pp. 334–343.

Herrenkohl, E.C., Herrenkohl, R.C. and Egolf, B., 1994. Resilient early school-age children from maltreating homes: Outcomes in late adolescence. *American Journal of Orthopsychiatry*, 64(2), pp. 301–309.

Hirblinger, A.T. and Simons, C., 2015. The good, the bad, and the powerful: Representations of the 'local' in peacebuilding. *Security Dialogue*, 46(5), pp. 422–439.

Jensen, P.M. and Jacobsen, U.C., 2020. Augmenting proximity theories: including other proximities in the transnational travel of Danish television drama. In *Danish Television Drama*, pp. 169–186. Cham, Palgrave Macmillan.

Justino, P., 2009. Poverty and violent conflict: A micro-level perspective on the causes and duration of warfare. *Journal of Peace Research*, 46(3), pp. 315–333.

Justino, P., 2012, September. Resilience in protracted crises: Exploring coping mechanisms and resilience of households, communities and local institutions. In *High-Level Expert Forum on Food Security in Protracted Crises, Rome, September* (Vol. 13), p. 14.

Kaplan, H.B., 2005. Understanding the concept of resilience. In S. Goldstein, R.B. Brooks (Eds.), *Handbook of Resilience in Children*, pp. 39–47. Boston, MA, Springer.

Krishna, A., 2002. *Active Social Capital: Tracing the Roots of Development and Democracy*. New York Chichester, West Sussex, Columbia University Press.

Lee, A.R., Hon, L. and Won, J., 2018. Psychological proximity as a predictor of participation in a social media issue campaign. *Computers in Human Behavior*, 85, pp. 245–254.

Liberman, N., Trope, Y. and Stephan, E., 2007. Psychological distance. *Social Psychology: Handbook of Basic Principles*, 2, pp. 353–383.

Lindström, B., 2001. The meaning of resilience. *International Journal of Adolescent Medicine and Health*, 13(1), pp. 7–12.

Lederach, J.P., 2005. *The Moral Imagination: The Art and Soul of Building Peace*. New York, Oxford University Press.

Longley, C. and Maxwell, D., 2003. *Livelihoods, Chronic Conflict and Humanitarian Response: A Synthesis of Current Practice*. London, ODI.

Lösel, F., Bliesener, T. and Köferl, P., 1989. On the concept of invulnerability: Evaluation and first results of the Bielefeld project. In Michael Brambring, Friedrich Lösel, and Helmut Skowronek (Eds.), *Children at Risk: Assessment, Longitudinal Research, and Intervention*, pp. 186–219. De Gruyter.

Masten, A.S., 2001. Ordinary magic. Resilience processes in development. *American Psychologist*, 56(3), 227–238. DOI: 10.1037//0003-066x.56.3.227. PMID: 11315249.

Newton, K., 1997. Social capital and democracy. *American Behavioral Scientist*, 40(5), pp. 575–586.

Ogbozor, E., 2016. Resilience to violent extremism: The rural livelihood coping strategies in the lake chad basin. *Households in Conflict Network Working Paper*, Vol. 237.

Osirim, M.J., 2008. African women in the new diaspora: Transnationalism and the (re) creation of home. *African and Asian Studies*, 7(4), pp. 367–394.

Putnam, R.D., 1993. *Making Democracy Work*. Princeton, NJ, Princeton University Press.

Radke-Yarrow, M. and Sherman, T., 1990. Hard growing: Children who survive. In J. E. Rolf, A. S. Masten, D. Cicchetti, K. H. Nuechterlein, and S. Weintraub (Eds.),

Risk and Protective Factors in the Development of Psychopathology, pp. 97–119. Cambridge University Press. https://doi.org/10.1017/CBO9780511752872.008.

Rauh, H., 1989. The meaning of risk and protective factors in infancy. *European Journal of Psychology of Education*, 4(2), pp. 161–173.

Reagon, B.J., 1986. African diaspora women: The making of cultural workers. *Feminist Studies*, 12(1), pp. 77–90.

Seibert, S.E., Kraimer, M.L. and Liden, R.C., 2001. A social capital theory of career success. *Academy of Management Journal*, 44(2), pp. 219–237.

Seligman, A.B., 1992. *The Idea of Civil Society*. New York, Free Press.

Shaw, A.T. and Gilly, J.P., 2000. On the analytical dimension of proximity dynamics. *Regional Studies*, 34(2), pp.169–180.

Simonse, S. and Kurimoto, E. (Eds.), 2011. Engaging 'Monyomiji', Bridging the Gap in East Bank Equatoria: Proceedings of the Conference 26–28 November 2009, pp. 2–129. Nairobi, Pax Christi Horn of Africa.

Sorenson, J., 1991. Mass media and discourse on famine in the Horn of Africa. *Discourse and Society*, 2(2), pp. 223–242.

Souffrant, E. (Ed.), 2016. *A Future without Borders? Theories and Practices of Cosmopolitan Peacebuilding*. Leiden, Brill.

Spence, A., Poortinga, W. and Pidgeon, N., 2012. The psychological distance of climate change. *Risk Analysis: An International Journal*, 32(6), pp. 957–972.

Tankink, M. and Richters, A., 2007. Silence as a coping strategy: The case of refugee women in the Netherlands from South-Sudan who experienced sexual violence in the context of war. In J-C. Métraux (Eds.), *Voices of Trauma*, pp. 191–210. Boston, MA, Springer.

Trope, Y. and Liberman, N., 2010. Construal-level theory of psychological distance. *Psychological Review*, 117(2), p. 440.

Tomlinson, J., 2000. Proximity politics. *Information, Communication and Society*, 3(3), pp. 402–414.

Wagnild, G. and Young, H.M., 1990. Resilience among older women. *Image: The Journal of Nursing Scholarship*, 22(4), pp. 252–255.

Vasquez, J.A., 1995. Why do neighbors fight? Proximity, interaction, or territoriality. *Journal of Peace Research*, 32(3), pp. 277–293.

Windle, M., 1999. Critical conceptual and measurement issues in the study of resilience. In M.D. Glantz and J.L. Johnson (Eds.), *Resilience and Development: Positive Life Adaptations*, pp. 161–176. New York, Kluwer Academic/Plenum Publishers.

Winter, J., 2006. Notes on the memory boom. In D. Bell (Eds.), *Memory, Trauma and World Politics*. London, Palgrave Macmillan. https://doi.org/10.1057/9780230627482_3

Winter, C., 2015. Ritual, remembrance and war: Social memory at Tyne Cot. *Annals of Tourism Research*, 54, pp. 16–29.

Zamyatina, N.Y. and Pilyasov, A.N., 2017. Concept of proximity: Foreign experience and prospects of application in Russia. *Regional Research of Russia*, 7(3), pp. 197–207. https://doi.org/10.1134/S2079970517030108

9 Summary and Conclusion

Introduction

This study's research aim was to explore the Nilotic Lwo (Dinka, Nuer, Acholi and Anyuak) indigenous mechanisms employed in conflict prevention, peacebuilding and peacemaking in the South Sudan civil war situation. As a conclusion, this chapter provides an overview of the main findings and recommendations based on the study objectives stated in Chapter 1. These main findings, discussed in the previous chapters, include:

i) Socialisation: The significance of relationships, food and drinks.
ii) Etiquette: The manner in which indigenous peacebuilding processes are conducted.
iii) Traditional roles of youth, women or mothers in indigenous peacebuilding.
iv) Cosmic relations: The significance of spiritual authority in peacebuilding.
v) The significance of resilience, proximity and social capital in national peacebuilding. These concepts were derived during the post-research period.

The research questions set out and answered include:

i. What indigenous peacebuilding approaches do the Nilotic Lwo (Dinka, Nuer, Acholi and Anuak) have to intra-ethnic and inter-ethnic disputes resolutions?
ii. How do people who have the knowledge and experience in both indigenous approaches to ethnic indigenous peacebuilding and the civil war understand them?
iii. How can these indigenous approaches be utilised to deliver sustainable peace during conflict and post-civil war situations?

Also, responses from interviews and literature on peace theories have helped shape the above research questions. For instance, work by Lederach (1996, 1997, 2012), Galtung (1990, 1996, 2004) and Ramsbotham et al.

DOI: 10.4324/9781003133476-10

(2005) demonstrates the significance of localised solutions. The Nilotic Lwo approaches to peacebuilding have been described throughout the book. In addition, the use of Douglas' cultural theory, Gramsci's hegemony and Asante's Afrocentricity (Douglas, 1966, 1970, 1973, 1992; Sedgwick and Edgar, 2002; Gramsci, 1992; Asante, 2003; Jeong, 2005; Latigo, 2008) as lenses through which Nilotic Lwo peace cultures should be viewed.

Through these lenses, the book explained how significant people, institutions, norms, customary laws, beliefs and practices are to resolving the South Sudan civil war. Also, this work has provided an understanding of the Nilotic Lwo indigenous peace cultures or approaches and helped narrow the gap with the westernised methods of Lederach (1996, 1997, 2012), Galtung (1990, 1996, 2004) and Ramsbotham et al. (2005). Eurocentric ideas presented by Ramsbotham et al. place third-party involvement at the core. However, the analysis ignores communities and indigenous cultures, particularly in the national peacebuilding processes. Yet this book argues indigenous approaches align with Afrocentric cultural theories, which are pragmatic and contextual.

Some ethnographic and anthropological concepts of the cultural theory were utilised in the narrative inquiry process. In addition, the analysis of the literature and interviews contributed critical information. The interviewees told stories about their life experiences (i.e. their involvement in customs, beliefs, practices, conflicts and conflict resolution). Further interviews were conducted on other concepts (social capital, resilience and proximities) crucial in uniting the diasporas and locals to achieve national peacebuilding. The broader themes of these Nilotic Lwo peace cultures are summarised as follows:

i) Socialising. The significance of relationships, food and drink. In view of cultural theory (Douglas, 1970; Cashmore and Rojek, 1999), these practices help organise people at all levels to achieve a social goal.
ii) Etiquette. The manner in which indigenous peacebuilding processes are conducted. Considering Douglas' (1966) work, etiquette influences people's behaviour through oaths and symbolic acts of purification, such as 'stepping on an egg' (Nyono Tong Gweno). These cultural acts are contextual given Afrocentric ideas (Asante, 2003) and, therefore, significant regarding South Sudan civil war resolution.
iii) Traditional roles of youth. In the light of Gramsci's hegemony (Gramsci, 1992), the youth (Monyomiji) is a traditional institution through which socio-cultural control and moral leadership in the civil war resolution can be achieved.
iv) Subtle roles of women or mothers in indigenous peacebuilding. For instance, taking note of Douglas (1992), Nilotic women's motherhood roles help us understand specific new perspectives that may shift the social positioning in the conventional male-dominated areas of national peacebuilding. According to Afrocentric arguments, women's

204 Summary and Conclusion

knowledge of culture and facilitation roles imply that the Nilotic Lwo interests, values and perspectives predominate peacebuilding (Asante, 2003).

v) Cosmic relations. The significance of spiritual authority in peacebuilding. Considering cultural theory (Douglas, 1966), beliefs reinforce social pressures. Belief in the supernatural is a significant aspect of Nilotic Lwo cultures, which all members observed. Beliefs are an essential unifying feature in the civil war resolution (see Figure 9.1).

Considering the theoretical conceptualisation, this book argues that indigenous features, or Nilotic Lwo cultures, are crucial to a contextual resolution of the civil war. However, the conventional/international approaches embedded in standard peace theories and the past and existing conflict resolution attempts (see Chapter 2) focus on Eurocentric ideas which do not incorporate indigenous cultures. Therefore, a significant conclusion is that Nilotic Lwo cultures should take a central place in national peacebuilding. Third parties should understand and support the cultural (Nilotic Lwo) structures and practices (see Figure 9.1).

Most of South Sudan's ethnic communities live traditional lives in traditional settings (Jok et al., 2004). Therefore, subtle roles played by societal groups are crucial in keeping societies at peace. This thesis highlights that colonialism led to the breakdown of some of these traditional institutions and structures of

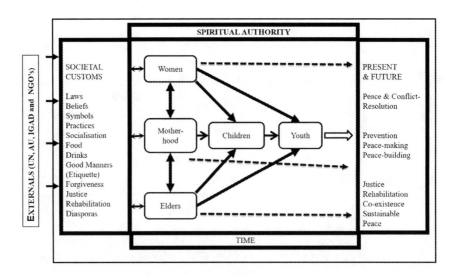

Figure 9.1 The Proposed Sustainable Indigenous Peacebuilding Model

power and authority (Poku and Mdee, 2013). While some indigenous methods have been revived to deal with civil war crimes, for example, in Acholi communities Latigo (2008), they are mainly implanted at local, not national levels.

This research sits firmly in the information domain instead of the public administration domain but may be used to inform current policies. It does not seek to impose a theoretical policy framework but proposes a pragmatic theory—the indigene-centric approach to peacebuilding. Given cultural and Afrocentric theories, Nilotic Lwo peace cultures are sensible, suitable and efficient. This study is not intended to test the efficiency of the current South Sudanese or conventional peacebuilding systems, methods and interventions. It is specifically about highlighting the potential for indigenous peacebuilding processes in resolving a national conflict. It provides a robust learning framework from which knowledge can be drawn because these indigenous approaches analysed here are capable of dealing with civil war crimes. Other African governments are utilising similar approaches. For example, the concept of Ubuntu runs throughout Botswana government institutions, as documented by the Presidential Task Group (Bedigen, 2017). Further evidence presented on the utilisation of Gacaca courts in Rwanda indicates that indigenous peacebuilding concepts can be fully incorporated into the justice system to help deal with post-civil war crimes (Bedigen, 2019). A similar example, the Ujamaa in Tanzania, provides learning and potential for local approaches to societies' political, social and economic development (Nyerere, 1968).

Considering the above, this research was inspired by the concern that inter-ethnic conflicts, which feed into civil wars, have persisted in South Sudan. Despite numerous conventional resolution attempts, national peace remains elusive. This is due to the marginalisation of indigenous approaches that are instrumental in local peacebuilding. For instance, the regional government's Intergovernmental Authority on Development (IGAD) negotiations, the UN peacekeeping force and the AU mission and mediation have intervened majorly politically (Bedigen, 2017). In addition, there have been government (Sudan and South Sudan) interventions, which include counter-insurgency, diplomacy and power-sharing (de Waal and Flint, 2005; Prunier, 2005; Bedigen, 2017). Summarised by Bedigen (2019), other small-scale (inter-ethnic) local-level interventions include the Wunlit Dinka–Nuer peace conference of 1999, organised by the NSCC; the Waat convention of 1999 and the Liliir peace conference of 2000.

However, despite conventional peacebuilding attempts, millions of lives have been lost and millions more people displaced internally. Intermittent conflicts have continued since 1983, and refugees have fled to neighbouring countries (Ogot, 1999; de Waal and Flint, 2005; Prunier, 2005; Iyob and Khadiagala, 2006; Allison, 2016). These failures highlight that the methods utilised by international and regional governments are not singly effective in situations where inter-ethnic conflicts feed into civil wars—thus, the need to include indigenous methods.

206 Summary and Conclusion

This research was conducted on conflicts among ethnic groups under study to understand the usability of Nilotic Lwo indigenous peacebuilding methods in the civil war, plus the origins and linkage of inter-ethnic conflicts and the civil wars (in Chapter 2). Other grassroots peace writers, such as de Waal and Flint (2005), indicate that disputes between two ethnic groups spill over into other ethnic communities, regions and neighbouring countries. This analysis strongly suggests that inter-ethnic conflicts and the national conflict (civil war) are distinct but connected. Therefore, any resolution attempt has to target both separately and consistently. The findings show that indigenous approaches to local-level conflicts or inter-ethnic peacebuilding have distinctive features. Note that national, regional and conventional peace processes have generalised approaches to peacebuilding, exacerbating elusive peace. It is recommended that peace actors make careful choices by considering the peace culture of the ethnic community/communities in question.

Figure 9.1 model proposes what indigenous peacebuilding should look like and how externals can be involved. It places the externals (UN, AU, IGAD and NGOs) or peace actors from foreign countries at the periphery. Actors must become involved via communities and their societal customs, not directly. The diagram emphasises that externals' involvement should be through indigenous systems or structures. These systems include the community members' (i.e. women/mothers and elders) institutions. These structures draw indigenous peacebuilding knowledge from the members of the societal customs. The model demonstrates that women, motherhood and elders influence children, who grow into youth who become instrumental in conflict prevention, peacemaking and peacebuilding.

The long-term plan must be based on community projects that encourage and support indigenous education in societal values. These values enable youth (Monyomiji) to take control of their community's future, including peacebuilding. Shorter (1974:77) explains this further in his work, indicating that 'in traditional society, the child was introduced to wider responsibility within society through progressive, formal instruction and ritual.'

Given the nature of the inter-ethnic conflicts and civil wars in South Sudan, it became necessary to review the literature and explore peacebuilding attempts that have been implemented since 1983. This is because crimes from this period are similar to those committed during historical inter-ethnic conflicts. Johnson and Anderson (1995) elaborate on these crimes. Historically, these conflicts/crimes grouped under murder, assault or property (see Chapter 2) were resolved locally, using indigenous peacebuilding methods (Jok et al., 2004; Bradbury et al., 2006; Harlacher, 2009). Thus, the argument here is that they can be applied in civil war situations.

As analysed in the previous chapters, indigenous institutions resolve historical inter-ethnic conflict. They include Monyomiji/Honyomiji, Mato

Oput, Gurtong, Gomo Tong, Mabior, Ekisil and others. Despite their existence, peace actors seem not aware that they are alternatives. They have consistently implemented more conventional methods, despite their failures. For instance, these conventional measures do not address the root causes of conflicts in the manner that the indigenous process does. Also, they have not encouraged inter-ethnic or national peacebuilding, which is central to indigenous systems analysed here.

It concludes that all the conventional peacebuilding attempts consist of broadly constructed features and events unfamiliar to South Sudanese conflict contexts and indigenous reconciliation cultures. For example, they involve seminars, workshops and conferences that aim at signing peace deals that never last. These formal processes have excluded the fundamentals of indigenous processes. For instance, grassroots peacebuilding processes such as the Waat convention and the Wunlit Dinka–Nuer and Liliir conferences reveal some significant indigenous peacebuilding features such as meetings, speeches, timing and prayers. At the same time, it excluded critical features such as sharing, visitation and relationship building. Yet, conventional elements are incorporated into 'grassroots' peacebuilding processes without carefully examining their effectiveness and value.

From their work, it appears that the NSCC identified this gap and then took upon itself the task of organising local peace processes, as well as representing culture and religion, during political peacebuilding negotiations. Alex de Waal (2014) points to the work of the NSCC under William Lawrey, which led to the Wunlit agreement. It is essential to point out that, contrary to its claim to represent culture, the NSCC did not recommend or campaign for any traditional customs to be utilised (Bedigen, 2019). Thus, its claim to represent culture is less convincing and dissuades communities from standing up for indigenous peacebuilding processes. This matches an argument by Ogot that the locals can be deprived of opportunities (1999), particularly by certain actors who are not in favour of indigenous cultures. This research suggests that, before any peacebuilding attempt, peace actors should consult with the locals and suggest approaches that reflect familiar community interests that are embedded in indigenous institutions and societal customs (customary laws, beliefs and practices).

In addition to the above, an Anyuak interviewee, Deng, sums up the core argument in this thesis—placing indigenous practices at the foundation of sustainable peacebuilding. He writes:

> We say, '*Te okono obur pe luputu*' – 'You must not uproot the pumpkin in the old homestead'; and 'he who rejects the mother stone starves to death'. They both mean the same thing. You cannot cut yourself off from your origin or culture; you cannot reject your mother, even if she is blind or disfigured, because if you do so, you die; never to be buried or remembered. Your relatives will be ashamed to bring your

208 Summary and Conclusion

bones back home to bury. This is us now; we said we wanted to govern ourselves, our own African culture, different from that of Arabs in the North, so we gained independence. But we forgot all about what makes us South Sudanese: culture ... and we are killing each other again.

(Deng, 15 August 2014)

The above highlights that while protracted conflicts have many dimensions, any resolution measures that are alien to the community, or exclude these cultures, remain unsuitable to the local contexts and therefore fail. Moreover, it points out that civil war crimes are similar to historical inter-ethnic crimes. Thus, implementing unfamiliar conventional peacebuilding concepts is not entirely necessary. In light of the theoretical conceptualisation, it is crucial to include useful features such as beliefs in the supernatural, symbols, manners, the use of food and drink in peacebuilding, in particular, cosmic relations (spiritual authority), socialising, etiquette and the traditional roles of youth and women/mothers (see Figure 9.2). This book noted an existing gap in the representation of these indigenous systems at national levels. It stressed that to realise sustainable peace, subtle norms could be recultivated through education in societal values.

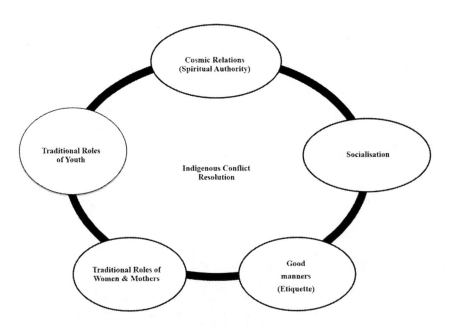

Figure 9.2 Components of an Indigenous Conflict Resolution

Socialising—The Significance of Relationships, Food and Drink

Conventional peacebuilding attempts in South Sudan have excluded traditional cultures that include socialising, food, drink, the restoration of relationships and co-existence (Machar, 2015; Latigo, 2008). Such cultural practices implemented during peacebuilding processes include socialising by the victim's and perpetrator's families/communities through food and drink (Douglas, 1973; Cashmore and Rojek, 1999). This book has shown that customary practices that encourage socialising through food and drink are deeply embedded in indigenous cultures, so they are the preferred course of action in South Sudan. Yet, there is no evidence of their meaningful application in the civil war political conflict negotiation, mediation and agreements by external actors (Wol, 2014). By deconstructing socialising in the Nilotic Lwo practices, three things can be achieved, that is, conflict resolution, restoration of relationships and co-existence (Latigo, 2008). Examples include women from neighbouring communities coming together to weave, wearing Loketio to prevent conflicts and engaging in joint celebrations of conflict prevention and conflict resolution marriages. This resonates with p'Bitek's (1966) views which demonstrate the significance of traditional lifestyles in addressing societal issues. The findings show that socialising features can be contextualised within contemporary national peacebuilding.

Further, the findings demonstrate that Nilotic Lwo's socialising practices include ceremonies and rituals that include animal and crop sacrifices. Examples of such ceremonies and rituals relevant to the civil war are discussed, including the significance of specific crops or food, such as sesame, wild honey, millet and black-eyed bean leaves. Interviewee narratives reveal that these crops are eaten with reverence and belief in a positive outcome during ceremonies. Biologically, these crops offer healing and nutritional values, and they are a symbol of peace, as they are shared after ceremonies/rituals have taken place. A unique attribute of food crops in indigenous peacebuilding is that they help reignite community peace meetings or communication. Additionally, they contribute to post-conflict rehabilitation.

Therefore, in utilising food and drink for socialising, conflict prevention, peacebuilding and peacemaking are achieved. As is demonstrated in Deng's account (seen earlier), this is an aspect that cannot be separated or uprooted from indigenous peacebuilding processes. It is concluded that indigenous methods that embrace the utilisation of crops are inclusive, practical and widely acceptable among the South Sudanese. They are also relevant in modern contexts. The danger is that sacrifices of food crops are not considered significant aspects of grassroots peace initiatives where externals are involved—for example, in the Wunlit, Waat and Liliir conferences. No emphasis was placed on what kind of food should be available for these processes.

210 Summary and Conclusion

This book concludes that the politics of governments (national; regional—IGAD; and international—the USA and China) affected how the origins of conflicts were perceived or addressed through socialising and the 'one culture' the South Sudanese possess. In view of inter-ethnic conflicts and civil war resolution attempts, government politics in Sudan, South Sudan and the region (the Horn of Africa) have crippled inter-ethnic relationships and national unity, even before 1983. Further, we saw the 'spirit of togetherness' Ubuntu or Ujamaa or Diel or Cieng or Nyuak or Kacoke Madit, the Nilotic Lwo concept of 'brotherhood,' has, in many ways, contributed negatively to reconciliation processes. It has hindered moves towards cohesion due to its political manipulation. For instance, the findings demonstrate that 'brotherhood' has at times caused or escalated conflicts because in most instances, kinsmen are politically inspired to support each other. Moreover, traditionally, it is considered taboo not to help a clan member, irrespective of who the perpetrator is. Kin loyalties in ethnic communities are significant, as indicated by Shorter (1974). In addition, although historical inter-ethnic disputes exist, politics 'provoke' and resolutions that exclude socialising are politically pursued. Thus, resolution attempts excluded subtle norms—making sustainable peace elusive (Prunier, 2005). As demonstrated in Deng's narrative below, any political or non-political peacebuilding attempts that ignore subtle norms remain precarious. Deng narrates:

> We are from the same stalk; we are *brothers*. This peace, without consideration of our ancestry, will not be realised. We all believe in and respect our culture, so it should be the foundation. Anything else, like politics or democracy, should be rooted in it. Otherwise, our country will never achieve peace or exploit its potential; South Sudan will be like a tree with withered roots or an anthill without the queen.
> (Deng, 12 December 2014)

As indicated in the above account, socialising is productive when all actors and partnerships get to understand each other. Further in Chapter 2, selected theories (i.e. the bottom-up theory, Peacebuilding from Below and Galtung's model) attempt to explain what indigenous peacebuilding should be. Yet, such theories exclude local socialising methods that strengthen peacebuilding, i.e. sharing food and drink. For instance, they explore local resources and cultures but do not go deep enough to explore what these local resources or cultures are, nor how they should be implemented in indigenous processes through socialising.

This book notes that the bottom-up, peacebuilding from below and Galtung's model peace theories mainly focus on promoting partnerships and third-party involvement in grassroots peacebuilding, most predominantly the partnerships between local elites and external organisations, not disputants and the state (Ramsbotham et al., 2005; Lederach, 1996, 1997, 2004). Such theories exclude the practice of partnership and socialising between the communities in conflict. In reality, these theories help expose the wide gap between theoretical models, peace actors/actions and what is practical in a proper indigenous process. They place peacebuilding in a 'technical' context, not a social one as indigenous processes.

When these theorists and western peace actors talk of partnerships, the inclusion of local resources, cultures and religion, they refer to cultural/ traditional leaders but not the culture(s) to which these leaders belong (Ramsbotham et al., 2005). Once they have identified such leaders, they advocate for robust third-party involvement based on conventional principles and approaches, not local/traditional methods.

Practically, these western-oriented theories place local resources or leaders in the hands of externals with minimal knowledge of the local cultures—thus leading to the coercive 'education' of community leaders in conventional models of peacebuilding. In the South Sudan civil war, 'local approaches' framed on conventional models only suit external actors' ideals. Given this, findings suggest that third-party, or externals', involvement has at most contributed to conflict settlement rather than peacebuilding (Bedigen, 2017). This book suggests that actors in national peace processes limit their control and liaise with the whole community instead of hand-picking leaders. This is because, in indigenous perspectives, a partnership is about the entire society.

A hybrid peacebuilding approach similar to Truth and Reconciliation Commissions (TRCs) was proposed as a potential approach to South Sudan's peace—this time, named Transitional Justice/Reconciliation, where a hybrid court would be established. Its judges would be appointed by the African Union Community (AUC), Bedigen (2019) document. In reality, TRCs convey something of the mixed traditional–western principles of peacebuilding and, therefore, cannot represent a proper indigenous process. Their focus commands reconciliation, but it is a political showcase that can mainly replicate failures. In support of the above, balancing justice and community unity and co-existence can be complex when applying TRCs. TRCs float between retribution and restoration (Bedigen, 2017). Yet this work suggests that what can work well, with minimal influence from TRCs, are traditional institutions and practices.

Given the theoretical conceptualisation of the study (Douglas, 1966, 1970, 1973, 1992; Gramsci, 1992, 1995; Asante, 2003), cultural practices implemented during socialising encourage participation, partnership, social interaction and communication, which, in the long run, contribute to peace sustainability. Therefore, cultural norms, practices and beliefs must be central to indigenous peacebuilding—thus the development of an indigene-centred approach to peacebuilding (see Figure 9.1). For example, Turo chogo 'breaking the right thigh bone,' Gurtong 'to blunt the spear' and the use of blood and liver are appropriate ceremonies. Peace actors may try their best, but subtle features such as customary practices embrace socialising, a feature often excluded in national peacebuilding.

In previous interventions in other African countries, conventional methods and TRCs have approached peacebuilding by praising traditional institutions. Thus, they include the victims, perpetrators and traditional leaders but have excluded the culture itself. Generally, conventional methods and TRCs are concerned with restructuring governments, policies and political leadership rather than grassroots institutions. Thus, this book suggests they start by re-establishing indigenous values. This might call for the adaptation of relevant local aspects rather than the importation of methods from further afield.

In this section, the book pointed out that socialising through sharing food and drink can refresh stale relationships. This section has indicated how conventional approaches have ignored this aspect and instead have dwelt on technical aspects. For instance, traditional theories that encourage working with the local people never mention socialising. Additionally, politics has worsened these processes over the years because it aims at signing agreements, not rebuilding social cohesion. Thus, if socialising is to be considered by external actors, they ought to be educated on its cultural significance to avoid introducing other methods from further afield. For instance, the TRCs often partly embrace aspects of local cultures, excluding its holistic application.

Good Manners (Etiquette)

This section analyses behavioural codes during indigenous peacebuilding processes. In East African traditional families, much emphasis is placed on cultural behaviour, both home and away (Shorter, 1974). The findings demonstrate that what international peace actors consider indigenous etiquette is less of its content. Additionally, it noted that community-based peacebuilding traits are misunderstood or misrepresented by certain western actors (de Waal and Flint, 2005; Prunier, 2005; Bedigen, 2017), including some African writers (Jok et al., 2004). Moreover, interviewee accounts indicate that the failure of a disputant to observe the other's etiquette during peacebuilding can lead to communication breakdown and the withdrawal of the offended party from the process. For example, Wibo mentioned that the failed Wunlit agreement was due to a lack of employment of indigenous behavioural code (Wibo, December 2011).

Further, Asante's (2003) work on the black perspective demonstrates that etiquette is at the core of African cultures and makes a unique contribution to peacebuilding. The reason being, these cultures encourage hospitality, friendliness, empathy, modesty, cleanliness, humility, kindness, language use, brotherly love and the unity of mind and purpose. These cultural aspects are not highly regarded in national peacebuilding processes.

This study found that what constitutes local peace processes must include etiquette associated with how peace actors dress, talk, sit, eat and generally interact with local communities. It agrees with Asante (2003), who indicates that behavioural codes (i.e. dress, dance and language) are an outward

Summary and Conclusion 213

demonstration of what one likes or treasures. The manner in which the process is handled has a significant bearing on the resolution outcome. As explored in Chapter 2, 'good manners' have historically enabled sustainable indigenous peace processes among the Nilotic people and their neighbours. Drawing from the Wunlit conference report (of 1999) and the discussions in Chapters 4–6, any peace processes that do not adhere to the cultures of those in conflict are destined to fail. For example, in Chapter 4, Rosie's and Samwiri's stories highlight how mannerisms can negatively influence peace processes. These two stories—one representing a conventional, the other an indigenous setting—demonstrate that etiquette is not a unique concept in peace and peacebuilding. This has since been found to be true in the case of South Sudan. No holistic traditional process (that embraces traditional etiquette) has been applied nationally (Bedigen, 2017).

This research highlighted how customary practices, which include mannerisms, have been utilised to resolve issues that could not have been dealt with in any other way. In these cases, the research discussed only customary laws or practices related to and useful for civil war crimes. Various peace obligations in traditional institutions, ceremonies and practises useful at community, inter-community and national levels are discussed. It is important to note that while these customary obligations may be relevant at all levels, the possibility of implementing them at a national level remains unexplored, as evidenced in the South Sudan national peacebuilding agreement (Bedigen, 2019). This research emphasises that relevant peace agencies should include etiquette in indigenous processes to develop a workable solution to the South Sudan situation. In support of this, Edelstein (2011) suggests that ignoring or violating cultural customs (e.g. etiquette such as dress code) can inadvertently result in the rejection of essential information.

Wearing decent clothes is considered morally right or good behaviour, such that externals (for example, NGO peace actors) or locals (such as Grace) who refuse to comply, for instance, by wearing trousers, would be breaking the law. The dress code does not only apply to local women but also to outsiders who engage in women empowerment and development projects. NGO community peace and reconciliation members working on Dinka–Nuer community dialogue initiatives were underlooked due to some staff's non-native dress code. Dogra (2011:345) argues that western-style dressing by local women and NGO workers 'connotes development and modernity brought by the NGO .... through the vehicle of the NGO local staff, whose dress symbolises her status as being closer to Western women, thereby giving her legitimacy' to empower others through western-initiated development and empowerment programmes. Moreover, a strict dress code may not be an issue in urban settings where western types of dressing, particularly trousers, are perceived as expressions of empowerment and traditional dresses repressive (Dogra, 2011:342). In adhering to the community's strict dress code, individuals submit to a culture from which cultural norms are used to inform societal rules that empower them. In many respects, this dual submission enables women to voice their opinions and be heard—thus, the significance of self-representation in indigenous empowerment.

Adding to the above, indigenous etiquette is consistent with its past and present. Behavioural code is reflected and meditated upon during the peacebuilding socialising processes through folk songs, stories and jokes (see Efo's interview). For instance, songs that encourage peace are composed about how attractive the other community generally presents itself. Such expressions of behavioural codes define societies and promote peaceful co-existence. This is contrary to western approaches, where the focus is on the technical aspects of negotiation, mediation and the signing of agreements (de Waal, 2014).

This book suggests that any peacebuilding process that ignores a given community's positive historical indigenous behavioural code ignores its future. This view is supported by Ogot (1999) and Mbiti (1970) in their discussions of African concepts of time, indicating that all significant events in an African setting are marked into seasons. Therefore, there must be coherence in behavioural code and time, as one can inadvertently affect the other. The reason is that behavioural code has to be linked to the community customs.

While it is noted that etiquette is not a unique aspect of peace processes and that it applies to both modern and traditional contexts, customary behavioural codes are sidelined at foreign-led and national levels of peacebuilding. It is argued that cultural behaviours that are regarded as morally right or sound in a given community are ageless and so must not be ignored or regarded as obstacles to peacebuilding but should be included.

Subtle Roles of Youth in Peacebuilding

Traditionally, youth are trained in societal behavioural codes and are expected to undergo some purposely designed trials, administered according to their respective age groups. The Monyomiji is an ethnic youth and traditional youth governance or leadership system. The term translates as the 'owners or fathers of the village' who manage the community's political, social and economic affairs (Bedigen, 2019:2). It is a crucial indigenous institution that makes decisions on land disputes and protects the community's interest (Grawert, 2014:144)—thus ought to be included in national peacebuilding. It is tasked with preserving these societal behavioural codes for future generations as an institution. While this particular youth role is less written about, authors such as Simonse and Kurimoto (2011) have explored youth's political leadership role within a traditional setting, for example, their participation in signing the 2005 CPA that took place in Kenya (Bedigen, 2017). Also, findings indicate that their role extends far beyond a political one—interviewees indicate they fight against marginalisation.

Since their return from the front line in the 1980s, the youth have become a formidable force, invigorated through the Monyomiji structure, in those communities that practise this traditional leadership system. In the broader context of the South Sudan conventional peacebuilding processes, the significance of grassroots youth actions has been redefined in different ways, such as the Monyomiji conferences, seminars and workshops. For instance, Monyomiji as a conventional-style youth conference was attended by the Tombe Monyomi of Central Equatoria. Moreover, this traditional holistic structure itself has never been officially included in the IGAD peace processes (Bedigen, 2019). Interviewee stories, and Sellie's in particular, reveal how the Lulubo community is solely dependent on the Monyomiji social, economic and political system. This is a view supported by Bedigen's (2017) argument that, when faced with conflict situations, we often tend to revert to past experiences.

While, at times, its security roles can be compromised in that village defenders become neighbours' aggressors, the Monyomiji system brings to light the significance of traditional youth participation in peacebuilding. Such is achieved through apprenticeships, campaigns, provision of security and defence of culture or community's future. Bedigen (2019) indicates that youth must be involved in conflict resolution processes. As is illustrated in Figure 9.1, youth are instrumental in ensuring transformation and sustainable peace.

Next, this book discusses the role of women/mothers, who are often well equipped for peacebuilding.

Subtle Roles of Honyomiji Women/Mothers in Peacebuilding

Bedigen (2021) highlights the significance of women's participation in conflict resolution processes and stresses their social role functions within a local women's institution (Honyomiji). Findings demonstrate that, much as women are not visible at the national political negotiation table, they play subtle roles in the family, intra-ethnic and inter-ethnic peacebuilding. Regarding the everyday challenges that women in war zones face, it is necessary to look into ordinary women's cultural beliefs, practices and experiences. Women have contributed much to local ways of preventing, discussing, managing and resolving armed conflicts. Also, various alternative lenses through which these cultures can be observed and developed for national peacebuilding have been highlighted. The most challenging obstacle is represented by the possibility of implementing these traditional roles and finding a package through which they can fit into mainstream contemporary conflict contexts. Therefore, this book concludes and recommends that the most transformative project is to invest peace efforts in motherhood and the subtle roles of women. These are found to encourage social cohesion, cultivation and transmission of a peaceful culture (Bedigen, 2021).

Despite being patrilineal, women/mothers are the backbones of Nilotic Lwo traditional communities (Shorter, 1974; Latigo, 2008). Various ways in which women's traditional roles are intertwined in all societal values, including peacebuilding, have been discussed. Interviewees' stories also demonstrate that tensions and disunity within a family, or a community, can persist if women are not culturally rooted in peace values. It has indicated that Nilotic Lwo women's peace roles commence when they are little girls, as learners; once they grow up, it progresses in their marital homes and community. Unlike the conventional approaches, where women participate within the dominant protocols of mediation and negotiation, indigenous processes offer 'unrestricted' creativity. For instance, women utilise their femininity, personal items (Loketio, bangles and beads), the environment and everything in their power for the purposes of peace. Also, it highlights the significance of motherhood in peacebuilding, conflict prevention and peacemaking. This book argues that such beliefs and practices are engineered by women and mothers who sustain peace in a particular community. On the other hand, conventional peace actors perceive women's roles as a dichotomy. That is, those women considered capable are selected and instituted into leadership roles, whereas the majority remain uninvolved in the peace processes (Bedigen et al., 2020).

To empathise, women's pivotal subtle roles in community peacebuilding stress that their relationships with children, men and spirits (through rituals and sacrifices) enhance social cohesion and support sustainable peace.

Next, spiritual authority, the highest power in indigenous peacebuilding, is discussed.

Cosmic Relations—Spiritual Authority

This study recommends that spiritual authority be included in peace processes. It influences forgiveness, healing, examination of conscience and control which are crucial. It influences forgiveness, healing and self-examination. Expounding on this, belief in the supernatural being (God) as the most significant authority makes sense to the Nilotic Lwo because it controls the community's economic, social and political aspects (p'Bitek, 1966; Mbiti, 1970). Such a belief is community derived. Also, such beliefs are derived from people's own experiences, reinforcing the social pressures that bond people (Douglas, 1970; Cashmore and Rojek, 1999). Adding, Asante (2003:5) indicates, 'All people create their religions out of their histories.' In resolving community issues, including peacebuilding, belief in the supernatural helps the Nilotic Lwo integrate their experiences, meaning and purpose of life. Given these views, the Nilotic Lwo cultural practices are incomplete without a supernatural involvement and according to Mbiti (1970).

Peace offerings are conducted to ensure that the relationship between humans and the supernatural is not stale. Interviewee narratives demonstrate that customary beliefs (religion and/or symbols) are a significant aspect of Nilotic Lwo indigenous processes. Their omission only results in something less authoritative and thus not respected. This view is supported by Bedigen (2022), who indicates that ethnic communities hierarchically organise themselves under a hierarchy of authority, including spirituality. In Chapters 2 and 4–6, arguments and perspectives demonstrate that beliefs and spiritual connections are essential for a community to thrive. While all good is believed to originate from a supernatural being, all evil is believed to originate from evil spirits, Nueer (the Dinka word for evil spirit) or Lacen (an Acholi word for evil spirit) (Bedigen, 2021). The philosophy here is that evil deeds, or crimes, are spiritually influenced—thus, a need for a spiritual remedy.

The findings demonstrate that spiritual ways to resolve civil wars are never considered or discussed at conventional or IGAD negotiation tables. It is not that the disputants are ignorant of the usefulness of spiritual authority in their communities; the problem is that the resolution processes are not influenced by the disputants or the locals themselves but by the external agencies (Bedigen, 2017). Yet, Bedigen (2022) identifies spirituality as one of the authorities to be included in the South Sudan conflict resolution process. Whereas the locals revere spiritual authority, their peacebuilding representatives have not called for or exploited the potential of spiritual power. Yet, they seem to have exploited the same beliefs to their personal advantage as politics have at times been used to influence spirituality issues.

Further, the findings demonstrate that spiritual beliefs are inseparable from customary practices as similarities exist between Nilotic Lwo cultural–religious practices and biblical scriptures on war and peace. Notably, specific animal body parts are used in the resolution and restoration rituals and ceremonies. For example, the Mabior undefiled or young bull sacrifice and Ekisil have been utilised in resolving war crimes. The challenge here is that conventional or IGAD peace actors are sceptical of religious beliefs and practices and have not explored their potential at the national level of negotiations.

Previous discussions indicated that Christianity, under the NSCC, is the body that represents both culture and religion (Christianity and Islam). Although it would be significant for an influential body such as the NSCC to identify and promote traditional beliefs, (Bedigen, 2017) points to the NSCC's political neutrality in some local peace processes, i.e. the Wunlit, Waat and Liliir conferences. The NSCC work has helped advocate for self-determination. It relentlessly campaigned for South Sudan to separate from Sudan due to the cultural and religious differences and the marginalisation of the southern ethnic communities. The NSCC has advocated forgiveness but has not promoted any other religious beliefs or any of the cultural practices discussed in this thesis. Perhaps this is because they are not actively in favour of indigenous practices. It should be noted that forgiveness might be possible through South Sudan's own TRC framework, as indicated by

Ackerman (1996) in his work on theological and psychological reflections on truth and reconciliation.

Further, beliefs are a matter of conscience that translates into cultural practices where forgiveness is embraced. For instance, Okot p'Bitek (1966) questions the action of Ocol, an Acholi man, who had become a political leader. He hated his brother for belonging to a different political party (Okot p'Bitek, 1966). In his explanation, Ocol's conscience (murderous thoughts) towards his own brother is not right and requires cleansing through the Mato Oput ritual (Bedigen, 2017). Almost all Nilotic Lwo rituals focus on cleansing evil spirits that influence human minds and lead them to do wrong. The involvement of the victim or his family in an indigenous process focuses on forgiveness, letting go and moving on. Conscience and forgiveness are the most powerful tools that can produce genuine peace in any given peacebuilding situation. It is significant to note that these two principles match biblical teachings on conflict, reconciliation and peace. Considering the loss that most South Sudanese have suffered since the start of the civil war, meaningful peace can only be restored through an examination of conscience (by the perpetrators) and forgiveness (by the victims), through their beliefs and practices (Bedigen, 2021).

Psychologically, the conscience of the perpetrator is purged when he/she tells their story in front of the elders. In the process of storytelling, he examines his conscience and repents of his wrongdoing. He or his community pays compensation and then the victim forgives him. This implies that peace begins inwardly through the body and psychological healing. Following, outward peace is evidenced in peace with the environment or involvement in humanitarian activities. Unlike the IGAD process which focuses on the outward political outcomes mostly achieved at the national levels. Others such as Jok et al. (2004) focus on cultural rights, not conscience and human behaviour (Blumberg et al., 2006). Above all, the move by the International Criminal Court (ICC) in hunting for perpetrators demonstrates limitations. This is because implementing justice in South Sudan complex cases requires a spiritual approach or Lacen, who avenges if the perpetrator is unknown or in complex cases beyond human comprehension.

Resilience, Proximity and Social Capital

This chapter discusses three main concepts (i.e. resilience, proximity and social capital) in relation to migrant perspectives, thus providing additional information to the original research. These subtle concepts are less known in peacebuilding, yet they are of significance in everyday lifestyles of the subjects. Their crucial contribution links diasporas' views and attempts at peacebuilding to local approaches. While it seeks to demonstrate that resilience and proximity concepts are inbuilt in peoples' cultures, beliefs and everyday peace practices, and that these two are strengthened by social capital, it recognises that these concepts can promote western approaches and exclude indigenous knowledge and locals.

This 'indigene-centric' or the core set of indigenous institutions, customs and practices underpins the historical and foundational peace values existent in the Nilotic Lwo ethnic groups and the South Sudan justice system. Arguments here utilise migrants' perspectives; reflections of their past, current and future concerns; and the steps some South Sudanese refugees in the Diasporas have taken in contributing to peacebuilding at local levels in their home country. While South Sudan national peacebuilding has been politically led, these discussions demonstrate that resilience and proximity concepts are inbuilt in peoples' cultures, beliefs and everyday peace practices. Adding, it shows that these two are strengthened by social capital in South Sudan and among South Sudanese in the diasporas.

Summarily, the analysis of resilience, proximity and social capital concepts in indigenous peacebuilding is significant in many ways. (1) Ethnic communities under study have historically experienced intermittent conflicts but prevailed, indicating their latent resilience (Bedigen, 2017). (2) At conflict intensities when government or peace agencies are absent (Bedigen, 2019), local resiliences demonstrated through cultures of proximities have enabled inter-ethnic peacebuilding to happen. (3) These concepts are quite well analysed in other disciplines, but remain less discussed in peacebuilding—thus their analysis here contributes new knowledge to peacebuilding. Arguments presented here conclude that interviewees' perspectives (of those at home or in the diaspora) are essential in maintaining networks for local and national peacebuilding.

Summary of Contribution to Knowledge

This book's theoretical contributions are many. First, it suggests that peacebuilding in post-conflict environments should be indigene-centred at local and national levels. Second, by utilising the qualitative narrative method, this book provides a close link that has been forged between theory, method and data—contributing to ethnographic and anthropological methodologies. It argues this particular method is crucial in researching indigenous communities. Third, by exploring intra- and inter-ethnic conflicts, civil wars and subtle peacebuilding norms, this book successfully integrates the research results into existing bottom-up peacebuilding theories—arguably leading to sustainable peace at national levels. It adds that the sociological contribution of norms, including resiliences, proximity and social capital, is clearly shown to contribute to sustainable peace, unlike the politically led measures. Fourth, the indigene-centric focus redirects empirical research in peacebuilding to commence from the local/community level or the disputants' cultures/beliefs/practices. It suggests that the new initiatives 'westernise' indigenous peacebuilding by excluding these key attributes.

Summary of Recommendations and Conclusion

1) Everyone involved in the current peace processes in South Sudan makes careful choices based on consultations with, and the involvement of, whole ethnic communities, with due consideration of their peace cultures.
2) The governments' political influence on the peace process is examined and ways through which politics can benefit peacebuilding are explored and implemented, with solutions being derived from traditional methods.
3) The most transformative project is to invest peace efforts in motherhood or subtle roles of women to encourage social cohesion and the cultivation and transmission of a peaceful culture.
4) Spiritual authority is included in peace processes, as it influences forgiveness, healing, examination of conscience and control of all aspects vital in achieving sustainable peace.
5) South Sudan national peacebuilding processes should include the diasporas.

Future Plan

The significant aspects that define the existence, functionality and sustainable peacebuilding are key contributions from this research. These include the local languages, etiquette, stories, music, food and subtle roles of especially local women. Filling these gaps and further contributing to knowledge implies that this research will expand on these areas—particularly by focusing on contextual and sustainable peace and development issues in the post-conflict communities. This includes the empowerment of locals as core actors.

Bibliography

Allen, T., 1994. Ethnicity and tribalism on the Sudan-Uganda border. In K. Fukui and J. Markakis (Ed.), *Ethnicity and Conflict in the Horn of Africa*, pp. 112–139. London, James Currey.

Allison, S., 2016. South Sudan's rebel leader: 'I am a hero. I am a victim' Maverick, South Africa. Retrieved April 21, 2014, from http://South Sudan's rebel leader: 'I am a hero. I Am a vi … (dailymaverick.co.za).

Asante, M.K., 2003. *Afrocentricity: The Theory of Social Change*. Chicago, IL, African American Images.

Bedigen, W., 2017. Traditional conflict resolution. The Nilotic Lwo of South Sudan (PhD thesis). Leeds, Leeds Beckett University.

Bedigen, W., 2019. Youth (Monyomiji) and conflict resolution in the South Sudan civil war. *Journal of African Cultural Heritage Studies*, 2(1), pp. 18–35.

Bedigen, W., 2020. Significance of societal customs in the South Sudan civil war resolution. *Journal of Peacebuilding & Development*, 15(1), pp. 3–17.

Bedigen, W., 2021. Honyomiji: The local women's peacebuilding institution in South Sudan. *Peacebuilding.* doi: 10.1080/21647259.2021.1895613.
Bedigen, W., 2022. A quest for sustainable peace in South Sudan: The role of everyday religious practices, ceremonies and rituals in robust peacebuilding. *Journal of the British Academy*, 10(Supplementary Issue 1), pp. 55–77. Retrieved from https://www.thebritishacademy.ac.uk/documents/3698/JBA-10s1-04-Bedigen.pdf.
Blumberg, H. H., Hare, A. P., and Costin, A., 2006. *Peace Psychology. A Comprehensive Introduction.* Cambridge, Cambridge University Press.
Bradbury, M., Ryle, J., Medley, M. and Sansculotte-Greenidge, K., 2006. *Local Peace Processes in Sudan: A Baseline Study.* London, Rift Valley Institute.
Cashmore, E. and Rojek, C., 1999. *Dictionary of Cultural Theorists.* London, Hodder Arnold.
de Waal, A. and Flint, J., 2005. *Darfur: A Short History of a Long War.* London, Zed/International African Institute.
de Waal, A., 2014. When kleptocracy becomes insolvent: Brute causes of the civil war in South Sudan. *African Affairs*, 113(452), pp. 347–369.
Dogra, N., 2011. The mixed metaphor of 'third world woman': Gendered representations by international development NGOs. Third World Quarterly, 32(2), pp. 333–348. doi: 10.1080/01436597.2011.560472.
Douglas, M., 1966. *Purity* and Danger: *An Analysis of Concepts of Pollution and Taboo.* London, Routledge and Keegan Paul.
Douglas, M., 1970. *Natural Symbols. Explorations in Cosmology.* New York, Routledge.
Douglas, M., 1973. *Natural Symbols: Explorations in Cosmology.* London, Barrie & Rockliff.
Douglas, M., 1992. *Risk and Blame: Essays in Cultural Theory.* London, Routledge.
Edelstein, S., 2011. *Food, Cuisine and Cultural Competency for Culinary, Hospitality and Nutrition Professionals.* Mississauga, ON, Jones and Bartlett Publishers.
Galtung, J., 1996. *Peace by Peaceful Means.* London, Sage.
Galtung, J., 1990. Cultural violence. *Journal of Peace Research*, 27(3), pp. 291–305.
Galtung, J., 2004. *Transcend and Transform: An Introduction to Conflict Work.* London, Pluto Press.
Gramsci, A., 1992. *Prison Notebooks (Vol. 2).* New York, Columbia University Press.
Gramsci, A., 1995. *The Intellectuals and the Organization of Culture.* Turin, Giulio Einaudi.
Grawert, E., 2014. *Forging Two Nations Insights on Sudan and South Sudan.* Addis Ababa OSSREA.
Harlacher, T., 2009. *Traditional Ways of Coping with Consequences of Traumatic Stress in Acholi Land: Northern Uganda Ethnography from a Western Psychological Perspective* (PhD thesis). Freiburg, University of Freiburg.
Iyob, R. and Khadiagala, G.M., 2006. *Sudan: The Elusive Quest for Peace.* Boulder, CO, Lynne Rienner Publishers.
Jeong, H.-W., 2005. *Peacebuilding in Postconflict Societies.* London, Sage.
Johnson, D.H. and Anderson, D.M., 1995. *The Prophet Ngundeng and the Battle of Pading. Revealing Prophets: Prophecy in Eastern African History.* Oxford, James Currey Publishers.

Jok, A.A., Leitch, A.R. and Vandewint, C., 2004. *A Study of Customary Law in Contemporary Southern Sudan*. Rumbek, South Sudan, World Vision International.

Latigo, J.O., 2008. *Northern Uganda: Tradition-Based Practices in the Acholi Region*. Stockholm, International Institute for Democracy and Electoral Assistance.

Lederach, J.P., 1996. *Preparing for Peace: Conflict Transformation across Cultures*. Syracuse, NY, Syracuse University Press.

Lederach, J.P., 1997. *Building Peace: Sustainable Reconciliation in Divided Societies*. Washington, DC, United States Institute of Peace Press.

Lederach, J.P., 2012. The origins and evolution of infrastructures for peace: A personal reflection. *Journal of Peacebuilding and Development*, 7(3), 8–13.

Machar, B., 2015. *Building a Culture of Peace through Dialogue in South Sudan*. Juba, South Sudan, The SUUD Institute.

Mbiti, J.S., 1970. *Concepts of God in Africa*. London, SPCK.

Nyerere, J.K., 1968. *Ujamaa: Essays on Socialism*. London, Oxford University Press.

Ogot, B.A., 1999. *Building on the Traditional: Selected Essays 1981–1998*. Nairobi, Anyange Press Ltd.

p'Bitek, O., 1966. *Song of Lawino and Song of Ocol*. Oxford, Heinemann Educational Books.

Poku, N. and Mdee, D.A., 2013. *Politics in Africa: A New Introduction*. London, Zed Books Ltd.

Prunier, G., 2005. *Darfur: The Ambiguous Genocide*. London, Hurst & Company.

Ramsbotham, O., Woodhouse, T. and Miall, H., 2005. *Contemporary Conflict Resolution: The Prevention, Management and Transformation of Deadly Conflicts*. 2nd edition. Cambridge, Polity Press.

Sedgwick, P.R. and Edgar, A. (Eds.), 2002. *Cultural Theory: The Key Concepts*. London, Routledge.

Shorter, A., 1974. *East African Societies*. London, Routledge and Kegan Paul.

Simonse, S. and Kurimoto, E. (Eds.), 2011. Engaging Monyomiji: (Bridging the governance gap in East Bank Equatoria). Torit, South Sudan. Proceedings of the Conference, Nairobi, Pax Christi Horn of Africa. 26–28 November 2009.

Wol, D.M.D., 2014. South Sudan conflict: IGAD fights, mediates and negotiates. *Sudan Tribune*. 10 September. Retrieved from http://www.sudantribune.com/spip.php?article52349 [Accessed: 15 January 2015].

List of Interviews Cited in the Text

1) Deng, 15 August 2014
2) Wibo, December 2011

Index

Acholi 14–32, 114
actual time 38–40
adulthood 135–137
African traditional religion 148, 179
Afrocentricity 125, 203
age-grade 99, 139, 140, 142
ageless 214
age-set 98, 99
Akigath 20, 125–127
Akobo 40, 116
Amangat 162
Anuak, Anywaa or Anyuak 22–24
apprenticeship 9, 99, 139–141, 148, 177, 192, 215
arbitration 139, 163, 176, 178
Aruko Jwi 99

beads 89, 100, 167, 168, 191, 216
behaviour 39, 45, 92, 99–104, 212
beliefs 35, 36, 87–103
bending the spear 3, 20, 207
bitter herbs 3, 91
blood, a blood relatives 111–114
blood relations 111–114
Bonyo feast 99
Boo 91–96
bottom-up theory 40–43, 210
boys 99
breaking of bones 125–126
bride 110, 168, 171–172
brotherhood 29, 107–111, 210
bull 3, 21, 102, 127, 138, 149, 168, 180, 217
bull names 102

cattle 15–19, 139, 141, 149, 150, 160, 176–179
cattle camps 15, 176
cattle raiding 16, 57, 110, 139, 141

ceremonies 119–128
chief 133, 138
chieftaincy 1, 147
childhood 51, 67, 108, 135, 148, 153
Christian 180
Christianity 47, 217
Cieng 3, 5, 94, 102, 109, 110
civil war 24–28
clan 1, 14, 28–29, 37–38, 41–42, 44, 51, 56–57, 94, 102, 125, 138, 147, 154, 156, 162, 164, 171, 210
clan head 37, 55
clan leader 41, 43
cleansing of ex-combatants 9, 144–157
co-existence 2, 47, 94, 107, 110–111, 142, 173, 174, 181, 198, 209, 211
colonialism 25, 29–30, 99, 182, 204
community 2, 3, 6, 22, 35
community service 141–144
conflict 14–31
conflict-resolution 36, 39, 40, 69–77, 209
conscience 218
context 142–155
contextual 177, 197, 203, 220
conventional 2–4, 6, 7
cosmic relations 202, 204, 208, 216, 218
counter-insurgency 4, 205, 206
crimes 205–218
cultural proximity 196, 197
cultural theory 41–42, 48, 59, 63, 83, 89, 92, 125, 203, 204
customary law 51, 58, 59, 87, 114, 127, 147, 149, 151, 161
customs 1–3, 5–11, 36–38, 41
customs, (societal customs) 35, 37, 58, 87–88, 156, 206–207
cwi 92–93
Cwiay 23–24, 92

Index

Cwiay-gol 23–24, 92–93
Cwiny 23–24, 92–93

daho 153
dako 153
dang 46, 67
data sources 64, 67, 70, 71
DDR 127
defence 24, 46, 140, 216
diaspora 164, 188–194
diel 68, 110, 119, 210
Dinka 14–32, 217
diplomacy 4, 176, 205
dispute 52–57
divination 161
diviners 164, 181
dowry 153–154, 172
dress code 100–101, 213
drinking bitter herbs 3

education 161–162, 164, 174–175
Ekisil 8, 119, 121, 125–128
emotional proximity 195–198
empowerment 140, 174, 213–214
entity 50, 155
etiquette 202–203, 209, 212–215
eurocentric 41–42, 48, 152, 162, 203–204
ex-combatants 42, 50, 59, 111, 120, 122

Fambul Tok 1, 144, 145, 156
family 37, 49, 52
family head 38, 112
fathers of the land and river 23
femininity 173, 216
food 8, 15, 27, 87–104
food for peacebuilding 92–97, 103
forgiveness 123, 125–126
funeral dance 151–152

Gacaca 54, 72, 151
Gipir 21
girl 70, 140, 151–156
god 87, 91, 95, 123, 127, 138, 148, 179, 216
gol 92–93
Gomo Tong 3, 20, 207
grassroots 29, 31, 35
Gurtong 3, 63, 207, 212

Heerin 154
herbalists 164
heredity 147

immigrants 81, 190–191
indigene-centred 60, 211, 212, 219
indigene-centric 1, 4, 10, 36, 118, 128, 198, 205, 219
indigenous 87–92
indigenous (empowerment) 101, 140, 155, 174, 191, 213–214, 220
indigenous cultures 4, 20, 203–204, 207, 209
indigenous customs 182
indigenous institutions 1–2, 15, 25, 27, 35–36, 43, 48–49, 59, 99, 103, 113, 116, 119, 162–163, 165, 177, 182, 190, 196–197, 206–207, 219
indigenous peacebuilding 1–35
indigenous practices 6, 8, 87, 89, 94, 98, 208, 217
institutions 94–104
Islam 46–47, 218

Jabwor 98, 112
jewellery 190
Jodong Lweny 20
Judiyya "local Muslim justice system" 1, 3, 47, 57, 180
justice system 1, 5–7, 35–36, 43, 48–54

Kaal 95
Kacoke Madit 119, 210
kasurube 111
Katiba Banat 166
kinship 22, 41, 87, 110, 170, 179, 189
kwaaro 22
Kwero Merok "cleansing of ex-combatants" ritual 154–155

laberna 171
Labongo 21
Lacen 120, 121, 124, 125, 155, 180, 217, 218
Lanyim 95
leadership 95, 99–100, 114, 128, 132, 136–147
Liliir 40, 72, 116, 145, 156, 180, 205, 207, 209, 217
liver 23, 88, 91–94, 211
liver-eating ritual 92–94
living peace village 142
Logedio 167, 171–173, 182
Loketio 167, 171–173, 182
Lord's Resistence Army 1, 20, 28, 50, 116, 195
Lotuho/Lotuko 132, 134, 164, 178

Index

Luo 14, 70
Luwo 14

Mabior 4, 5, 7, 138–140, 144, 150, 180, 182, 207, 217
Machar, Riek 27, 46, 91
marriage 2, 17, 20–21, 40, 75, 83, 127, 134, 141, 152–154, 171, 172, 209
Mato-Oput 69, 100, 119–123
mediation 2, 4, 9, 42, 47, 153–154, 156, 163, 176, 178–179, 205, 209, 214–215
medicine man 138, 149–150
messengers 166, 168
migrants 188, 190, 194
millet 91, 95, 209
Monyomiji 100–101, 116, 119, 132–156
mother 161–163, 167, 174
motherhood 161–163, 167, 174
Murle 15, 21, 23–24

national peacebuilding 31, 44, 81, 92, 94, 116, 134, 138–139, 141, 143–144, 146, 161–163, 165
native 3, 30, 35, 48, 102, 190–191
negotiation 2–4, 26, 41–43, 47, 49, 53, 71–72, 99, 108, 110, 115–116, 119, 126, 129, 132, 138–140, 146–153, 209, 215–217
network 188–189, 193
network structures 189, 193
Ngundeng Bong 46
Nilotic-centred approach 89
Nilotic Lwo 90–92
Nilotics 14, 24, 164
Nilots 14
Nueer 155, 180–181, 216–217
Nuer 21–32
nyieya 23
Nyono Tong Gweno 122–125, 154
Nywak 109

Obok lok 68, 70
Odonge 98, 127, 138, 140, 148
offender 37, 55, 81, 87, 109, 112–113, 123–124, 155
Oput 112, 119–121
Owiny Ki-Bull 21–22
ownership 17, 28, 75–76, 90, 189, 194

partnership 43–44
passage 99, 150

pastoralists 101, 149–150
patriarchy 172
patrilineal 216–220
peace 216–220
peacebuilding 36
peacebuilding food 83, 87, 90
peacebuilding from below 210
peaceful culture 216, 220
peace market/market places 55, 92, 142
Pigio 22
power-sharing 2–4, 27, 175, 205
practices 29–31
pragmatic 139, 143–144
pregnancy support belt 167–175
princesses 175
proximity 189–200

queen 176, 210
queen mother 176

rain chief 43, 133, 138, 149, 179–180
rainmakers 164
rainmaking 179
refugees 188–189, 193, 195
regional governments 2, 4, 48, 53, 205–206
reintegration 127, 139, 143–147
relationships 153, 173–174, 179–182
religion 196, 207, 211, 216–217
resilience 188–198, 219–220
resolution 202–207
rituals 87–196
Rod 47–52

Saza 38
scars 168
self-representation 101, 214
Shilluk 5, 15–18
skin 68, 89, 91, 100, 103, 127, 168, 177
social capital 218–220
social cohesion 212, 215, 220
social support 82, 162–164, 174–175, 181–183
socialising 51, 70–78, 87–104
societal 87, 91, 101, 103
songs 67–68, 92, 95, 108, 145, 151–152, 166–168, 170–171, 176–178, 197, 214
South Sudan Justice System 1, 5, 7, 35–36, 51–60, 198, 219
The spear and the bead 21, 33, 126, 138
spirits 57, 87, 90, 91

spiritual authority 148, 203–204, 208, 216–217
Stepping on Egg 8, 122–125
storyteller 67–70, 82, 92
supernatural 39, 57, 141, 180, 204, 209, 216–217
sustainable 204–209

Tali Lanyim 95
Tedo Kidi 98–99
time 38–39
To blunt the spear 3, 211
Toposa 5, 151, 167
traditional institutions 113–115

Ubuntu 109, 119, 205, 210
Ujamaa 109, 117, 119, 205, 210

victim 36–37, 50

war chief 16, 43, 93, 138, 149–150
warrior class 144
warriors 45, 127, 168
White bull 3, 149
wife 166, 172, 176
witches 27, 175, 182
women 161–183
Wunlit 20, 39–40, 205, 207, 209, 212–213, 217

youth 151–156

Zamani 38